Please return/renew this item by the last date shown.

North
Somerset
C O U N C I L

The Book of the Eclipse

David Ovason did postgraduate research into the influence of hermetic thought on late mediaeval literature. He is a teacher of astrology, and has been a student of Nostradamus for over forty years. His first book, *The Nostradamus Code*, was published by Arrow in 1998 and his third, *The Secret Zodiacs of Washington DC* is now available from Century.

THE BOOK OF THE
ECLIPSE

———◦⊱⊰◦———

The hidden influences of eclipses
DAVID OVASON

ARROW

Published in the United Kingdom in 1999 by Arrow Books

1 3 5 7 9 10 8 6 4 2

Arrow Books Limited
Random House UK Ltd,
20 Vauxhall Bridge Road, London SW1V 2SA

Random House Australia (Pty) Limited
20 Alfred Street, Milsons Point, Sydney,
New South Wales 2061, Australia

Random House New Zealand Limited
18 Poland Road, Glenfield,
Auckland 10, New Zealand

Random House South Africa (Pty) Limited
Endulini, 5a Jubilee Road, Parktown 2193, South Africa

Random House UK Limited Reg. No. 954009

A CIP catalogue record for this book
is available from the British Library

Papers used by Random House UK Limited are natural,
recyclable products made from wood grown in sustainable forests.
The manufacturing processes conform to the
environmental regulations of the country of origin.

ISBN 0 09 94 0633 0

Typeset in Ehrhardt by MATS, Southend-on-Sea, Essex
Printed and bound in the United Kingdom by
Cox & Wyman Ltd, Reading, Berks

Contents

THE SOLAR ECLIPSE OF 11TH AUGUST 1999

The solar eclipse of 11th August, 1999 will be visible from all parts of the British Isles, but will be seen as a total eclipse only from the southern tip of Cornwall and South Devon. The central line of totality will pass between Falmouth and Helston, in Cornwall.

The northern-most limit of visibility of the total eclipse will be south of the line from Port Isaac to the south of Teignmouth. Times of visibility will vary slightly, south of this line, but (for example) at Falmouth, totality will begin at 11:11:20 AM, and will last for 2:05 minutes. At the northern-most point of this totality, the eclipse will last for 30 seconds, but, around the southern-most point, at Penzance, St. Ives, Falmouth, and so on, it will last for over two minutes.

The further north the viewing point in the British Isles, the less close to totality will the eclipse appear – at London over 96% of the Sun will be obscured, at Manchester about 90%, at Newcastle about 85%. In Edinburgh, it will be about 83%. In Dublin, it will be about 90%, and in Belfast, about 87%. Most of the partial eclipses will begin shortly after 10:00 AM. For example, in London, it will begin at 10:03, in Edinburgh at 10:05, and in Belfast at 10:01.

The line of totality will pass through northern France (south of Amiens, and almost touching Laon), Germany (south of Saarbrücken), and through central Europe, northern Turkey, parts of the Middle East, and through central India.

Introduction

Whether we be young or old,
Our destiny, our being's heart and home,
Is with infinitude

(William Wordsworth, *The Prelude*, Bk. vi.)

The solar eclipse which will be visible in parts of southern England in August 1999 has caught the imagination of many people. It will take place on 11 August, at 11:11 am, and will be visible in parts of Cornwall, the coastline tip of south-western England, in parts of France, Central Europe and Turkey. Its duration will be 2 minutes and 23 seconds, and, as far as astrologers are concerned, it will take place in 18.21 degrees of Leo.

As the media tap into the popular interest, a lot of nonsense will be spoken and written about this particular eclipse, as about other eclipses. Researchers working for broadcasting stations have contacted me even before I started writing this book, seeking my opinion, quite convinced that the great French savant, Nostradamus, predicted this eclipse – and that he predicted death and destruction in its wake.

This book is an attempt to set the record straight. My purpose is to show that eclipses can and do have effects on people, but rarely in the ways that are popularly believed. I shall also show that Nostradamus had not the slightest interest in this eclipse, and that eclipses (even visible total eclipses) are not as rare as people seem to believe.

In order to demonstrate these truths, I have taken the horoscopes of over sixty famous individuals, and attempted to show how their lives were dramatically affected by eclipses. I have selected most of these charts because of their intrinsic value as horoscopes: this explains why the list contains so many artists, writers and poets. However, the charts were also

1

selected because I happen to believe that soon – when modern astrology comes of age, and emerges from the subcultural nonsense with which it is mixed up at present – it will be seen that the traditions of astrology may throw unexpected beams of light on art, literature and poetry.

I have not gone out of my way to choose these examples simply because they demonstrate the truth of eclipse-lore. Such a selective approach is scarcely necessary, for the lives of virtually every individual may be influenced by an eclipse, indeed by several eclipses. My choice was partly determined by a wish to deal with so unfamiliar a subject within the context of people who are likely to be familiar to the general reader. Even so, as this book will make abundantly clear, eclipses do seem to work most dramatically and thoroughly through the lives of the great and famous – through the aspirations of the talented and those blessed or cursed with genius. Whether this is because people born in the shadow of powerful eclipses are destined for greatness, or simply because eclipses in the charts of the great and famous are most easily remembered by historians such as myself, I cannot tell. In writing about such questions, I cannot help thinking of the Chinese poet who could not decide whether the wind moved the trees, or whether the swaying of the trees caused the wind.

I have written this book for the layperson, who has no special knowledge of astrology. To lend help to such people, who may at times encounter words or phrases which puzzle them, I have appended a glossary of terms. In addition, I have attempted to explain each technical-seeming word when first I use it in the text. Thus, if a reader perseveres with the text from beginning to end, then it is unlikely that he or she should have any trouble in following my argument.

In order to keep things simple, I have adopted two conventions. First, I have decided to summarize all important eclipse-positions for ease of reference. For example, in regard to the chart of Prince Charles, the heir to the British throne, I have condensed the eclipse data and data from his chart in the following form:

SOLAR ECLIPSE OF 21 JUNE 1982:	29.47 GEMINI
URANUS IN THE CHART OF PRINCE CHARLES:	29.56 GEMINI

My purpose in using such a convention is to show that the two cosmic elements – in this case, the solar eclipse and the planet Uranus – were within the same degree of Gemini. At this stage, it does not really matter whether you know what Uranus is, or what Gemini is – or, for that matter, what a solar eclipse is. My hope is that all such terms will be explained as they arise. Even so, a reader who admits to being entirely uninformed in the matter of astrology, and yet who remains anxious to learn something about this fascinating subject, might do well to glance through the first page of the glossary, where the names for the planets, zodiacal signs, and their corresponding symbols, are set out in a simple form.

Second, wherever possible when discussing personal charts, I have presented an actual horoscope alongside a table of data. The example below is the chart of the Russian Czar, Alexander II, whose involvement with eclipses is discussed on page 126–7.

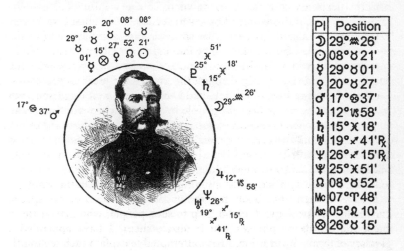

Pl	Position
☽	29°♒26'
☉	08°♉21'
☿	29°♉01'
♀	20°♉27'
♂	17°♋37'
♃	12°♑58'
♄	15°♓18'
♅	19°♐41'℞
♆	26°♐15'℞
♇	25°♓51'
☊	08°♉52'
Mc	07°♈48'
Asc	05°♌10'
⊗	26°♉15'

It does not matter, at present, if you do not know what the symbols and numbers in this figure mean: the sigils (as the symbols are called) are also explained, on page 260. However, as an introduction to the basics of astrology, here are the corresponding names of the planets and zodiacal signs from the above chart.

Moon in Aquarius	☽ 29°♒26'
Sun in Taurus	☉ 08°♉21'
Mercury in Taurus	☿ 29°♉01'
Venus in Taurus	♀ 20°♉27'
Mars in Cancer	♂ 17°♋37'
Jupiter in Capricorn	♃ 12°♑58'
Saturn in Pisces	♄ 15°♓18'
Uranus in Sagittarius	♅ 19°♐41'℞
Neptune in Sagittarius	♆ 26°♐15'℞
Pluto in Pisces	♇ 25°♓51'
Dragon's Head in Taurus	☊ 08°♉52'
MC in Aries	Mc 07°♈48'
Ascendant in Leo	Asc 05°♌10'
Part of Fortune in Taurus	⊗ 26°♉15'

3

If you compare the positions of the planets in the horoscope with those in the table, you will see that the two sets of data correspond exactly. This close correspondence of chart and table is not always found in other examples of horoscopes which I give in the book. In many cases, I have elected to choose historically interesting charts which may not be as accurate as modern computing methods now permit. However, in every case, the tables are computer-originated and are as accurate as possible. This means that, if one is concerned with accuracy, one must consult the tabulations of data, rather than the sample horoscopes I provide: the horoscope figures are to be regarded as being merely of historical or astrological interest. When I draw comparisons between birth-data and eclipses, I do so in terms of the tables, rather than the horoscopes.

I should observe that astrologers use a very simple method of abbreviation for denoting the position of planets or such planetary phenomena as eclipses. They indicate these positions against the zodiacal belt, in terms of degrees and minutes (in some cases, also in terms of seconds). Thus, the abbreviation 'Saturn in 16.20 Aries' means that the planet Saturn was located in 16 degrees and 20 minutes of the zodiacal sign Aries. You can see from the table on page 3 that the convention is to show the sigil for the sign with the degree to the left and the minute to the right.

Although I have written this book for the layperson, I am all too aware that a few of the claims I make may need some sort of justification or development which cannot properly be made in the body of the text. At times, I feel the need to be in a position to make a few technical observations – for example, about the accuracy or source of certain famous horoscopes, and whence I derived the data. In order to do this in a way which will not obtrude on the general readability of the book, I have kept almost all such specialist references to footnotes.

Eclipse-lore is not widely studied by modern astrologers, yet I happen to think that it is one of the most interesting of all the many areas of this art of astrology, which wise men in past times (bearing in mind its inner content) joined with the secret science of alchemy, and called the Royal Art.

In fact, as this book will show, eclipse-lore has enthused and inspired poets and artists through the ages, with the consequence that the meanings in many works of art – especially, paintings and engravings – remain obscure to those who are not familiar with the symbolism of eclipses. Artists of the last two centuries have been influenced by three major symbolic forms derived from eclipses, all of which I shall examine in this book.

The most important graphic convention in regard to eclipses is one in which the artist represents the dark Moon exactly over the radiant Sun. A very simple example of this is in an engraving by the Italian Jacopo Guarana, of 1792 (figure 1).

This shows the dark lunar globe over the Sun, above the head of the prophetess, Albunea.

Technically, this is a solar eclipse, and it is a device which is represented in several paintings, in one variant form or another.

A painting by the nineteenth-century English painter, Dante Gabriel Rossetti (see page 70), represents the Moon by the second convention. It is still overlaid on the Sun, but the crescent Moon is not dark.

Of course, this arrangement of Sun and Moon is physically impossible, since the crescent is a consequence of the Moon being some distance from the Sun. It is merely a graphic convention, allowing both to be visible. Rossetti was by no means inventing this symbol of an eclipse by drawing together Sun and Moon into an unlikely union: as we shall see, this was a widely used convention in art (and in alchemical symbolism) for almost two thousand years.

A similar, but different, convention was used in the title-page of Jacopo Guarana's collection of engravings for his *Oracoli* of 1792. This depicts the ancient Greek gods and goddesses on Mount Olympus, in conference (figure 2). In the foreground is a zodiacal band, and in the heavens is a Sun with a crescent Moon very close to it. The remarkable thing about this crescent is that *it is oriented away from the Sun*. Since the Sun is supposed to light up the crescent under normal circumstances, there is something abnormal about this arrangement.

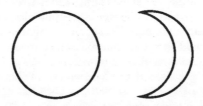

In other words, just like the Sun of the Rossetti painting, this detail is physically impossible. Here, then, is another painterly convention by which the artist shows either that there is something at odds in the cosmos (are the gods in the picture having an argument, for instance?) or that the Moon is itself being eclipsed by the Earth, which is throwing its own shadow upon the satellite. This orientation was often used by the painter-poet, William Blake, whose connection with eclipses is discussed on page 134. The Dutch painter, Vincent van Gogh (an eclipse-struck soul, if ever there was one), also used the technique of 'wrong' lunar orientations widely in his work – see page 171.

Few artists have actually incorporated diagrams of eclipses into their art, but the modern artist, Max Ernst (whose life was deeply influenced by eclipses – see page 162) did precisely this in a number of paintings. The remarkable picture by Ernst, 'Of This Men Shall Know Nothing', which I discuss on page 163, is one of the most sophisticated commentaries on cosmic influences painted in the twentieth century.

It is one thing to inquire whether eclipse-lore has influenced art, but it is another thing to ask if eclipses influence human lives. In fact, the answer to such a question must be fairly obvious, since everything which occurs in the noumenal and phenomenal world influences our lives in one way or another. For all the nonsense which is talked in the modern world, our destiny is with what the poet Wordsworth called *infinitude*, and not merely with the material world. There is no-one alive who does not feel in some way the ripples of air at the fall of a sparrow or leaf, for this is the language of infinitude. This is not an expression of Wordsworthian mysticism or pantheism, but of common sense idea realized even by modern science. If, as Einstein showed, gravity bends even light, then our own inner weight must constantly work upon and change the changing world which is revealed to us chiefly through the action of light. If, as the German scientist, Frau L. Kolisko showed (see page 43), eclipses influence liquids, then our own inner being must be constantly hemmed in by changes within our physical frame. *Of course eclipses influence our lives.* How could it be otherwise? This book is intended merely to present evidence in demonstration of that truth.

Yet such a realization that eclipses can change lives in the twinkling of an eye should not lead us to fatalism or a supine despair. If there is any danger that the reader should misunderstand my thesis, then it is better that he or she should thrust the book aside. The astrological theory of eclipses does not lead to fatalism, but to realization of the infinitude and creative power of the Spiritual. The antidote to that fatalism which a misunderstanding of astrology sometimes encourages is the realization that we are all children of a creative Cosmos.

Just as there are eclipses in the space beyond us, so there are eclipses within our beings, for these vast spaces are contained within our selves. We each of us at some time in our lives experience a darkening and a coldness equivalent to the experience of a lunar or solar eclipse, and I hope that this book enables the reader to see why this should be. At its very worst, the inner eclipse reminds us that we are children of the gods – yet it would be sacrilegious to believe that we are the playthings of the gods.

It is reasonable for a reader to ask where the horoscopes of famous people used in this book come from. Almost since the tenth century, when astrology was reintroduced into Europe by the Arabs, astrologers have constructed lists of horoscopes – partly for their own instruction, and partly for posterity. Tens of thousands of horoscopes are preserved in astrological manuscripts in such collections as the British Library, and the Manuscript Department of the British Museum, or the Bodleian (Oxford), and in astrological magazines which have been published in most European countries for almost two centuries, and in America for about a century and a half. These range from John Varley's chart of his friend the artist-poet, William Blake, in the magazine *Urania* (see page 135), to modern horoscopes for the so-called 'Millennium Bug', as set out in the January 1999 edition of the American astrological magazine, *The Mountain Astrologer*.

The sources are vast, and we owe the attempt to make representative collections of charts to a few astrologers who have gone to the trouble of setting down their own collections of horoscopes, in the hope that these will be of interest to aficionados. Some of these 'collectors of births' are well known in astrological circles, even today.

The sixteenth-century Florentine scholar, Franciscus Junctinus, drew up and published a great number of charts of the mighty and famous of his own day, and these, still available in his *Speculum Astrologiae* of 1583, are a wonderful source for historians of the art: among them, the chart of Michelangelo is particularly famous. While Junctinus is renowned as a scholar and scientist in areas other than astrology, his reputation in popular books on the arcane arts is poor. A nineteenth-century wood-engraving by Leon Trouvé (figure 3) portrays him as a Faustian figure, with black cat at his feet, magical symbols on his table, and a stuffed crocodile hanging overhead. However, even Trouvé was compelled to depict the astrologer's planisphere on a stand, while in the background he has shown the magic square of Mars, hinting at Junctinus' prowess as an horoscopist. The seventeenth-century English astrologer, John Gadbury, told a story of how Junctinus died:

Franciscus Junctinus, an Italian, of the City of Florence and a most ingenious Artist [astrologer], from some unhappie constellation in his own Nativity, foretold that he himself should die some violent death;

and upon the very day (as he before had predicted) was knocked on the head by the Books in his Studie falling upon him.

Gadbury was too good an astrologer not to have recognized that Junctinus would have been able to foretell his own death (which occurred in 1590), from the effect of an eclipse of the Moon in that year. In the astrological jargon with which both Gadbury and Junctinus were familiar, the eclipsed Moon of 17 July 1590 fell on the astrologer's Jupiter, while Saturn was in opposition to his Ascendant – astrologic-talk which indicates a promise of death in a chart.

Some astrologers (like the seventeenth-century antiquary, Elias Ashmole) have preserved horoscopes in private diaries, now fortunately archived in libraries. In the case of Ashmole, these are mainly in the Bodleian at Oxford, together with many of his other arcane and astrological writings, and those of his friends.

In the same seventeenth century (which marked the heyday of English astrology) the English astrologers, William Lilly and John Gadbury, left an enormous number of horoscopes. Usually, these charts are in manuscript form, but Gadbury went to the trouble of publishing woodcuts of the most interesting and instructive of his natal charts in *Collectio Geniturarum* (1662) and *Cardines Coeli* (1686) – perhaps the most important in the latter collection was the horoscope of the prophet

Nostradamus, whose death was also self-predicted (see page 203). Much of this data, and the accompanying figures, are of great interest to us, even today; however, experience has taught the modern astrologer that it is generally wise to recast the figures from the data provided by these late mediaeval sources, whose tables of planetary and stellar positions were not as accurate as those now available.

In an age less supportive of the astrological tradition, the eighteenth-century astrologer, Ebenezer Sibly, adapted some of the more interesting famous charts from earlier sources, and added to these horoscopes from his own considerable collection. His 'portrait-charts' (see opposite and figure 4) are justly famous among historians of astrology, even if they are not always as accurate as one would wish. Sibly cast some very original horoscopes: for example, he was the first to publish a pictorial engraved chart for the Declaration of Independence in America, and certainly he provided some graphically interesting charts for such events as the decapitation of Louis XVI and Marie Antoinette during the French Revolution (figure 4). Within the context of our interest in eclipses, his chart for the Crucifixion of Christ is interesting, in that it equates the darkness which fell over Golgotha – the hill of Crucifixion – with a lunar eclipse.

As the popularity of astrology increased, during the nineteenth century, astrologers began to publish the charts of interesting births, or of famous individuals (including, of course, royalty) in their own textbooks. In the United States, for example, Luke Broughton – a doctor by profession – published a considerable number of horoscopes in his astrological magazine (his famous chart of Lincoln served as a front-page advertisment for this magazine, figure 5). His major work on the subject, *The Elements of Astrology* (1898), also included a fair number of horoscopes of famous Americans.

At about the same time as Broughton's pioneering work was coming to an end, Alan Leo began to publish *Modern Astrology* (figure 6), which, besides introducing a new seriousness to the ancient art, has established itself as a useful quarry for horoscopes – especially, of course, for late-nineteenth-century charts.

'Alan Leo' was in fact, a pseudonym. He was an English astrologer, William Frederick Allan, whose horoscope (above), with four planets in the sign Leo, explains the choice of pen-name. Leo accurately predicted the moment of his own death from a heart-attack in August 1917: he recognized the coming of the end, in the January of that year, when a lunar eclipse fell upon his planet Venus.

Leo was more of a popularizer of astrology than a pioneer who extended the boundaries of the art, but in his magazines and books he would frequently copy horoscopic data from earlier sources – an example, the horoscope of Oliver Cromwell, in figure 7, which he borrowed from the seventeenth-century John Partridge. Leo, who was never especially careful with his facts, wrongly imagined that Partridge had been a physician to Queen Elizabeth I. Eventually, Leo put together (one might add, without too much care) a collection of horoscopes under the title of *1001 Notable Nativities*, followed by *More Notable Nativities*, which are still used by modern astrologers.

A more carefully researched approach to the idea of a massive collection was made by the American astrologer, Marc Edmund Jones. His *The Sabian Symbols in Astrology* (1953) contains a thousand useful horoscopes.

In the following pages I have reproduced some of these charts in antique style where possible from the original sources – because these are historically or graphically interesting. In some cases, I have had to make do with copies – for example, Nell Gwyn's chart (figure 8) is not the original and famous cast by William Lilly or Ashmole, now preserved in the Ashmolean, but a graphic equivalent, in a seventeenth-century manuscript style. Similarly, the horoscope of Leonardo da Vinci (figure 9) is an instructive pastiche of Leonardo's chart over which has been superimposed the zodiacal rulership over parts of the body – a curious image which I use in lectures.

Of course, it is true to say that one has no need to hunt for charts through lists of horoscopes in old books and magazines. With the advent of computers, it is now a relatively easy matter for anyone to cast horoscopes, even though the more difficult art of reading them remains just as elusive as before. However, the major problem nowadays is the one which has faced astrologers in all times: that is, the acquisition of accurate data – which is to say, the locating of reliable sources for exact time, place and date of birth. In this work I have made considerable effort to check birth data against reputable biographies. In those cases where such data remains doubtful, I have attempted to rectify the chart against the known events in the life of the person concerned. This method is widely used by modern astrologers. Such rectification allows one to formulate uncertain birth-charts which would otherwise be effectively lost: for example, the time of Beethoven's birth is not known at all, yet by means of rectification, it has been possible to establish a workable horoscope figure (see page 132).

It is sometimes said that cosmic phenomena *cause* certain events to unfold on earth through the lives of individuals. I am very uneasy with this idea: in the esoteric astrological tradition, it is taught that the relationship between the Cosmos and the realm of mankind is not that of causation at all. According to this tradition, the two worlds *parallel* each other, and influence each other, but do not cause events reciprocally. I might liken the relationship between the higher and the lower to that which exists between the Sun and plants. When a plant grows, and flowers

11

– perhaps into a rose of extraordinary beauty – it is quite correct to seek the source of that plant in the action of last year's sunlight, for all plant-forms owe their growth and existence to the action of sunlight. In truth, the seed which eventually flowered as a rose might have lain around for some years before the gardener planted it: do we therefore seek the cause of the rose in that seed, or in the planting of the seed? If in the latter, do we seek the cause of the rose in the soil around it? This would be foolish in the extreme, for you cannot isolate a part of the soil from the entire earth: do we, therefore, seek the cause of the rose in the globe of the earth? This would be foolish for without the seed, the earth could not engender the rose. Again, at some point that seed must have been part of a previous rose: can we rightfully say that the previous rose caused the flower to grow? And if we answer yes to this question, how many generations of roses must we go back in our search for the origins of the seed? Do we go back to the first seed to be engendered by that mythical Big Bang of creation? The seed was planted by a gardener: may we say that the gardener caused the seed to grow?

When we begin to look into such issues, it dawns on us that the entire cosmos conspires to enable a rose to flower – just as the entire Cosmos conspires to enable a human being to exist and develop to spiritual maturity. When the poet, John Donne, wrote 'No man is an island', he was surely thinking in esoteric terms (in terms of what he would have called the Macrocosm-Microcosm theory) – no man is an island, for all men live within a Cosmos, as permanently dependent upon it for life as a new-born babe is dependent upon its mother. Within such a context, it is perhaps short-sighted to suggest that eclipses *cause* events, yet the limitations of our language (which reflects certain trends in our thinking) scarcely permit any other approach. It would be linguistically clumsy for me to continue to write 'such and such an eclipse paralleled in a macrocosmic way such and such an event'.

In this work, I have written at some length about the mediaeval plagues and their relationship with eclipses. I have been tempted to do this because the mediaeval astrologer was in some ways more simplistic than some modern astrologers – the mediaeval astrologers seem to have had little doubt that the relationships between the heavens and the earth were causal. They did not doubt that a specific eclipse (or perhaps a major planetary conjunction in the heavens) caused an outbreak of the plague. Within the framework of the more sophisticated astrology which exists today, this was myopic vision, for it did not take into account (for instance) the nature of the seafaring trade during the period in which they lived. It did not take account of the nature of the fleas that infest the skin and fur of rats. It did not take into account the design of mooring ropes in ships at that time – failing to recognize that such ropes did not prohibit rats from climbing aboard ships when moored in harbours . . . Are we to follow such a mediaeval myopic vision by claiming that the design of mooring cables caused the plague? All we can say is that the plagues which spread through Europe with such devastating consequences in the late mediaeval period appear to have been a consequence of the fleas carried by rats, along sea-trading routes that extended as far as China and India. But then, what caused the rats? and what caused the fleas on rats? and so on, interminably.

There is also another factor that we should take into account. Not everyone died from the plague. This implies that there must have been certain propensities within the souls or bodies of those who did attract the plague to facilitate that attraction. In the esoteric tradition, this facility to attract specific contagions and diseases has been linked with certain attitudes of fear and apprehension encouraged by experiences in previous lifetimes. Now, whilst this belief is held in the face of what modern science presently happens to hold as true, it does at least offer a possible explanation of how certain diseases may strike down some people and not others. These issues reinforce my view that it is very difficult to say what causes what: it seems that the Cosmos is such a unified whole that every event – the fall of a sparrow – is just as involved with the actions of the whole Cosmos as (say) a major plague, or a major war. In sum, when I say or imply in this book that an eclipse *causes* a particular event, the reader should be alert to translate this verb into the linguistically clumsy parallels, bearing in mind that the Cosmos overshadows the material realm in a creative way, but does not issue fiats of causal command.

For all it may seem complicated, eclipse-astrology is actually one of the more simple adjuncts of astrological studies, and may be easily assimilated by the layperson who is prepared to learn the basic alphabet of astrology. I hope that the following pages will both entertain and instruct – and perhaps alert the reader to the importance of eclipses in the reading of personal destiny.

Eclipses and Us

It is said that when the Norwegians – so used to the bitter cold – first saw roses, they dared not touch them. They imagined that the rose-trees were budding flames.[1]

This delightful story reflects on how our knowledge of things can condition our attitudes. If you had never seen a rose tree, then the sight of red flames among its green leaves would appear to you as a great wonder.

So it is with eclipses. Eclipses are not rare phenomena – there can be as many as seven in a single year, yet the solar eclipse is visible from only a small area and is as evanescent as the wind; only two total eclipses of the Sun have been seen in England during the entire twentieth century. For those in England who have not the opportunity to travel overseas in search of such things, the total eclipse of the Sun which will be visible in Cornwall for two minutes and 23 seconds on 11 August 1999 will offer an opportunity to see the budding flames in roses which they can neither touch nor understand.

This image of light and fire might seem a strange metaphor for an eclipse, which seems a thing of shadows and darkness, yet I choose it with some conviction. The real experience of the eclipse is that we stare into a temporary shadow of the Earth or Moon – into a shadow which is made possible only by the pyrotechnics of the Sun.

The absence of light is one thing: the coldness, the silence, and the unaccustomed view of the stars at midday, is another. When I have watched eclipses I have never found it difficult to believe the mediaeval accounts which tell how, as a solar eclipse became total, birds would suddenly drop in fear from the sky. In a history of his own times, Ristoro d'Arezzo wrote of his personal experience of the total eclipse of the Sun, on 3 June 1239, which he had witnessed from his native town.

> One Friday, towards the sixth hour of the day, the Sun was in 20 degrees of Gemini. The weather was serene and clear. Then the sky began to turn yellow, and we saw the entire body of the Sun obscured step by step, and it became night. And we saw Mercury near the Sun; and we saw also all the stars that were above the horizon (of Arezzo);

and all the animals were terrified, as were the birds. And the wild beasts could be captured with ease . . . and we saw the Sun remain completely covered for that space of time during which a man could take 250 paces.[2]

Not exactly a world in upheaval, yet a world under tremendous emotional pressure, and – if the writings of later astrologers are to be believed – one which saw disastrous consequences. This solar eclipse of 1239 was almost certainly the same as the one Peter of Abano mentioned in his arcane work *Conciliator*, which he finished in Padua during 1310. According to Peter, this same eclipse (which had been witnessed throughout Europe) was followed by a weakening of human nature, an increase of avarice and cupidity, and a proliferation of both good and bad demons over the face of the Earth.[3]

With such promises and threats, it is not surprising that the hotels and boarding houses in Cornish villages in the south-west tip of England have been booked up for months, and even years, in anticipation of the 1999 eclipse. For some people, it will be the first time that they have really had an opportunity to luxuriate in the wonders of the heavens. When caught up in real life, it is easy to forget about the Sun and the Moon.

When the Greek poet Theoclymenus observed an eclipse for the first time, he fell into a poetic panic at such a portent, lamenting that 'the Sun has perished out of heaven, and an evil mist has spread over all.'[4] Times have changed, and with them our fears. It is unlikely that anyone who witnesses a lunar or solar eclipse at first hand in modern times is likely to be frightened. They may well be deeply moved, yet they are unlikely to fall on their knees in fear, as so often happened in ancient times.

Even so, the immediate experience of an eclipse can be very disturbing: the sudden darkness and cold are quite palpable, and one has the distinct feeling of loss. One has the sensation that it would not be possible to live under these conditions for very long. When, in the seventeenth century, the astrologer William Lilly, wrote of three eclipses which would be visible in England in 1652, he felt it incumbent upon himself to attempt to allay the fears of the peasants and farmers who might witness the phenomenon. Even so, like Ristoro d'Arezzo, Lilly could not contain his excitement at the idea that the stars he loved so much would be visible in the day-time:

> Whereas I find a generall feare possessing mens spirits, concerning the darknesse which the Eclips portends, and some queries whether it threatens not danger unto those people who are either in the Fields about their labouring occasions, or other wayes occupied without

dores on their Domesicall affaires; I say it threatens no Man or Cattle with danger in that consideration; nor will the Darknesse it selfe be of so great or long a continuance as many imagine ... the darknesse it selfe will not last hardly one quarter of an houre; I mean its greatest obscurity will last little longer; yet I beleeve ... so great it will be for the time that we shall behold the fixed starrs.[5]

William Lilly did not need to pause to ask if an eclipse would have an effect on history. He had written at great length in several books on particular eclipses, and had even provided on a title page of one of his books[6] what was to become the most famous of all seventeenth-century woodcuts of a triple eclipse – those which were visible in England in a twelve-month period beginning in the 'Dark Yeare' of 1652:

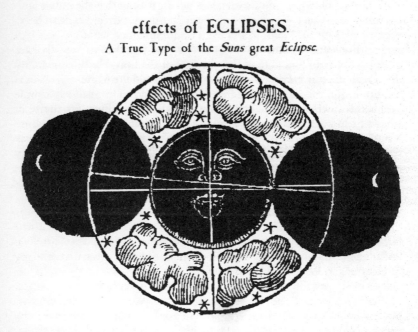

effects of **ECLIPSES**.

A True Type of the *Suns* great *Eclipse*.

Lilly knew, from his vast experience of astrological prediction, that eclipses always have an effect on history, even if they do not immediately influence every chart.

Those people who are not astrologers, and who have never studied eclipses in such a context, are less certain. Such people may legitimately question if, in general, eclipses influence or reflect upon the lives of individuals. They may even have questions concerning the effect of particular eclipses upon humanity. For example, they may ask, what effect will the solar eclipse of 11 August 1999 have on the world population?

The surprising answer to this question is, *almost* no effect at all! It is relatively easy to give this answer because astrologers recognize that eclipses work only through individual charts – through the sensitive points established between eclipse and horoscope. When we study the effect of eclipses on human beings, we shall discover that it is possible to see influences working into history only through the charts of individuals, or through events regulated by people – even in such large-scale activities as the founding of buildings, the launching of ships like the *Titanic*, or the dropping of atomic bombs.

When considering the answer as to what effect the 1999 solar eclipse would have on most people, I had to write '*almost* no effect', for the fact is that *some* people will experience a great effect of the August 1999 eclipse in their lives, just as others will experience the effects of the earlier solar eclipse of 16 February of the same year. We shall examine why this should be so shortly, as these effects have been classified in the astrological tradition, and the rules of the effects can be set down in relatively simple terms. Meanwhile, I should observe that, while it is difficult to arrive at statistics in such matters, in terms of predictive astrology any eclipse (including the eclipse of 1999) is unlikely to affect in any significant way the lives of more than one in twelve people! Even in such a limited number of cases, the effect will be slight, and in some cases it can be beneficial. In sum, I doubt if more than one in 200 people are likely to find their lives dramatically influenced by the eclipse of 1999. Nevertheless, in total this amounts to a huge number!

How do I arrive at these rough estimates? In order to understand these figures, we must glance at the theory of eclipse-interpretation in astrology, and the underlying rules which govern the art of making predictions about the effects of eclipses.

It does not matter one jot, in astrological terms, whether the eclipse is seen or not seen, and whether it is visible or invisible. In terms of the astrological theory of eclipses, the *syzygy* (as the ancient Greeks termed the eclipse alignment of Sun, Earth and Moon) influences the entire spiritual atmosphere of the Earth, and works upon all sublunar creatures equally, according to the nature of their births.

If we are to assume that the astrological tradition is correct, and eclipses work through degrees in individual horoscopes, then it would be absurd to imagine that an eclipse would be limited only to those areas on the earth where the eclipse was visible. In the case of the thin band of visibility in the 1919 solar eclipse (map on page 30) only a very small number of individuals would have been affected, if visibility were an important factor in such influences. Yet there is much evidence to show that the 1919 eclipse had influences on individuals very far removed from this band of visibility.

This observation brings me back to the oft-repeated rule of chart-interpretation, which is that an eclipse has personal significance only when it falls upon a degree already activated in the personal horoscope. This important rule has nothing to do with eclipse-visibility. Even so, there is a popular belief that a visible eclipse can have a powerful, and even dire, influence on a person who gazes upon it. In astrological terms, this is nonsense. Queen Elizabeth I of England must have been aware of this truth, for many of her courtiers believed that it was harmful to look upon an eclipse, yet when a lunar eclipse occurred, the Queen personally drew back the curtains from the palace window to gaze upon it. Perhaps she had been taught something of the reality of eclipse-influences by her astrologer, John Dee?

What is the power which keeps these two cosmic globes – so conveniently of the same optical size when viewed from the earth – hanging in space? Newton might have used the word gravity to explain this silent display, yet the word explains nothing. Before Newton, Dante had suggested that the globes were held in their magical balancing act by love.[7] I am not proposing that Newton is wrong, and Dante is right – merely that there are different ways of looking at the question. It is curious that we have to wait for these two great orbs to move together before we recognize that we know almost nothing about them.

Like the Norwegians with the flaming flowers, we all see different things. The astronomer will see how the Moon occults the solar disk and perhaps leaves visible the chromosphere and corona flames which are the froth of the perpetual hydrogen-bomb explosions within the body of the Sun. He may use a solar eclipse to confirm Einstein's theory that gravity bends light.

The artist may stand in wonderment at the glorious pyrotechnics of the solar eclipse Corona (figure 10), such as those drawn and photographed during the total eclipse of the Sun in August 1868 and June 1871 (opposite), and recognize the depth of symbolism in this union. As we shall see, William Blake and Vincent Van Gogh were just a few artists who used the symbolism of eclipses to deepen the cosmic significance of their works.

The poet, and even the theologian, may see in the eclipse a culmination of the fight between light and darkness – the conflict of those ancient

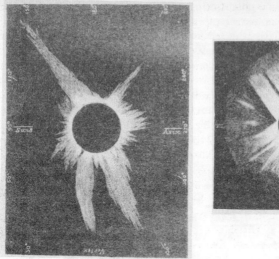

dualities which the wise men of old turned into gods of light and demons of darkness. During that fight, the poet and the theologian may sense something of the darkening horror which would come upon the earth if the demons should ever win.

The hermetic tradition states that an eclipse offers an inner entrance to the spiritual realms, even within the soul of Man. A person steeped in this arcane lore may see the dark body of the Moon boring a hole into space, creating a safety-valve for human passions – a tunnel leading towards the world of the gods. He or she will know that the hermetic teachings are right, and the two luminaries (the Sun and Moon) are inside Man himself, for what is above is also below.

The astrologer may allow his fancy to play with this miracle which is at once so miraculous and ordinary that it almost benumbs the senses. Yet he or she will know, with a quiet satisfaction, that when the eclipse is over, the zodiacal band itself will be different. Where the eclipse took place, there will remain a stain much like an invisible burn-mark, which will continue to influence in some small way the sentient world below.

The primitive man, who lived in the degenerate remnants of a once-magnificent knowledge, retained the sense of wonder which has long-since fled civilized man: such people may view the eclipse in fear and trembling on their knees. That they should fear eclipses is under-standable, for in their cosmoconception the Sun and the Moon are recognized as mighty gods and goddesses, tended by the lesser gods, who demand propitiation. Perhaps those primitives who saw the Sun and

19

Moon as living creatures possessed of intelligence, and guided by spiritual beings, were wiser than ourselves?

It is said that on their fourth voyage to the Americas, Christopher Columbus saved himself and the lives of his companions because of his foreknowledge of an eclipse. Columbus had carried with him a number of calendars, among which was the two-colour *Calendarium* of the astrologer Regiomontanus, issued in Venice by Ratoldt in 1485 (figure 11). The detail below reproduces the relevant section from the six blocks of eclipses marked down by the printer for the period between 1497 and 1504. This section shows the eclipse of the Moon for 29 February 1504, which was expected to last for 1 hour and 46 minutes:

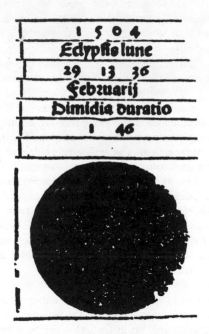

As it happened, Columbus and his men were captured by Indians, and it was only the leader's memory of this plate which gave him an edge over the hostile natives. With a foreknowledge of the imminent eclipse, he was able to save his own life, and those of his companions, by reason of the fear he inspired among the Indians, who saw his knowledge of the Cosmos as something god-like.[8] Just as Joshua had once commanded the Sun to stand still, it seemed that Columbus had commanded the Moon to darken.

At least the Amerindians who released their European captives displayed a sense of wonder, and recognized that knowledge of such things was indeed a sign of spirit. How different is this account from that offered by a missionary, William Wyatt Gill, concerning an eclipse he witnessed in Rarotonga. The natives in his charge had been converted from their 'heathenism', and although they watched the eclipse for almost one and a half hours, until sight of it was obscured by clouds, the natives (much to the delight of Gill) practised none of their pre-conversion rituals to prevent the darkening of the Sun. Their priests did not begin their accustomed rhythmic chant, begging the solar god Tangaloa to give them back their beloved Sun. They seemed no longer to believe that the hungry demon Gangarod had swallowed up the Sun, and might be persuaded by prayers and rituals to vomit the bright morsel up again.[9]

A similar victory of intellect over emotions (we might also call it supression of imagination) was displayed much earlier than in nineteenth-century Rarotonga. The Roman Army had frequently been sent into panic by both lunar and solar eclipses – especially by those which occurred before or during battles. The fears of the soldiery had been fed by a multitude of superstitions which would have made Shakespeare's description of the prodigies preceding Caesar's death seem tame. Knowing that there was to be a solar eclipse on his birthday in AD 45, Claudius wisely decided to limit any panic by issuing a proclamation which predicted the precise time of the eclipse. The official document announced the duration of the eclipse, explained the mechanism involved, and gave an account of why it was inevitable.[10]

It took almost two thousand years for the fear to be replaced by romance, and the romance to be replaced by that sort of nonchalance that looked to other things than the eclipsing bodies themselves. Writing in 1886, Sir Robert Stawell Ball, Andrews Professor of Astronomy at Dublin and Royal Astronomer of Ireland, was interested only in the value of the eclipse to science, and seems to have lost the feeling of sanctity the experience carried in earlier times.

> The few minutes during which a total eclipse lasts are of the most priceless value to the astronomer. Darkness reigns over the earth, and in that darkness rare and beautiful sights can be witnessed.[11]

Somehow, the attitude of the Amerindians who permitted the eclipse of 1504 to save Columbus seems more spiritually healthy – more human – than the scientific and mechanistic diagrams favoured by such astronomers as Ball – diagrams which really explain nothing at all about the miracle of these cosmic alignments. Professor Ball was not to know that in 1913, one of the five eclipses of that year would fall on a planet in his own horoscope, presaging his death.[12] This was a language of eclipses which the professor never learned.

The story of Columbus and the Amerindian natives has a curious relevance, for, almost before I begin to look into these mysteries, I must define an awkward word. This is the term *native* which, even when used in an astrological context, often leads to confusion. The word is from the Latin *natus*, 'birth', which gave us our familiar modern word 'nativity', and reminds us that the Italians still call the birthday *il natale*. In astrology, the *native* is the person for whom a chart has been cast. Horoscopes themselves are sometimes called 'nativities', yet, as we shall discover, not all horoscopes are cast for the moment of birth.

It is likely that the earliest documented eclipse was that which took place on 19 March 721 BC. This was a lunar eclipse, visible from Babylon – at that time the most important centre of astronomical studies.[13] Although it is clear from surviving documents that the Babylonians understood the mechanism of eclipses, this did not rid the world of superstitious notions about what caused them.[14] Even the later Greeks seem to have been constantly surprised by these cosmic events, and often either regarded them as spiritual happenings worthy of fear, or interpreted them as special omens: 'Zeus, father of the Olympians, made night from mid-day, hiding the light of the shining Sun, and sore fear came upon men.'[15]

This is from a fragmentary survival of a lost poem by Archilochus of Paros. Some scholars take it to be a reference to his first-hand experience of the total eclipse of the Sun that took place on 6 April 648 BC.[16]

In a later Pythian Ode, which Pindar addressed to the Thebans, the poet takes an eclipse of the Sun as his theme, opening with the lines which connect the all-seeing eye of the Sun with human sight – a tradition which still pertains in modern astrology, but which was ancient even in the days of Pindar among the Egyptian priests.[17] Pindar also recognizes in the poem that what happens in the heavens affects events on the mortal plane:

> Beams of the Sun! O thou that seest far . . . O mother of mine eyes! O star supreme, reft from us in the daylight. Why hast thou perplexed the power of man and the tenor of wisdom, by rushing forth on so darksome a track?[18]

It is likely that the poem concerns the solar eclipse of 30 April 463 BC, which was almost total at Thebes.

Besides observing eclipses, and expecting their poets to lament the passing of the Sun, the ancients also used eclipses. Few things can be more supportive of the fact that the ancients regarded eclipses as windows of opportunity than the traditions relating to the founding of Rome by Romulus, for this was involved with eclipse lore. According to the Roman astrologer, Tarutius, the founder of Rome was conceived while the Sun was in total eclipse,[19] while Plutarch recorded that Romulus was supposed to have founded the city when the Sun was eclipsed by the Moon.[20]

Perhaps the most famous of the ancient eclipses was the total solar of 28 May 585 BC. According to some people, it was the first eclipse of ancient times to have been predicted, by the philosopher Thales, but it seems that Thales merely indicated the year when it would happen, rather than its time or date.[21] Thales certainly knew that the Moon was eclipsed when it passed through the shadow of the Earth.[22]

This same eclipse has a double fame, for it was mentioned by Herodotus as taking place during a battle between the Lydians and the Medes. The event was so frightening to the soldiers that they stopped fighting.

There is a fine wood-engraved illustration by V. Le Campion to a modern edition of the works of the Greek historian, Herodotus, which depicts an eclipse (figure 12), and which may point to this very incident.[23] However, in his *Histories* Herodotus mentions several eclipses as having influenced battles, and it is also possible that the illustration may relate to the eclipse of 17 February 478 BC, which Xerxes, the leader of the Persian hordes, witnessed shortly before mounting his expedition against Greece. The Persian commander called his soothsayers to ask them the meaning of the portent. They said that the eclipse was prophetic, and was foretelling the destruction of the Greek cities. According to these wise men, the Sun was symbol of the Persians, while the Moon was symbol of the Greeks.[24]

Le Campion's illustration (figure 12) arranged the graphics in a cosmically inaccurate way, yet in one which dramatically conveys the startling power of an eclipse. By revealing the rim of the Sun against the dark radiants, and by surrounding the intense lunar body (if you look closely at the eclipse in figure 12, you will see that this is formed by concentric circles) the artist successfully caught something of the intense drama of the eclipse.

I am reasonably certain that the lady in this picture is Clio, the goddess of History, and I suspect that she is portrayed signalling to the combatants that their conflict should end.[25] On the other hand, the figure could represent a prophetess, predicting the success of Xerxes against the lunar Greeks.

In fact, Clio would be most appropriate, given how eclipses play such an important role in writing the personal history of many individuals. This will be seen later in the examination of a number of horoscopes of the famous – all of which demonstrate in one form or another the dramatic workings of eclipses.

The one thing which astrologers seem to agree about concerning

23

eclipses is that their effects are dramatic – often awesome. At one time, the reputation of eclipses was linked with more than drama – it was widely believed that eclipses caused most of the ills of mankind. This was possibly one reason why eclipses were so dreaded in early times.

In the fourteenth century, many European astrologers traced the beginnings and duration of the terrible plague of 1345, which we now call the Black Death, to the lunar eclipse which occurred on the evening of 18 March 1345. Following astrological tradition, few astrologers of the day claimed that the eclipse actually *started* the plague, yet some at least were convinced that its explosive charge came merely at a difficult cosmic moment.[26]

The eclipse was exact at 9:28 pm, with Moon in 7 degrees of Libra. I have calculated these figures for Oxford, England, in order to compare them with the data recorded by the thirteenth–century French astrologer, Geoffrey of Meaux, who paid especial attention to the Black Death.[27] One contemporary manuscript by Geoffrey (or, at least, a fourteenth–century mediaeval copy), is still in Oxford, in the Bodleian Library: from his writings, it seems that Geoffrey was studying, and perhaps observing the skies, in this city. Geoffrey tells us that the eclipse took place one hour after the rising of the Moon, and was visible for a considerable time.[28]

The difficult cosmic moment was represented by powerful groupings of the remaining planets into two zodiacal signs.[29] Curiously, the several astrologers who have left records relating to this day do not appear to have seen its underlying significance, which is that, when the eclipse was first formed, the planets (with the exception of the Moon) were huddled together either in the sign Aquarius, or in Aries.[30] In fact, had the mediaeval astronomers been aware of the existence of the planets discovered since, Uranus, Neptune and Pluto, they would have been tempted to read even more doleful consequences into the effects which this eclipse sparked off. The chart opposite illustrates the skies at the time of this lunar eclipse, with the planets disposed in two massive groups in the airy Aquarius (♒) and the fiery Aries (♈).

Modern planets or not, it is unlikely that anything more doleful than the Black Death had been experienced in late mediaeval Europe, and it is not surprising that many astrologers of that period had something to say about its cosmic origins and likely consequences.

Spreading along the trade–routes from China, the plague had reached Egypt by 1348, and very quickly spread into Europe. In the same year it was rampant in Weymouth, and by the next year it had killed off a third of the population of England. It lasted in Europe for four years. In fact, the Black Death was the most important event in Europe during that century, and its effects lasted for several decades due to the huge reduction in population. It left Europe with more casualties than were

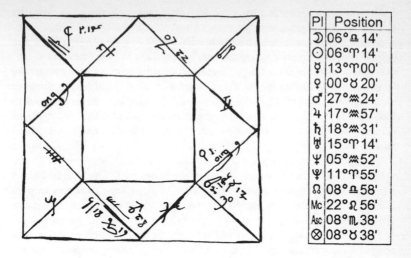

Pl	Position
☽	06°♎14'
☉	06°♈14'
☿	13°♈00'
♀	00°♉20'
♂	27°♒24'
♃	17°♒57'
♄	18°♒31'
♅	15°♈14'
♆	05°♒52'
♇	11°♈55'
☊	08°♎58'
Mc	22°♌56'
Asc	08°♏38'
⊗	08°♉38'

seen in the two major wars of the twentieth century. In England and France alone, at least one third – possibly over a half – of the population died. It is claimed that between 1347 and 1351, 75 million people died of the disease.

Of course, the Death (as it was called) did not reach Europe until some time after the eclipse of 1345. Under normal circumstances this might lead us to question if it were correct to link the eclipse with an event which materialized just over three years later. In fact, as we shall see, this discrepancy in times is quite in accord with the mediaeval astrological theory of eclipse-prediction.

According to Geoffrey of Meaux, the eclipse lasted for 3 hours, 29 minutes and 54 seconds. This precision of timing, in an age when the mechanical clock had not been developed to any standards of precision, should encourage us to ask, why was the astrologer so keen to determine the duration of the eclipse?[31]

As we shall see, the astrological tradition has always insisted that, from a knowledge of the duration of a particular eclipse, a good astrologer would be able to work out just how long it would continue to exert an effect on the mundane, or earthly, plane. In other words, given that Geoffrey could foresee the effect of the eclipse, he was keen to establish just how long it would be before the terrible scourge of the Death would begin, and how long it would last.[32]

Geoffrey's own method of calculating this period is not one that would be used by modern astrologers, but he concluded that the plague would last for five years and five months. In actual fact, he seems to have been out by about one year.

Had Geoffrey applied the traditional rules – that the effect of the eclipse will last for an equivalent number of years as hours of duration in the eclipse itself – then his prediction would have been more accurate. Give or take a month or so, the three hours and twenty-nine minutes would project into three and a half years. The plague is generally said to have begun in 1347, and to have come to an end in 1351. In terms of eclipse-theory, then, it began within the prescribed period, and ended within a similar period.

The question remains, was the Black Death actually *predicted*, from the eclipse? It is difficult to answer this question with any certainty, for although several fourteenth-century manuscripts lay claim to the prediction, it is not always possible to determine which of these were written after the event.

I should point out right away that a prediction of such an event as a plague, based merely upon a study of an eclipse, is very unlikely. It is, of course, quite possible to predict from a personal chart whether a person might suffer from, or die from, a particular disease or illness, but it is quite a different thing to predict mass contagions merely from eclipses.

Generally speaking, fourteenth-century predictions based on even less dramatic horoscopes than the one we are considering were fairly doleful. John of Bassigny appears to have predicted for the middle of the thirteenth century 'a general mortality and pest' which would carry off two thirds of the population, and last for 35 years. The basis for his predictions is far from clear, yet he does mention the conjunction (not the eclipse) of 1345. At least one of his predictions – that, in 1356, the King of France would be captured – seems to have come true when Jean II of France was captured at Poitiers by the English.

The fifteenth-century Abbot Trithemius – one of the great scholars of arcane lore, who was intimately familiar with the astrological literature of the preceding centuries – was of the opinion that the Black Death *had* been predicted. From his extensive record we note the dramatic prediction of 'pestilence and terrible and incalculable loss of human life through the whole world'. The modern historian, Lynn Thorndike (who recorded the Trithemius summary) noted that one remarkable feature in it was the suggestion that the spread of the plague was due to 'tiny beasts'.[33] In the fourteenth and fifteenth centuries, it was believed that the contagion was carried in the air (hence the importance of the lunar eclipse in the air-sign of Libra, and the gathering of planets in the air-sign Aquarius). It was not until medical investigations into a plague that ravaged Bombay in 1896 that scientists recognized that the bubonic plague was transmitted by fleas.

The striking thing is that the eclipse of March 1895 (when the Indian plague is said to have started) was in the same degree as that eclipse which is claimed to have begun the mediaeval Black Death which, from 1345 onwards, wiped out millions of people in Europe.

SOLAR ECLIPSE OF 26 MARCH 1895:　　　　　05.31 ARIES
SOLAR ECLIPSE OF 18 MARCH 1345:　　　　　06.14 ARIES

Very little study has been done of the relationship between eclipses and diseases, yet there does appear to be some connection between this degree of the Aries-Libra axis and epidemics. In 1876 there was an outbreak of plague in India, which became so virulently epidemic that it even attracted a special report from the bureaucracies of the British government in India. On 25 March 1876, there had been a solar eclipse in 5.32 Aries. The year 1894 saw a vast sweep of plague through Iran and central Asia, through Russia, as far as China. Although this had begun late in the previous year, there was a solar eclipse on 29 September 1894 in 6.04 Libra, on the same Aries-Libra axis.

Nowadays, with our advanced knowledge of medicine, it might be foolish to suggest that eclipses are in any way connected with epidemics, such as the Black Death. However, even while I agree that much of the super-stition attached to eclipses should be discounted, I have to say that all too often the symbolic language in which astrologers of the past expressed themselves is not always fully understood in modern times. What may appear as rank superstition to us was often nothing other than intelligent symbolism to them.

An example of this may be seen in accounts of the gem called the *glossopetra*. This magical stone was said to be shaped like a human tongue, and was believed to fall from the sky during a lunar eclipse. The stone was much sought after as an aid to *selenomancy*, the art of divination by means of the Moon.

The superstition may sound foolish now, yet there lies behind it an arcane meaning. It was once believed – and with good cause – that at the moment of eclipse the whole world changed for the duration of that eclipse. It was believed that during this period mankind had an oppor-tunity to communicate with the gods: the tongue-like stone was a sign that such communication was possible. The idea behind this symbolism seems to have been that the shadow-cone which anchored the Moon to the Earth was a sort of dark pathway, or tunnel of spirit, which offered an unusual opportunity to contact the gods.

I suspect that many of the old rituals connected with the recognition of the new Moon (over) are survivals of a time when priests signalled that the

pathway to the gods had been closed – a closure announced cosmically by the emergence of the new crescent.

This idea of there being a periodic 'pathway to the gods' explains why some occultists have insisted that eclipses are cosmic safety valves, which periodically allow evil forces to escape into the Cosmos, where they will be of no harm to mankind. At the solar eclipses, such contact and communication with the gods was believed to be of an altogether different order – even more sacred and powerful. According to certain occult theories, the shadow-lane of the solar eclipse permitted initiated priests to communicate with the higher gods, and put to them questions of profound importance. Some scholars maintain that this was the underlying reason why the ancients built the mysterious stone circles which are still scattered through parts of northern Europe (figure 13). By means of these circles, the priests were able to predict with great accuracy the coming of eclipses, and at these august times communicate with the gods. The idea of human sacrifices (which are now inexorably linked with such stone circles) may have been a degenerate idea that at the sacred moment when the cosmic pathway was opened, the gods should be propitiated.

28

It is only in relatively modern times that astronomers have begun to realize that the ancient stone circles and megaliths which are found in such abundance in Europe are astronomical observatories. This discovery, which seems to have dawned on several individuals at approximately the same time, has led to some extravagant and imaginative claims about these ancient circles. For example, it has been suggested that the more complex circles, such as Stonehenge, Avebury and Callanish, are megalithic computers. This is far from the truth, yet there may be no doubt whatsoever that such circles were constructed to serve (among other things) as predictors of solar and lunar phenomena. While scarcely megalithic computers, the circles and related structures do appear to have been designed as sophisticated solar and lunar calendars.

Because they are calendars, the more complex of the circles (and this includes the famous Stonehenge) are inevitably linked with the phenomenon of eclipses. This truth was recognized by intelligent arcanists in the nineteenth century, long before modern astronomers began to suspect that the circles were linked with solar-lunar phenomena. The esotericist Rudolf Steiner[34] indicated that the ancient Northern Mystery schools made use of the stone circles to study cosmic phenomena. He argued that it was important that they should be able to predict eclipses because they recognized the special relationship that priests had with the spiritual world during them.

Of course, in terms of modern thinking, this idea seems far-fetched, yet it is probably much nearer to the truth than the degraded image we have of the Druid priests offering human sacrifices on the stones, for their own sacerdotal purposes (figure 13).

The secrets of the ancient stone circles may never be revealed now. Not only has our view of the purpose of life changed, but it is very evident that the human psyche has also changed considerably in the past four or five thousand years. The one thing we may be sure about is that the circles and cairns of the ancient world were all attempts to build links between man and the cosmos by way of Sun and Moon. Since such structures measure with extraordinary precision the positions of these luminaries (and in some cases important fixed stars), we may be certain that they also were used to predict eclipses.

While by means of advanced mathematics it is possible to calculate the times of eclipses, there is no simple eclipse cycle by which astronomers can predict total solar eclipses for a given place, or locality. If there is a vast cycle of eclipses *that pertain to place as well as time*, these have not yet been recognized. It would, therefore, be foolish to imagine that Stonehenge or any stone circle would serve in ancient times as an accurate 'computer' of eclipses. Even so, it is reasonable to assume that the circles, outliers and movable sticks or stones (which could be lodged in holes, as markers) would permit the ancient astronomers to work out the extreme positions of Sun and Moon, which are important for gaining some approximate idea of the timing of eclipses.

In ancient times, it must have been far from easy to predict the timing of visible lunar eclipses,[35] while the timing and siting of visible solar eclipses must have been even more difficult. Something of this difficulty may be gleaned from a diagram drawn to represent the area of visibility of the solar eclipse of 1919.

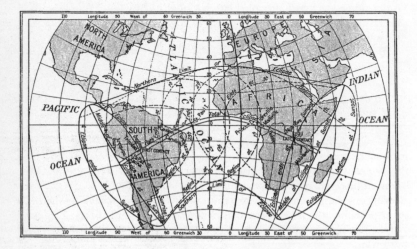

This eclipse, which occurred in 8 degrees of Gemini, has become famous because it was used to prove Einstein's theory that light was subject to the pull of gravity. Accordingly, the pattern it left on the surface of the Earth has been reproduced in many astronomical journals and books.[36] The path of the shadow traced by the eclipse ran across Africa, the Atlantic and South America (above), lasting for a brief 6 minutes 61 seconds. What is important about this diagram is that it indicates the very narrow path along the longitudinal curvature of the Earth in which the eclipse would appear to be total: this is the narrow yet extensive arc in the centre of the diagram above.

The visibility of a lunar eclipse is entirely different, for it is apparent wherever the Moon can be seen. If one compares this limited locality of the solar eclipse with what happens during a lunar eclipse, one immediately sees why the ancients would be more likely to be successful in recording, in their stone monuments, the recurrence of lunar eclipses than the solar eclipses. This comparison suggests the stone monuments, in so far as they were used to anticipate eclipses, were probably more concerned with lunar eclipses than solar ones.

In the early 1960s, the astronomer Gerald Hawkins, using computer programs, realized that an eclipse (of Sun or Moon) occurred when the full Moon, near to the time of the winter solstice, rose above the Heel Stone to the north-east of the main circle of sarsens at Stonehenge:

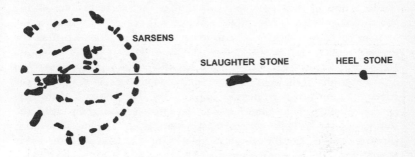

In the diagram, the straight line from the centre of the sarsens circle, running along the so-called Slaughter Stone and the Heel Stone, indicates the line of visibility of such a full Moon. Less than half the eclipses that followed this Heel Stone rising would be visible from the Salisbury plains. However, since a considerable number would be visible, Hawkins was led to suspect that this Heel Stone winter rising might be regarded by the priests (or astronomers) who constructed the circle as a kind of eclipse-warning.

After considerable research, Hawkins came to the conclusion that the arrangement of upright stones and 'Aubrey holes' (noted by the antiquary John Aubrey in 1666) around the site, were linked with three lunar periods of 19 + 19 + 18 years – that is a cycle of 56 years. This periodicity was reflected in the number of Aubrey holes, which was exactly 56. Although Hawkins's theory is fairly complicated (and has not gone without substantial criticism in astronomical circles), the upshot of his proposal was that the megaliths and the holes were used in ancient times for computing future eclipses, and as an indicator of lunar cycles.[37]

There are the remains of about 500 stone circles and avenues in Europe (the majority sited in Britain). Many of these reveal to investigators a glimpse of extraordinary astronomical knowledge of lunar and solar phenomena, suggesting that the ancient megalithic builders had a more sophisticated grasp of cosmic rhythms than is generally realized. Familiarity with these ancient structures suggests that the ancients had some system for predicting eclipses which we have not yet reduplicated. I can make this claim because of the quite extraordinary sophistication of

31

the measurements involved in so many of the megalithic solar and lunar observatories.

In fact, some of the refinements in the system of megalithic solar-lunar measurements are so precise as to be almost beyond belief. In consequence, a few of the ancient circles, temples and cairns of Europe are among the unacknowledged wonders of the ancient world. Almost every one of these megalithic calendars has its hidden mystery.

For example, it is now recognized that the 'solar temple' of the megalithic complex of Mnajdra, in Malta, was designed to measure the extreme solstitial positions. The following simplified ground-plan of the massive stones in this single temple, which is part of the Mnajdra complex, indicates the nature of this orientation. The first rays of the Sun on the morning of the Winter Solstice throw a vertical slit of light on the edge of the northernmost marker stone at WS. The first rays of the Sun on the morning of the Summer Solstice throw a vertical slit upon the southernmost edge of the vertical marker stone at SS. The line which runs through the centre of the temple (S) marks the direction of the first rays of sunlight at the Equinox, from the east:

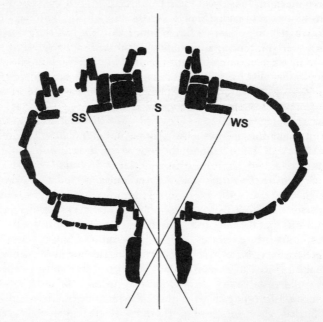

Now, this sort of precision of building is one thing, for it is quite possible (over a number of years) to construct such a monument purely by means of direct measurements of the annual solar extremes. However, quite a different level of cosmic awareness is involved in the marking of stones (within the same solar temple) which takes into account the slow movement of the solstice point due to a decrease in the declination of the Sun over a vast period of time.

Yet – remarkable as it may seem, such a difficulty was overcome by these megalithic builders, who foresaw and made provision for changes in these periodicities. At Mnajdra, the need to allow for this slow solar displacement is reflected in the arrangements the builders made to allow the first light-slit of the solstitial winter sun to move gradually across the flat surface of an upright stone (WS in the diagram). The annual effect is quite marvellous. When the Sun is half risen over the horizon to the south-east of the temple, on the morning of the Winter Solstice, a vertical slit of sunlight (channelled by the upright stones framing the south and north of the entrance to the temple) falls on the edge of stone WS.

As the astronomer Paul Micallef has shown, the displacement of this vertical slit of light (after a period estimated at 5,689 years) was 15.6 cms.[38] This eventual displacement must have been recognized by the ancients, because the outer edge of the stone was positioned to mark the most northerly slit, and the east-facing vertical face of the stone was designed to receive the subsequent movement of this slit, with the passing of millennia. It will take approximately 9,500 years for the slit of light to move to its extreme southerly position, before beginning the slow return journey (of about 12,600 years) back to its original position, at the very edge of the stone, occupied in 3700 BC. These periods of time are vast, yet it is evident that the displacement was accommodated by the megalithic builders.

The designation 'solar temple' used for this part of what is an intricate observatory system at Mnajdra is modern, and probably not altogether accurate. While it is quite clear that the orientation of the huge stones is intended to serve as a solar calendar, the small porthole 'windows' in its fabric imply that on very rare occasions the same 'astronomical instrument' would be a measure of lunar phenomena, *including lunar eclipses.*

An equally impressive, and no less ancient, use of light-magic may be seen in an even more sophisticated astronomical stonework in one of the cairns at Loughcrew, in Ireland. Long thought to be burial mounds, these cairns are now seen for what they were – solar predictors. The passages have various symbols incised upon them, but the most impressive series is on the backstone of the 17-foot long Cairn T, which is richly incised with solar symbols and leaf-patterns (over). Modern research has confirmed that these were designed to record minute fluctuations in the patterns of sunlight that fall upon this stone at certain times of the year.

During the 5,000 years of the Cairn's existence, the position of the Winter Solstice has moved about one degree further north from its original position, and therefore the beam does not fall with quite the precision as before. Even so, as Tim O'Brien has shown, the patterns on the stones still record the daily fluctuations of direct sunlight, according to a precisely drawn series of vertical and horizontal lines.[39]

I have attempted to reconstruct one of these effects from photographs I made at Loughcrew a few years ago, showing a corner of the sunlight, falling on what at first appear to be 'leaf-patterns', but which the sunlight effects reveal to be spatially interlinked ladders, or calibrations. The two relevant patterns incised on the backstone look like this:

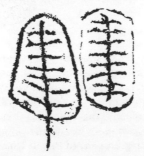

On certain days of the year, the sunlight is thrown down the long passageway of the cairn, to fall in an oblong of glowing light upon the backstone. The patterns, such as ladders, sunbursts and circles, incised on the backstone (of which the two 'leaves' above are samples) are designed to record various stages in the diurnal passage of this oblong of sunlight.

In effect, the four sides of the oblongs of light which are thrown upon the patterns of this back-wall are marked by the calibrations within these patterns. In the diagram below I have represented the way in which the two adjacent 'ladders' combine to record the passage of the Sun during two adjacent days. This record is made by means of two markers - one of which is vertical, the other horizontal.

The two schematic diagrams below show the corner of the lighted oblong which is thrown upon the patterns on consecutive days (15 and 16 September, in modern times). The movement of the sunlight on the two days is marked by two interlinked steps on the ladders. When the vertical of the lighted oblong falls on the vertical of the left-hand leaf, on the first day, the top horizontal of the oblong of light is at the topmost 'step' of the ladder. On the following day, when the left-hand vertical of light falls on the same vertical of the left-hand ladder, the sunlight is measured two 'steps' lower down on the adjacent ladder.

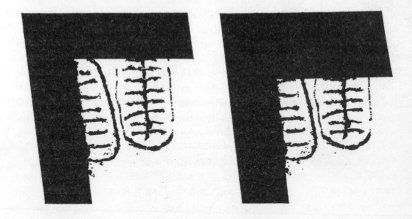

O'Brien's careful study of these patterns has shown that the equinoctial solar pattern incised on the backstone is so carefully designed that it reveals the minute solar fluctuation of the equinox cycle of four years.[40]

The incredible precision of measurement involved in the two astronomical devices which I have studied here, in places as widely separated as Malta and Ireland, reflect an ancient knowledge of astronomy that is quite extraordinary. In view of this, it would be foolish to imagine that the ancients had not developed some method for predicting the timing of solar and lunar eclipses – even if the precise viewing-sites of the solar eclipses were beyond their reach.

There is an important reason why I have chosen to illustrate the fact that, in spite of all the difficulties attendant upon such construction, the stone circles and cairns were built as eclipse-predictors. This reason is connected with the fact that the arcane literature insists that the ancients recognized the effects and importance of eclipses in their spiritual lives. The cairn passageways were themselves little more than constructed shadow-cones, which paralleled in their operation the shadow-cones which cause both lunar and solar eclipses. The porthole systems (such as we see in Mnajdra) and the passages we see in such places as Loughcrew are little more than sophisticated cameras, working not with chemically stilled images, but with living and moving ones, and in this context we must see them as the most extraordinary survival of ancient astronomy.

This idea of eclipses providing 'tunnels into the spiritual world' is expressed very graphically in the most ancient of the hermetic literature that has survived from Egyptian occult lore. In the writings of the priest of Delphi, Plutarch, we find a statement that a lunar eclipse is viewed as the equivalent of the god Osiris being laid in his coffin.[41] The same text reveals that 'the shadow of the earth into which they think the Moon has fallen and is eclipsed' is called Typhon. The significance of this becomes clear when we learn that Typhon was one of the names for Set, the chief deity of the powers of Evil, who manifested in the form of a serpent, named Apep. It seems that even the ancient snake – the Old Serpent – that dwelt in the garden of Eden was linked originally with the lunar eclipse, and with the shadowy lightless tunnels in which such eclipses take place.

The later Roman historians seem to have come closer to the earth, and often regarded eclipses in almost anthropomorphic terms. In their view, an eclipse was a sign of the distress of Nature at the calamities of the Earth. Around this idea of a weeping Nature, there grew many curious tales: the Roman historians insist that there was a darkness for six hours when Romulus, the founder of their city died. Just so, the darkness which fell over the Earth at the death of Christ on the hill of Golgotha was said to last six hours. What these Roman stories had in common with the Egyptian is that emphasis was placed on the darkness – upon the shadows – rather than upon the eclipse itself.

It may well be that the so-called 'solar eclipse' that is supposed to have occurred at the Crucifixion of Christ is more than symbolic of the occulting of the Light. In hermetic literature, it is pointed out that just as the star which led the Magi to the new-born Jesus was not an ordinary star[42] so the darkness which shrouded the Earth at the death of Christ was caused by no ordinary eclipse. This hermetic thought is important, for it reminds us that at the moment of this sacrifice – unique in the history of the world – the Earth was literally darkened, as the evil which had been overcome by Christ's death fled the world. We are reminded of this unique cosmic moment by tens of thousands of paintings and woodcuts that show Sun and Moon on either side of the crucified Christ.

A similar, if less dramatic link is drawn between the lunar eclipse and demonic powers in a considerable body of pagan literature. In one of the Mayan chronicles, it was said that during a solar eclipse, 'a monster plunged head down towards the earth during the time of darkness'.[43] It is of course possible to regard this description as arising from poetic licence – but suppose that it was not poetic licence? Suppose that the initiate priests who conducted the Mayan rituals could see on the Astral plane – suppose they had this 'vision of the tunnel'? If they had this vision – and if they had or pretended to have magical abilities – they would no doubt use that period to propitiate the demons or spiritual beings involved. It would therefore be of paramount importance that the priests should have some idea as to when eclipses were going to fall.

Of course, this approach to eclipses is not one favoured in modern times – perhaps, indeed, that interior vision or faculty which permitted priests to converse with the Cosmos by means of eclipses is no longer accessible to modern man. We are all too easily persuaded to think of the megalithic builders as being backward versions of ourselves – when, in truth, the evidence suggests that the most highly evolved among the ancients had an extraordinary knowledge of the skies, as of architectural principles and engineering. Perhaps, along with these talents, they also possessed an inner spiritual vision which we have lost?

The remarkable Henry Wansey, who seems to have been the first to explore Stonehenge as an astronomical calendar, had intuited this truth in 1796. He wrote that 'learned Brahmins' (at that time believed by Europeans to be highly respected savants versed in higher magic) might comprehend more of the design of the famous circle than Wansey's contemporaries.[44] Wansey was recognizing that the real mystery of Stonehenge lies not merely in its stone structure, but in the spiritual purpose which must have lain behind its construction.

This feeling for the relationship between man's vision and the power of eclipses may be seen in a very simple woodcut from the title page of a Spanish book on optics, published in 1623.[45]

The pair of spectacles which dominate this woodcut are inset with images of Sun and Moon. This is quite in accord with the arcane astrological tradition, which held that the right eye of men and women is ruled by the Sun, the left eye by the Moon – a tradition that may be traced back to the hermetic lore of ancient Egypt. What is quite fascinating about this woodcut is that between the two spectacles is a curious arrow,

CON PRIVILEGIO.
Impreſſo en Seuilla, por Diego Perez Año de 1623.

pointing to a small image of an eye, beneath the arch of the bridge. It might be tempting to link this tiny eye with the hermetic tradition of the third eye of inner vision, yet this would be a mistake. In this particular case, the middle eye is intended to refer to ordinary vision. The idea behind this crude-seeming image is that when we look into the world, with our Sun and Moon eyes, our brain creates the illusion of our *looking into the world with only a single eye*. Our brain makes a single order from the outer duality, which engenders the perceptive act. Thus, the symbolism points to a physiological and spiritual truth. We perceive reality aright only when our personal Sun and Moon align, in the equivalent of a single tunnel vision.

The implications behind this simple idea are quite remarkable, for the small central eye, which symbolizes the inner vision, points to a mystical chemistry that takes place in the brain – of which the physical eyes are extensions. The optic nerves which connect the eyes to the brain are in esoteric terms the equivalent of the shadow-tunnels which, in the outer cosmos, connect Sun, Moon and Earth in an eclipse.

This insight into the connection between vision and the eclipse has not been lost on esotericists. Within the deeper levels of esoteric thought, the eclipse in the macrocosm is the equivalent of a blink in the microcosm, or little world of man. Something of the implications of this connection between the blink of an eye and the more extensive periodic equivalent of the Cosmos has been explored by the modern esotericist, Rodney Collin, who pointed out that one thirtieth of a second is 'a moment of recognition', which is the time taken, under normal circumstances, to perceive and identify a physical object. It is also very close to the time of a blink of the eye.

Rodney Collin, after introducing the curious fact that at certain total eclipses the disc of the Moon fits exactly over that of the Sun, remarks that this is so well known that no-one even considers it extraordinary.[46] Yet, as he indicates, if the Moon were a hundred or so miles wider, or a few thousand or so miles further away from the Earth, this total eclipse would not be possible. The cosmos seems to have been carefully orchestrated to permit eclipses which allow Moon and Sun to cancel each other out.

I have already written about an eclipse being a shadow-tunnel: in a solar eclipse, the tunnel seems to lead through the body of the Moon into the Sun. In a lunar eclipse, the tunnel seems to lead directly to the dark Moon. It is this latter form of eclipse which has troubled esotericists, and enlivened the imaginations of poets. The lunar eclipse seems to represent the bewitching hour of the Cosmos, the death of the sun-god Osiris due to the machinations of the evil Set, when the fragile human imagination is subjected to a tremendous onslaught. Those who have attempted to feel the effect of a lunar eclipse, by means of directed attention or meditation, have no difficulty in appreciating why the ancients called such a phenomenon 'evil', or 'demonic'.

Even the two most dramatic colours of the lunar eclipse seem to betoken a presage of evil. The most disturbing is the red eclipse, closely followed by the disorientating black eclipse.

A red eclipse – sometimes called in mediaeval literature, an 'eclipse of blood' – is one in which the fully eclipsed Moon appears in a coppery-red colour. This effect is due to the refraction effects of the atmosphere which lies between the Earth and the Moon, yet it can have the effect of making the lunar face look dramatically bloody.

A black eclipse is a lunar eclipse that occurs when the Earth's atmosphere is heavy with suspended dust. Under such conditions, the refraction of sunlight in the upper atmosphere is absorbed and the disk of the Moon cannot be seen. The Moon disappears altogether in the shadow of the Earth. A black eclipse of this kind was that recorded on 19 December 1964, in 28 degrees of Gemini. In this case, the dust-pollution was from excessive volcanic activity.

The evil Set of the ancient Egyptian mythology was sometimes called the 'black god', and at other times 'the red-eyed god'. This nuance of lunar association is deepened in other attributes of Set, the shadow god. One of the magical amulets, which was contrasted in power with the Udjat, or 'Eye of Horus', was the 'Eye of Set', made from the left-eye, linked with the Moon. The importance of the Eye in Egyptian mythology, and its cosmic link with both eclipses and mysteries of perception, are attested in numerous images of the left or right eye. This example from

39

the Egyptian *Book of the Dead* is typical, showing the sacred eye in the hand of Thoth, the god of wisdom:

The significance of this Eye of Set was linked with one of the most important primeval symbols of the ancient Egyptians, the solar bird – the falcon. The right eye of this bird was said to be the Sun, the left was said to be the Moon. It has been pointed out by several Egyptologists[47] that behind the mystic cosmic falcon there stood an almost forgotten deity, called by the Egyptians 'the one who commands both eyes'. This hidden face seemed to be the inner man, the spiritual being, who reconciled the duality of Sun and Moon. The deity was the equivalent of the perceptive act, which welded together the two divergent streams of light which entered the two eyes, into one single perception. Within this ancient theosophy, the shadow lunar deity was as important as the light-filled solar deity.

Human recognition is a very complex process, involved with light streaming into the dark tunnel of the optic nerve, where by some alchemy which is not at all understood, it is translated not only into pictures, but into perceptions involving meanings. In former times, there was no doubt in the spiritual centres that guided mankind that there was an inner vision that was just as valid as the outer vision. Today, the inner vision seems to have almost atrophied, or to have become the subject of humorous pictures. That opposite illustrates the interiorizing effect of certain hallucinogenic drugs as a human vision, unaccustomed to the Astral plane, is compelled to swim within it.

Is it far-fetched to link the cosmic 'blink' of solar and lunar eclipses with the development of higher meanings – with that inner vision that could seek out cosmic meanings? If such a link is valid, then it would explain at least one reason why the ancient priests were so anxious to construct buildings which would reveal the lunar and solar rhythms behind eclipses.

The mystery of sight – of how the sunlight is transformed by the two shadow tunnels which link with the brain, so as to turn light into a meaningful vision – is one of the perennial mysteries of arcane literature and art. A most remarkable modern painting, by the Jewish artist, Fay

Pomerance, deals in compelling imagery with this arcane connection between vision and eclipses (above).[48] The underlying theme is progression from darkness to light – a parable for the evolution of humanity from a backward animal-like state to a more spiritual stage of human development. The dark, inchoate group to the left are the mass of undeveloped human souls, from which breaks loose a single human, who moves towards the lighted disk to the extreme right. As the figure moves, he plucks at a long fleshy tube which extrudes from his forehead, and which seems to be transformed in its descent to the earth from light into darkness.

This tube is a play on the inner vision, for it is nothing more than an extension of the optic nerve projected into space, rather than into the brain. Fay Pomerance seemed intent on portraying a man (who stands between the undeveloped mass of inchoate humanity, and the highly developed figure to the right) who lives as though immersed in an inner realm – as though for him the outer were the inner: he is a clairvoyant who is sustained by an inner vision. This is a symbol of the atavistic clairvoyance which is still found undeveloped in many individuals even today.

In contrast, the kneeling figure to the right has been plunged into the outer vision. The optic nerve now connects with the inner brain, and he worships the disk in the skies. But, what is this disk? In keeping with the theme of the picture as a whole – which deals with the progression from darkness to light – the disk itself contains darkness and light, for it is a portrayal of a solar eclipse. The disk is marked with the shadow of the lunar crescent, which indicates that the circle of light represents the Moon. Behind it (as in a similar eclipse in figure 1) the rays of the Sun stream out to indicate that the Sun itself is being occulted, in a total eclipse. The play on light and darkness, or inner and outer, on inner clairvision and outer vision, is entirely in accord with the deepest levels of hermetic speculation.

Does the world change in some way at the moment of an eclipse? Incredibly, scientific evidence suggests that it does. Modern research has shown that liquids and substances immersed in liquids change in some inexplicable way. The implications of this are extraordinary, bearing in mind that our physical bodies are vertical columns consisting of about 80 per cent water.

The science of capillary-dynamolysis was developed by Dr L. Kolisko in the 1920s, at the suggestion of the esotericist, Rudolf Steiner. Her painstaking researches showed beyond all doubt that filterpaper pictures of plant-saps changed fundamentally during eclipses.[49]

The many filterpaper pictures, or chromatograms, made during solar, lunar and planetary eclipses, demonstrate that at the moment of eclipse the absorption rate and pattern of saps change radically, and according to recognized rhythmic (that is, non-chaotic) cycles. This research seems to support the astrological tradition, which maintains that the effects of eclipses are not dependent upon their being visible. The filterpaper pictures made on 29 November 1955 when the partial lunar eclipse was visible in Switzerland (where the experiments were being conducted) showed no appreciable difference from other pictures made during eclipses that could not be seen from that part of the world.

Equally interesting is the fact that the occultations, or eclipses, of other

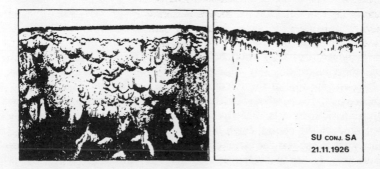

SU CONJ. SA
21.11.1926

planets with the Sun also had an effect on chromatograms, or sap-pattern pictures. The two images on page 43 contrast a normal precipitation of a lead solution on litmus paper (left) with that made during a conjunction of the Sun with the planet Saturn in 1926.[50] The precipitation pattern left during this cosmic change could hardly be more dramatically illustrated.

Dr Kolisko herself saw the results of her research as pointing to the activity of 'unknown forces' working within matter itself, in a manner which could not be grasped by ordinary chemical analysis. It is clear from some of her notes that she preferred to do her experiments during solar eclipses, and she would travel considerable distances to set up her laboratory to measure the effects of total solar eclipses where they were visible. Her study of the total eclipse of the Sun in Bordighera (Northern Italy) on 15 February 1961, and her studies of the effect of the eclipse of 1936 at Brussa (Asia Minor) on gold-chloride, were especially productive.[51]

An eclipse of the Sun takes place when the Moon passes between the Sun and the Earth, and a shadow of the Moon is projected on the face of the Earth. An eclipse of the Moon takes place when the Moon hangs in the shadow of the Earth.

The following diagram shows how an eclipse of the Moon takes place.

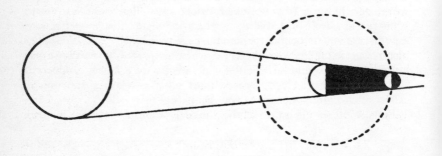

A sixteenth-century woodcut illustrates the principle fairly clearly, and in a more interesting way. The giant to the right is holding up what is in effect the shadow of the Earth, in the form of a cone. This shadow is caused by the Sun, which is in the bottom left, in the zodiacal sign Cancer. Its radiant light fills the whole Cosmos, save for that light which is occulted by the central earth (a dark mass of sky, houses and a bridge, intended to suggest the elements of Air, Earth and Water). The shadow cone extends into space. In this shadow is the darkened Moon, which is in

the sign Capricorn, opposite to that occupied by the Sun. The giant is pointing down to a vestigial tree, indicating that the Moon has dominion over the Earth, and over such things as vegetation and the growth of *physical* form.

The angel to the left of the zodiac is meant to contrast with the man, who is pointing down intently to the Earthly realm. This female angel seems to be overlooking the Sun, signifying that the Sun has rule over spiritual things. At her feet are a few buildings which are probably intended to represent a city: perhaps this detail is meant to indicate that eclipses have rule over history, and thus over human civilization?

At the mean distance of the Moon from the Earth, the shadow of the Earth is about 5,700 miles wide, hence much larger than the Moon itself. It can take well over three hours for the shadow to gradually cover the disk of the Moon, completely obliterate it, and then slip off the other side. However, the times of darkening vary enormously. For example, the total eclipse of the Moon which was visible on 6 July, 1982, lasted for 1 hour and 42 minutes. That which was visible on 29 November, 1993, lasted for only 50 minutes. The duration of the eclipse of the Moon on 16 July, 2000, will be 1 hour and 42 minutes. The reason for the variation of length is that the Moon does not always pass through the widest point of the conical shadow of the Earth. The nearer to the edge is its path, the shorter the eclipse.

In modern times, the convention is for the eclipse to be measured in terms of its totality. Many surviving records of observations by mediaeval astrologers indicate that they measured eclipses in terms of how long the entire phenomenon lasted, from the moment the Moon touched the Earth's shadow to its final separation. This may not sound a very important point, yet it is, bearing in mind that in traditional astrology it was believed that the length of an eclipse was a direct index of the length of time its effects would operate on the life of a native. An eclipse of three hours was supposed to have an effect of three years. An example may be taken from a chart cast by the English astrologer, A.J. Pearce, for the total eclipse of the Sun which was visible at Cairo on 17 May 1882:

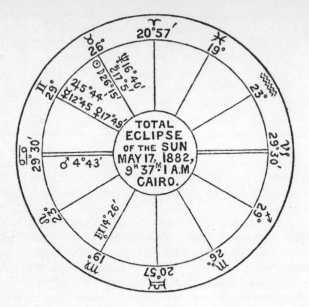

This eclipse lasted for three hours and twenty-five minutes, and Pearce (following astrological practice) read the history of its influence – through wars, a cholera epidemic and insurrections – for over three years and five months.[52] In passing, I should note that it was this same eclipse which led the remarkable astrologer Zadkiel to predict that the British would go to war in Egypt:[53] it was under the influence of this eclipse that General Gordon was sent to defend Khartoum, where he perished under the effect of yet another eclipse (see page 173).

The diagram below shows how a solar eclipse occurs, when the passage of the Moon around the Earth occults the Sun.

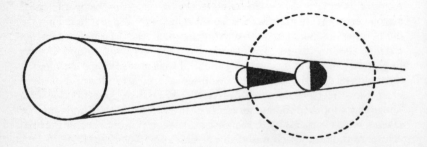

The shadow cast by the Moon, as it revolves around the Earth, throws a disk on to the surface of the Earth. The diagram shows this disk as though it were static, but since the Moon is revolving very rapidly around the Earth, and since the Earth is also revolving around the Sun, this disk of shadow also moves with incredible rapidity. From a human standpoint, the lunar shadow appears to trace a pathway over a part of the surface of the Earth: this pathway can be over 150 miles wide, and the shadow-disk travels over the surface of the earth at an enormous speed – much faster than the speed of sound. This means that solar eclipses last at most only a matter of minutes.

The maximum duration of the total eclipse is just over 7½ minutes, but most are much shorter. The solar eclipse of 11 July 1991 (visible from the Pacific Ocean and Central America) lasted for 6 minutes and 54 seconds, and was the longest in recent years. The solar eclipse of 11 August 1999 will last for 2 minutes and 23 seconds. The variation in the width of the path and the length of the eclipse is accounted for by the Moon's orbit not being at a constant distance from the Earth.

The centre of such a shadow-way traced by an eclipse will pass over a given place on earth only once or twice in about 350 years. However, the width of the path allows solar eclipses to be seen from a given place more frequently than this statistic suggests. Even so, visible solar eclipses are rare phenomena.

During the time of a solar eclipse, any observer in the centre of this pathway at the time of the eclipse will see the black shape of the Moon obscuring the Sun. Anyone who stands to the side of this pathway will see the Moon only partly obscure the Sun. Anyone who stands at a considerable distance from this pathway will not see the eclipse at all. Indeed, he or she will have to look into the ephemeris, or planetary tables, to know that there has been an eclipse.

Since the solar eclipse takes place when the body of the Moon passes in front of the Sun, and *occults* its light, the solar eclipse is sometimes called an *occultation* of the Sun by the Moon.

The solar eclipse can only take place at the New Moon, when the Moon comes between the Earth and 'transits' the Sun. Now while this 'transit' occurs once a month (since the Moon moves round the Earth in each month) this transit does not usually involve an eclipse. Even so, some astrologers do interpret this 'conjunction' between Sun and Moon as having some important bearing upon the life of a native, almost equivalent to an eclipse.

The representation of the thin shadow-line drawn upon the surface of the earth by a solar eclipse (page 30) is no modern thing. In a map of the southern constellations, designed about 1603 by Carel Allard of Amsterdam, there is a sophisticated representation of a solar eclipse with

47

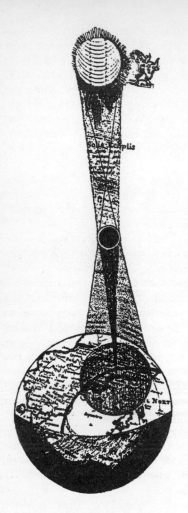

the black line marked upon the curvature of the earth's globe. This eclipse occurred on 12 May 1706, when the Sun was in 21.06 degrees of Taurus. Allard represented the eclipse in the familiar diagrammatic form, with the zodiacal position of the Sun indicated alongside by the stellar Bull of Taurus. The eclipse-shadow is shown running across Asia (alongside).

Eclipses in earth signs (such as Taurus) were believed to have a dramatic effect on the Earth itself. The lunar eclipses had a reputation for inducing earth-quakes, the solar for bringing about volcanic action. However, in this respect tradition is question-able, since both lunar and solar have been connected with earth-quakes, irrespective of the nature of the sign in which they occur. The total eclipse of the Sun on 29 August 1886 (in 06.04 of the earth sign, Virgo) was linked with the destruction of Charleston two days later, while the lunar eclipse of 1 June 1863 (in 10.52 of the fire sign, Sagittarius) has been linked with the destruction of Manila on 3rd of that month.[54]

Since the penumbra of the 1706 eclipse (above) was visible in Japan, it was blamed for the dramatic 'earth event' of the eruption of Fujiyama in the following year – the last time the famous volcano is recorded as being active.

Allard's map is interesting for other reasons than this representation of the solar eclipse. In designing it, the Dutchman introduced a number of new figures to take into account recorded observation of new stars and new stellar boundaries.[55] One of the constellations Allard introduced was the Unicorn, named by him with the over-kill title of *Unicornis al Monoceros* – 'Unicorn with a single horn' (opposite).

48

Allard's star-map was designed about 1603. By a curious twist of fate, about the same time that the unicorn was raised to the heavens by Allard, James VI of Scotland became James I of England. Because of this politically significant change, the white unicorn of Scotland was substituted for the red dragon of Wales. In 1707, the English parliament passed the Act of Union, which united the Scottish and English Parliaments, in consequence of which Scotland no longer had a separate Great Seal. It was because of this that the white unicorn of Scotland became the sinister supporter of the modern Royal Arms.

This heraldic unicorn is astrological in origin. In the ancient stellar tradition, Scotland is ruled by the sign Cancer, which is in turn governed by the Moon. The white unicorn is a lunar beast. Just as the lion of England is linked with the Leo of the zodiac and thus with the Sun, so Scotland is linked with the Cancer of the zodiac, and thus with the Moon. Since the heraldic pair are ranged opposite each other, across the armorial device, it is convenient to think of them as being in perpetual eclipse, with the horn of the unicorn an image of the shadow-cone cast by the body of the Moon.

In view of the connection which traditional astrology has drawn between the sign Cancer and Scotland, it is interesting to note that in 1603 – the year that James was invited to become king of England – a lunar eclipse fell over the Sun in his chart.[56]

SUN IN THE CHART OF JAMES I:	06.48 CANCER
LUNAR ECLIPSE OF 29 JUNE 1703:	06.27 CANCER

The solar eclipse can occur only when the new Moon is near the two points where the orbit of the Moon and Earth cross. In astronomy, these two points are called lunar nodes. In astrology, it is traditional to name these after a Dragon. In ancient times there was a widespread superstition that the solar and lunar eclipses were caused by dragons or serpents swallowing up the bodies of the Sun and Moon. This superstition has survived in some interesting imagery in Western, Eastern and Arabic astrology.[57]

Relevant to the sigils used in Western astrology are the late mediaeval illustrations which show the ecliptic in the form of a dragon. It does not require much imagination to trace in the diagram of the lunar dragon the origins of two sigils (☊ ☋) which represent the nodes, or meeting point, of the paths of Sun and Moon:

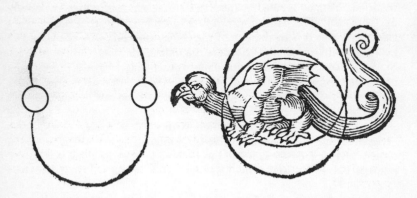

These nodes are intimately bound up with the theory of eclipses. In astrology, they represent the coming together of the Sun and the Moon in a personal chart (irrespective of where these bodies are in the chart itself)

and each node remains in the chart as a potential eclipse-point. We shall examine the way in which the nodes in astrology are linked with chart interpretation and predictive astrology at a later point.

Just as the solar eclipses trace a linear shadow across the surface of the earth, so the nodes trace a linear 'shadow' along the ecliptic in each horoscope. The nodes regress at approximately 3 seconds of arc each day, and this movement is involved, in certain forms of predictive astrology, with the dating of events in the life of the individual.

One image which appeared with many variations in mediaeval astrological books was the Lunar Dragon. This, in many variations, consists of two circles of similar size, intersecting, one at the head of the dragon, the other near or on its tail. One circle represents the path of the Sun, the other the path of the Moon. The two points where they intersect are called the Dragon's Head, and the Dragon's Tail.

The Dragon's Head is the ascending node – that which passes from the south of the ecliptic to the north: hence it is sometimes called the North Node. In astrology it is sometimes called by the Latin name, *Caput*, or 'head'. This nodal point is linked with beneficial events which (often quite unexpectedly) pour into the life of the native. We shall study some examples of these later.

The Dragon's Tail is the descending node – that which passes from the north of the ecliptic to the South: hence it is sometimes called the South Node. In astrology it is sometimes called by the Latin *Cauda*, or 'tail'. This nodal point is linked with difficulties and trials which (often quite unexpectedly) enter the life of the native.[58]

The symbol for the Dragon's Head has the curvature uppermost, the Dragon's Tail has it facing downwards. In astrology there is a hidden significance in this distinction, for, according to tradition, the Dragon's Head pours down (or bestows) benefits on the native, while the Dragon's Tail stores up unwanted spiritual darkness – the bad karma in a chart. The sigils themselves may be traced back to Greek astrology, and at one time were probably vestigial drawings of the path of the Sun or Moon, with the two crossing-point nodes represented as circles.

While astronomers and astrologers agree about what the Lunar Nodes are, they disagree on how they should be interpreted. Astronomers seem to be content to predict celestial phenomena, while astrologers have set themselves the equally difficult task of predicting earthly and human events.

The incorporation of eclipses in astrological theory is very ancient, and indications that it was used in Greek and Roman times are found in many early texts. Almost certainly, it was used as a technique in ancient Egyptian astrology, but was probably reserved for the exclusive use of priests who taught in the Mystery Schools. The Greek astronomer, Thales, who is reputed to have predicted an eclipse for 585 BC had studied under Egyptian priests.

The Mysteries of Isis were intimately bound up with the lunar mythology, and with the power of the serpent. This may have influenced some of the imagery and eclipse lore. Isis the goddess of lunar light, and her shadow–sister the dark Nephthys, were represented in the hieroglyphics as 'the two Snake-goddesses':

The glyph reminds us of the mythology of the devouring skysnake or dragon that was supposed to cause eclipses. It is a mythology which lives on even today in the widely–used astrological terms Dragon's Head and Dragon's Tail, but which was still very much alive in the seventeenth century when the Jesuit, Athanasius Kircher, represented a sequence of eclipses on a serpentine design:

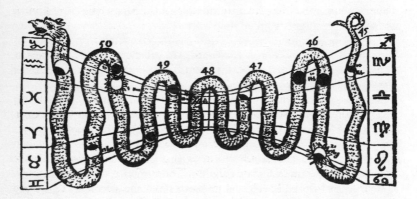

In this diagram, Kircher has attempted to show the ecliptic in the form of a sinuous snake, along which runs the eclipse points of Sun and Moon.[59]

One aspect of the symbolism in the Egyptian hieroglyph contains within it the notion that two serpents are connected with Light (with Isis) while two are connected with Darkness (with Nephthys).

This idea is well in accord with astrological theory, because this is

52

rooted in the idea that when, at birth, the spirit descends into the earth plane, it is itself a thing of light. By taking on a body, it becomes enmeshed in the darkness of earth. This means that, from an astrological standpoint, the human being is a mixture of light and darkness, living against a background of planetary forces which emphasize parts of this light as well as parts of this darkness.

In a sense, the four snakes of the hieroglyphic are early versions of the four small circles we find in the two sigils for the lunar nodes.

These nodes relate directly to destiny, or to what is often nowadays called *karma*.[60] The Dragon's Head is linked with the outflowing of good karma (symbolized as light), while the Dragon's Tail is linked with the outpouring of bad karma (symbolized as darkness). At a later point I shall examine in what way these highly sensitive nodal points manifest in the lives of individuals.

The lunar serpent of the ancient astrologies is, in one sense at least, the Serpent of Eden, that whispered temptation in the ear of Eve. A consequence of this temptation was that the Serpent brought Eve and her descendants down into the material world, placing them outside the light of the spiritual Eden. This is probably one reason why the Moon-bearing giant in the mediaeval eclipse-diagram on page 45 is pointing to the tree, and to the Earth, which is miraculously at his feet as well as at the end of his cone-shadow. This is almost certainly a reference to the Tree in the Garden of Eden, from which the fruit was plucked and eaten. In this sense, the gesture of the giant reminds us that the Moon rules over human destiny.

The sinuous serpents of the ancient astrologies were at least symbols of living things. The modern diagrams which demonstrate how eclipses work are somehow dry and banal.

Being an astrologer, I am disposed to think of the Cosmos as a living thing, and I find it somehow distasteful to describe celestial bodies in mechanistic terms, as though the cosmos were a clockwork device, rather than a spiritual organism, tended by spiritual beings. Even so, when attempting to describe another form of solar eclipse, it is easier to make use of a somewhat mechanistic diagram. The structure of the solar system is such that when the Moon is at its greatest distance from the Earth, the tip of its shadow falls short of the surface of the Earth by many miles.[61]

This results in what is called an 'annular' eclipse. The word has nothing to do with the idea of year (annual) but is derived from the Latin for 'ring' (*annulus*), for the annular eclipse is nothing more than an incomplete eclipse of the Sun by the body of the Moon, which leaves a bright ring of light around the surface of the occulting Moon.

A similar mechanism ensures that when the Moon is at the closest point to the Earth, the shadow it casts on the surface is about 165 miles wide.[62]

In those cases where the relative distances of the Moon from the Sun result in the apparent size of the Moon being slightly smaller than the apparent size of the Sun, there is an interesting phenomenon which is often called 'Baily's beads'. These are named after the English astronomer Francis Baily, who first described the phenomenon after observing the solar eclipse of 9 November 1836 in 16.43 Scorpio. The illustration below illustrates the phenomenon, which is caused by the light of the Sun shining between the mountainous silhouette of the edge of the Moon.

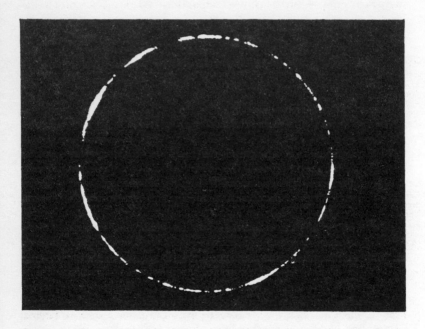

Some astrologers believe that the paths of the eclipse shadows are important in regard to the interpretation of the future. For example, it is often observed in modern textbooks that the path of the eclipse that took place on 5 May 1818 – the day that Karl Marx was born – swept across the Russian Empire.[63] Some have read the spread of Communism into Russia through this influence. My own experience has suggested that such shadows are irrelevant to interpretation. As we shall see, the importance of eclipses rests not in the shadows, but in the interaction of Sun and Moon with the degrees which mark the zodiacal belt. In my view, an eclipse of the Sun and the Moon has the same effect, whether total, partial or annular, and whether or not the person influenced by it is within or without the shadow trails these leave.

Some astrologers are inclined to place more emphasis on the solar eclipse (perhaps because both Sun and Moon are on the same degree of the zodiac), but this is not a distinction that I shall make in this present work.

In practical terms, this means that most astrologers will regard the partial lunar eclipse of 15 April 1995 (which was visible from the island of Fiji) as having the same interpretative significance as (say) the total lunar eclipse of 6 July 1982, which was visible from Easter Island. Furthermore, such lunar eclipses are usually accorded much the same significance as (say) the annular eclipse that took place on 22 August (visible from the Indian and Pacific Oceans) and the total eclipse of 11 August 1999, visible from India, Turkey, central Europe, France and England. As we study the case histories in this present work, we shall discover that these distinctions are not at all important so far as the astrological understanding of human destiny is concerned.

In any given period of eclipse-cycles, there are more solar than lunar eclipses – this may explain why some astrologers tend to read lunar eclipses as being more prophetic of darkness in the life of natives. This is not a distinction I make myself. I regard all eclipses as having the same force. This means that the seventy eclipses which (on average) fall during a Saros period of eighteen years and eleven days constitute opportunities of equal power for change, when these correspond to sensitive points in the charts of individuals. We shall glance at the Saros cycle shortly, but having observed that there are approximately seventy eclipses in such a period of eighteen years, we should note that this offers the opportunity for seventy crises, or changes, in a human lifetime of that period. The Cosmos is so arranged that no horoscope can ever accommodate so many changes – yet some people have more opportunities than others. In any given year, there cannot be more than seven eclipses. The year 1935 was a good example of this, for it contained five solar eclipses and two lunars. In 1982 there were four solars and three lunars. The fact that solar eclipses outnumber the lunars is counterbalanced by the fact that the number of solar eclipses visible from a given spot on the earth's surface is fewer than the number of lunar eclipses. No knowledge of three-dimensional geometry is needed to understand why this should be: while solar eclipses are visible from very small areas of the Earth's surface, a lunar eclipse can be visible from about half of the Earth's surface. These distinctions, of such importance to astronomers, are not of much importance in astrology.

What most astrologers regard as being important is not the type or strength of a given eclipse, but the degree of the zodiac in which it takes place. This is sometimes called the *sensitive degree*.[64] Thus, what was important for astrologers about the eclipse of November 1836 (see page 54 above) was not the fact that it was an example of the rare Baily's beads, but that it took place in 16.43 Scorpio, thereby rendering this degree of the zodiac sensitive.

It is here – with this notion of the sensitive degree – that the astronomers and astrologers part company in their views of the meaning of eclipses. The astronomers tend to deride the fact that astrologers look for the significance of an eclipse not towards the three 'planets' of Sun, Moon and Earth which 'produce' the eclipse, but beyond these, to the realm of the ecliptic.

The difference in attitudes really reflects intentions, rather than anything relating to superstitions. While the astronomer works on the reasonable supposition that the heavens manifest through complex rhythms which permit cosmic events to be predicted, the astrologer works on the equally reasonable supposition that the complex rhythms of the heavens are reflected on earth, and in the lives of individuals here on earth. Astrology, a tool which studies heavenly patterns, assumes an inner correspondence (in the psyches of human beings) with the outer rhythms of the stars and planets.

As the illustration we studied on page 16 revealed, in the period of a single year, during 1652–3, there were no less than *three* eclipses visible in England and parts of Europe, each of which challenged astrologers. Such eclipses – by which William Lilly meant, eclipses visible in England – were 'to be feared because of their infrequency'. The following data for the three eclipses in this dark year is that given by Lilly:

ECLIPSE OF THE MOON ON 15 MARCH 1652:   05.16 ARIES
ECLIPSE OF THE SUN ON 29 MARCH 1652:   19.15 ARIES
ECLIPSE OF THE MOON ON 7 SEPTEMBER 1653:   25.16 VIRGO

Of course, we should not be misled by Lilly's diagram. In the book which dealt with these eclipses, Lilly gave reasonably accurate horoscopes for the moment of the three eclipses. We need not study all three, even though it is interesting to record the horoscopes which Lilly gives for the moments of exact eclipse in each case (opposite)

It is the solar eclipse (that recorded in the centre chart) which proves to be of immediate interest to us, if only because it occurred in the same degree as that in which a solar eclipse of April 2005 will take place.[65]

SOLAR ECLIPSE OF 29 MARCH 1652 (OS):   19.10 ARIES
SOLAR ECLIPSE OF 8 APRIL 2005:   19.06 ARIES

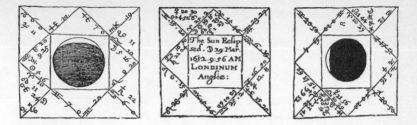

What may we learn from this? First, that Lilly tended to regard the *moment* of eclipse as being important. This is why he cast the horoscopes for the moment of the eclipses: he cast the equivalent of a *nativity* for this moment, almost as though he imagined that something was born, or initiated, at that second.

Most of the predictions which Lilly made from these three charts were based upon his reading not of the eclipses themselves, but of the horoscopes he had cast for the moment of these eclipses. This is a very different form of astrology from that which is practised today.

In modern times, very few astrologers interpret eclipses in the way Lilly did, with emphasis on the time of the eclipse.[66] Nowadays, the tendency is to regard the time-element as being of secondary importance, and astrologers prefer to concentrate on the space-element, the *sensitive degree*.

While we note that William Lilly's eclipse-interpretation was different from today's, what did Lilly have to say about the effect of the solar eclipse in that 'dark year' of 1652?

Typical of Lilly's style of writing, most of his text is taken up with scholarly-seeming quotations in support of astrology and eclipse-reading, garnered from the great authorities in this field. However, after establishing the credentials of astrology, he reminds us that a conjunction of Sun and Moon (let alone an eclipse) in the sign Aries is bound to bring difficulties between friends, often followed by death, 'from thence Warre and controversy, after which follows quarrels, and then Death and Destruction.' He then points out that England is ruled by Aries, and that an eclipse in that sign is bound to influence this country.[67]

Needless to say, the solar eclipse of that dark year was in Aries, from which it is reasonable to assume that Lilly is hinting at a catastrophe in England.

Why should Lilly be so insistent that great catastrophes follow on eclipses?

Is it true that eclipses are indicators of destructive or disruptive events? The answer to this question is quite definitely, no. The fact is that Lilly was temperamentally given to blood and thunder, and while his predictions for this year are not quite so dark or lurid as the title of his

57

book promises, he cannot help mixing a certain amount of negativity into his predictions – if only to meet the promise of the title. This predisposition to be lurid was partly supported by the expectations of his considerable number of readers: in the seventeenth century, it was taken for granted that eclipses promised dismal and dangerous things.

Modern astrologers are not always so concerned with the catastrophic, and research has shown that it is quite possible to trace the effects of eclipses as wonderful beneficiaries in life. In particular, eclipses seem to help artists in their creative self-expression.

The three eclipses took place in a sombre period in English history. The Civil War had ravaged the land for several years. King Charles I had been executed in 1649 – three years before the first of the dark eclipses – and it was presumed by many that England would continue as a Commonwealth, without a monarchy. In his eclipse-based prophecies, Lilly went along with this idea. Conveniently ignoring the fact that he had already predicted 'Death and Destruction', he interpreted one eclipse as meaning that the Commonwealth would continue in glory for three years. Indeed, he foresaw the 'rise or growth of the Common-wealth of England to a very high esteem all over the world'.[68] As it was, his prediction turned out to be correct, for the Commonwealth lasted for a further eight years.

In his ruminations on the first lunar eclipse of 1652 Lilly foresaw difficulties with the Dutch – because he was either a good astrologer or an astute politician. However, the astrological argument he presented for the prediction seems to be bound up with the fact that both Holland and Scotland were (and, indeed, still are) ruled by the sign Cancer:

> And this my conjecture I also conceive . . . some injury had been lately done unto some of our Nation, or is neer doing, either by some of the Dutch or Scotch Nation . . . I very much fear a War, or some Warlike attempts either by Sea or Land doe follow . . .[69]

In 1652, the first of the Anglo–Dutch Wars broke out, leading to the defeat of the Dutch by sea, off Dover, and the defeat of the British off Dungeness. In 1653, the Dutch were defeated off Portland, and then off the Frisian island of Texel, where the courageous Dutch admiral Tromp was killed.

The horoscope of Martin Harpertszoon Tromp had been widely published during his lifetime. However, it is certain that none of the astrologers of that time would have been able to predict the cause and time of his death in that battle, as neither of the two planets involved were known to them. In Tromp's chart, the planets Uranus and Pluto were together in 22 degrees of Aries. This was a dangerous placing for Tromp, since at the lunar eclipse of 1652 the planet Mars was very close to that degree. Lilly would have recognized the danger of the conjunction between an eclipse in Aries and a fiery planet which is itself prone to violent tendencies.[70]

The point I am making is that while it is difficult to predict such things as the political life of nations – for example, how long a Commonwealth will last after a regicide – it is fairly easy to gain some idea from an eclipse when a person will die, or face some kind of major change.

William Lilly was partly right in one respect – he was right to view eclipses as hinting at catastrophes, more frequently than at worldly beneficial events. Why this should be so raises very many difficult issues, some of which I shall deal with later.

How do eclipses influence a human life? Well, the answer is that the Cosmos is so arranged that not all human lives are directly influenced by – I might almost say *troubled* by – eclipses. Some people are more affected than others by eclipses. Some people – and this seems to include artists, poets, musicians and writers – are so often affected by eclipses that one might almost describe them as being Moon-struck. More accurately, they might be described as being 'eclipse people', over sensitive to solar/lunar influences – especially to eclipses. It is very rarely that one encounters the horoscope of a famous or prominent personality which is not in one way or another deeply influenced by eclipses.

To understand why this should be, we have to know something about what is called the Saros cycle. In the Saros period, eclipses are said to occur in very nearly the same order, when measured in terms of degrees. In human terms, the full cycle of the Saros is a sequence of four – that is to say, 4 x 18 years. This period of seventy-two years, or four Saros cycles, is regarded as being symbolically the length of a human life.

The period of seventy-two years is bound up into the esoteric numerology behind astrology, which need not concern us here. It is the period within which the stellar rhythm which we call precession meets with the solar-lunar rhythm of eclipses. Briefly, in seventy-two years, give or take a few days, the stars appear to fall back against the vernal point (the hypothetical zero degree of Aries) by one degree. In that same period there are four Saros cycles of a very distinctive character, in which the same degree of the zodiac is repeated.

Let us look at this Saros cycle in human terms.

Just suppose that you were born in London, on 12 August 1942, on which day there was a solar eclipse. This eclipse took place in 18.46 degrees of Leo. Now, the next time this same degree would be touched by an eclipse would be about eighteen years later. This eclipse would influence your life in some way – precisely how is not relevant to my present argument.

On 11 August 1961, there would be a solar eclipse in 18.31 degrees of Leo. Your life would be affected by three further eclipses in the 19th degree of Leo. Let me set out the sequence into the following century:

SOLAR ECLIPSE OF 12 AUGUST 1942:	18.46 LEO
SOLAR ECLIPSE OF 11 AUGUST 1961:	18.31 LEO
SOLAR ECLIPSE OF 10 AUGUST 1980:	18.17 LEO
SOLAR ECLIPSE OF 11 AUGUST 1999:	18.21 LEO
SOLAR ECLIPSE OF 11 AUGUST 2018:	18.41 LEO

If you managed to live for just under one century, you would experience five eclipses upon the same degree, simply because you were born on the day when the eclipse of 1942 took place.

Let us suppose, however, that you were born (say) three days later. Let us suppose you were born in London, on 15 August 1942. By then, the Sun will have moved on three degrees. Let us assume that you were born when your Sun was in 21.32 degrees of Leo. Surprisingly, there would be eclipses in only one year in this degree during your entire lifetime:

LUNAR ECLIPSE OF 11 FEBRUARY 1952:	21.19 LEO

If eclipses do influence the lives of people, then it is evident that a person born on 11 August 1942 is likely to have a richer (or, for that matter, a more troubled) life than the one born on the 15 August 1942.

As a matter of fact, had you been born on 16 August 1942, when the Sun was in 22.30 Leo, then your life would have been almost eclipse-free: there would be only one eclipse in this degree during the century in question – and this would be so far into your lifetime that it would – to speak periphrastically – probably mark your swan-song. The last eclipse in this degree was in 1757, and the next eclipse in that degree will be in 2017.

You see then that if we consider the position of the Sun alone, there is tremendous inequality in the quantity of eclipses that the Cosmos hands out to people. Of course, the Sun is not the only planet in the horoscope. Traditional astrology recognizes ten planets, and there are various other points in the horoscope that we shall examine, all of which are also sensitive to eclipses. This means that almost everyone is likely to experience the effect of at least one eclipse at some point in their lifetime. As my collection of case-histories, starting on page 126, indicates, other people will experience many eclipses. As we shall see, some lives are fructified by these eclipse contacts, while others are ruined. It is these inequalities in number and power which makes the study of eclipses so fascinating for the astrologer.

Perhaps we no longer need to ask ourselves why, for over 2000 years, eclipses have been regarded by astrologers as being so important? It must be clear why the finest astrologers of all periods have regarded eclipses as indices of individuals' destinies.

Perhaps now we are in a position to look at eclipses on a personal level, at how particular eclipses played into the lives – that is, into the histories – of two well-known individuals. I suggest this because I believe that before it is possible for anyone to develop an interest in eclipse lore, it is necessary for them to know just a little about what eclipses – the rhythmic play of Sun, Moon and Earth with shadows – mean on a human level.

With this in mind, let us examine the interesting chart of Charles, Prince of Wales, the heir to the British throne. Charles was born on 14 November 1948, at 9:14 pm, in London.[71]

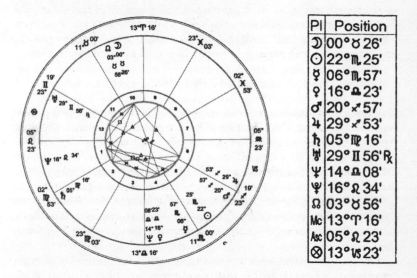

Pl	Position
☽	00° ♉ 26'
☉	22° ♏ 25'
☿	06° ♏ 57'
♀	16° ♎ 23'
♂	20° ♐ 57'
♃	29° ♐ 53'
♄	05° ♍ 16'
♅	29° ♊ 56' ℞
♆	14° ♎ 08'
♇	16° ♌ 34'
☊	03° ♉ 56'
Mc	13° ♈ 16'
Asc	05° ♌ 23'
⊗	13° ♑ 23'

Perhaps the most obvious feature in this horoscope is the fact that the two planets, Jupiter and Uranus, are in total opposition.

In astrology, the planet Jupiter (♃) represents the spiritual well-being of an individual. The planet Uranus (♅) represents changes (sometimes even violent change) which occur in a person's life. An *opposition* occurs between planets when they are directly opposite each other in the zodiac: this relationship of 'opposition' usually gives rise to tensions between the planets concerned, yet, in this context, we need not trouble ourselves about this.

You now have enough information to grasp the significant thing about Prince Charles's horoscope. In sum, the two sigils in the table above have the following meaning:

♃ 29° ♐ 53' means that Jupiter is in 29.53 degrees of Sagittarius

♅ 29° ♊ 56' means that Uranus is in 29.56 degrees of Gemini

The symbol ℞ , which comes after the entry for Uranus, means that the planet is *retrograde*. However, you need not concern yourself about the symbol, or its meaning, at any time while consulting the tables in this book, as it has no bearing on eclipse-interpretation.

As you will see, I have marked the chart to bring out this distinguishing feature of the opposition between these two planets. They could scarcely be more perfectly aligned in opposition: there is a difference of only 3 minutes of arc between them.

Now, as I have said, while Jupiter is a spiritually expansive planet, Uranus tends to work through change: whenever one considers Uranus in a horoscope, one is considering change. Whether the change will be dramatic and rapid, or slow and scarcely noticed – whether it will be joyful or sad – these are the things which an astrologer can learn from the position and condition of Uranus. Astrologers who are interested in this royal chart recognize that whenever the Uranus degree (that is 29.56 of Gemini) becomes operative, Prince Charles will undergo some major change in his life.

How does a degree become 'operative'? Generally, this happens when another planet or cosmic body chances to fall upon that degree.

One of the most dramatic ways that a degree will become 'operative', or influential in the history of an individual, is when an eclipse falls on such a degree. In this sense, an eclipse is rather like the descent of Fire from Heaven: either it can be something like a firework sparkler in the horoscope, bringing warmth and pleasure, or it can be a mighty flash of lightning which may strike with terror and an all-consuming con-flagration. It is because the eclipse can spark off such extremes that astrologers find them so useful in their predictive work. It is because of their power that those astrologers who study them in their interpretations usually take care to establish if and when eclipses will fall on specific planets in the charts they are studying.[72]

In astrology, eclipses (like planets) are recorded according to the degree of the zodiac on which they fall. Because an eclipse involves two powerful bodies – the Sun and Moon – it always enlivens, or sensitizes in an extraordinary way, a single degree in a most dramatic way. This sensitizing almost always parallels (I would prefer not to say 'causes') an

62

event in the life of the person concerned. An eclipse is the finger of Clio pointing at an individual, and selecting him or her for special treatment.

In considering the effect of an eclipse in the chart of Prince Charles, we shall concentrate on the position of Uranus.

In effect, we really have no alternative, as the planet Jupiter (in 30 degrees of Sagittarius) would not be touched by an eclipse in the whole of the Prince's lifetime. The last occasion when an eclipse fell exactly on the position of his Jupiter was in 1796: the last time an eclipse was even near to it was in 1853.[73] These dates give some idea of how rarely eclipse degrees become operative, as they slowly cycle the 360 degrees of the zodiac.

During the entire period of a hundred years following Charles's birth, there were only four eclipses near to 29.56 degrees of Gemini – that is, on the planet Uranus in his chart.

SOLAR ECLIPSE OF 21 JUNE 1982:	29.47 GEMINI
LUNAR ECLIPSE OF 21 DECEMBER 1991:	29.08 GEMINI
LUNAR ECLIPSE OF 21 DECEMBER 2010:	29.22 GEMINI
LUNAR ECLIPSE OF 20 DECEMBER 2029:	29.18 GEMINI

Let us see what happened in the life of Prince Charles at that time when the solar eclipse of 1982 took place. The eclipse of 21 June fell very close indeed to the planet Uranus in the Prince's chart:

SOLAR ECLIPSE OF 21 JUNE 1982:	29.47 GEMINI
URANUS IN THE CHART OF PRINCE CHARLES:	29.56 GEMINI

On that day – that is, on 21 June 1982 – Princess Diana gave birth to Charles's son, Prince William. Charles had an heir, and a stream of events were put into operation which will eventually influence the history of England. Besides the historical consequences of this royal birth, the arrival of his first-born was a considerable change in Charles's personal life, and it is reflected with remarkable clarity in his horoscope.

I have given this interesting example of the working of an eclipse because it is a very precise one. The eclipse was only 9 minutes of arc from being exactly upon Uranus. In addition, the birth of the son occurred *on the same day as the eclipse* itself.[74] Of course, not all eclipses work with such precision. As we shall see, in some cases, an eclipse can take months to work into a chart – even so, one may be confident that sooner or later, within a very specific period, the effect of a particular eclipse will be felt eventually, if it has occurred on a sensitive degree in the native's chart. We shall examine the rules that govern the limits of time through which eclipses work later, but for the moment we may regard the eclipse of 1982 as being a rather exceptional time-keeper.

The horoscope of Prince Charles has enabled us to grasp something of the principle behind the astrological approach to eclipses. It is no accident that I chose to examine the working of an eclipse through the horoscope of a prince. By definition, such people are to some extent removed from the ordinary levels of the world. They are, so to speak, in the spiritual limelight of history: it is as though Clio, the Muse of History, has singled them out for her personal attention. As we shall learn, this makes all such people in the limelight of history especially susceptible to the effects of eclipses.

Indeed, as we shall see later, Nature seems to select certain individuals and subject them to the profound influence of more than one eclipse in a single lifetime. Such individuals often exhibit genius in their lives, and some – writers and painters in particular – are constantly drawn to lunar and solar imagery in their work.

Among the outstanding people who were unwittingly obsessed with eclipse lore, and at whose horoscopes we shall glance, are the English mystical poet and painter, William Blake (see page 134) and the German artist, Max Ernst (see page 162). It is no accident that each of these artists were interested in alchemy.[75] The secret science of alchemy has adopted images of the Sun and Moon in a wide range of symbolic devices. In fact, the lore of eclipses has been adapted by alchemists to express some of their deeper thoughts about the inner nature of mankind – which is the proper study of alchemy itself.

The fascinating connection between human genius and eclipses has never received the study it deserves. Indeed, it seems to be one of the best-kept secrets of the hermetic philosophers. In so far as it is already set out in available literature, it is found in the writings of the alchemists, the so-called 'Fire Philosophers', who usually were as skilled in astrology as they were in the search for the inner stone, the magical *lapis* which every alchemist sought. This alchemical interest in eclipses is almost inevitable, for alchemy, as a science of spiritual research, is rooted in the idea that all human beings are composed of light and darkness, so often symbolized as Sun and Moon. The alchemists taught that a careful spiritual preparation was required to allow this polarity of Sun and Moon to unite in such a way as to give birth to the inner man. In traditional alchemy, the stages where the inner light and darkness come together and gestate this inner birth is likened to an eclipse.

Given this background, it is to be expected that the symbols of Sun and Moon play an extremely important role in alchemical illustrations. This is mainly because alchemists recognize that the outer is itself a reflection of the inner: for the alchemists, there is an inner Sun and Moon within the microcosm which is Man and Woman.

In simple terms, the Sun represents the external light of consciousness, while the Moon represents the internal light of the unconscious. When these two come together, in the inner eclipse, there is the potential for fructification. This idea of union – of conjunction – is one reason why sexual imagery plays such an important part in alchemy, for the coming together of the inner Sun and Moon can be expressed 'externally' as the 'coronation' of the king and queen, prince and princess, or as the coition of male and female (itself termed the *conjunctio*, a word lifted from astrology) which eventually gives rise to the birth of a Golden Child.

This kind of symbolism explains why, in many alchemical images, the coming together of male and female is represented in the form of an eclipse. Such images denote the necessary state of stasis (a temporary stillness), prior to a complete change, or redemption. It is the mysterious meeting of bodily fluids by which the child is conceived. A well-known image of this stasis (which is sometimes called *putrefaction* in alchemy) is from a plate in Daniel Mylius' book on alchemy.[76]

The skeletal symbol of death stands upon the eclipse, grasping in his right hand a black raven. The words Putrefaction, Death, *Caput Corvi* (Head of the Crow) and *Nigredo*, are alchemical equivalents – each pointing to that cosmic stasis during which purity is distilled, or separated from the dross, in preparation for an inner birth. Without this period of darkness, the purity cannot be extracted from the dross. Within the framework of this imagery, the copulation of man and woman, the 'marriage' of the king and queen, are equivalents of the cosmic eclipse.

A similar eclipse-imagery, still linked with the black crow, may be seen in a detail from an alchemical book by the German chemist, Libavius.[77]

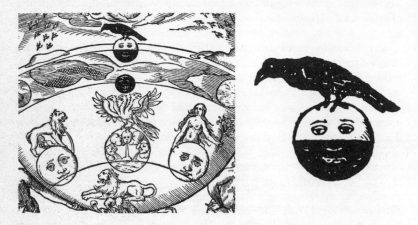

The black face above the three-headed bird is almost certainly a total lunar eclipse, while the half-dark Moon above seems to be in the throes of a lunar eclipse. These correspond to different stages of inner dissolution, prior to the development which offers spiritual freedom.

This alchemical symbolism has not usurped the astronomical image of the eclipse so much as recognized that just as there is a rhythm of eclipses in the Cosmos, so there is a rhythm of eclipses inside the spiritual being of man and woman. This inner eclipse is something akin to a temporary darkening, which is of necessity followed by a new influx of spiritual light.

The process of developing light from the inner eclipse is nowhere more clearly illustrated than in a series of details in plates drawn for the alchemist Johann Barchusen, in 1718.[78] These show various impossible unions of Sun and crescent Moon in a distillation jar. These are *symbolic* eclipses, or symbolic moments of darkness. In consequence of this union, the spirit (here symbolized as a bird, which is also the quicksilver of a newly-freed Mercury) can soar skywards (opposite, below).

One reason why I chose the detail of Prince Charles's chart was because the consequences of that particular eclipse of 1982 were so creative and beneficial. Unfortunately, however, the majority of eclipses do not bring happiness into the lives of the people they touch. We shall see this more and more as we examine some dramatic effects of eclipses in personal lives. For example, we shall see how a later eclipse touched the life of Princess Diana in a way which was quite tragic. Such an eclipse, from the stand-point of human life, certainly appears to work more through the lunar darkness than through the solar light. Examination of another chart will act as a sort of counterweight.

The artist-poet Dante Gabriel Rossetti was one of those artists who was touched by an inner feeling for the Moon, and for eclipses. One or two of his paintings actually portray eclipses. Among these, the most astounding must be that which he painted in 1877, the *Astarte Syriaca*.

Rossetti's painting represents the Babylonian goddess Astarte in flowing robe, facing the onlooker frontally. Behind her, and on either side, are two handmaidens, each clasping torches, and looking upwards to the heavens. Between their uplifted faces, and immediately above the head of Astarte, is an eclipse. However, to describe this union of Sun and Moon as an eclipse is in some ways misleading, for while the luminaries have come together, as in a solar eclipse, Rossetti has represented the Moon in crescent form.

In astronomical terms, this is a cosmologically impossible eclipse – what we might call a *symbolic* eclipse. Hovering over the head of Astarte (and perhaps part of her head-decoration) is an eight-rayed star set within a circle: this is derived from an ancient Babylonian symbol for Venus, of which Astarte was the planetary goddess. Since this Venusian symbol overlays the eclipse, it is possible that Rossetti was referring to a triple conjunction of Sun, Moon and Venus – a cosmologically important moment of love.

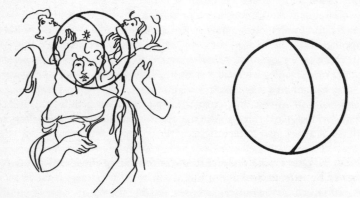

A superficial examination of the life of Rossetti might lead one to conclude that he was obsessed by women – or, at least by a particular type of woman. However, the truth is that Rossetti was obsessed by the Moon. Even Rossetti's name, Gabriel, evokes lunar forces, for in the arcane tradition Gabriel is the angel that rules the lunar sphere.[79] Inevitably, Rossetti's chart reveals the reason for this interest in the Moon, and in eclipses.[80] However, it is not this aspect of the horoscope which we shall deal with here.

Rossetti was born on 12 May, 1828, at 00:47 am, in London.

His horoscope is given on page 69.[81]

The detail in this horoscope to which I wish to draw your attention is the Part of Fortune (⊗) which is in 10.12 degrees of Capricorn.

The Part of Fortune is defined in the Glossary, but for the present purposes we need know only that it is a nodal point fixed by the angular distance between Sun and Moon. In a sense, it is therefore linked with eclipses, which are engineered by these two planets. It is reasonable to assume that an eclipse on this Part of Fortune would evoke very dynamic results. The astrological reasons for making this statement may sound a little obscure, but I shall put them in as simple a form as possible: the solar-lunar nature of the eclipse would be working on a sort of eclipse-equivalent, in the shadow-Sun and shadow-Moon in the Part of Fortune.

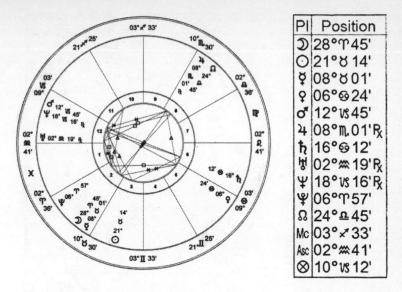

Pl	Position
☽	28° ♈ 45'
☉	21° ♉ 14'
☿	08° ♉ 01'
♀	06° ♋ 24'
♂	12° ♑ 45'
♃	08° ♏ 01' ℞
♄	16° ♋ 12'
♅	02° ♒ 19' ℞
♆	18° ♑ 16' ℞
♇	06° ♈ 57'
☊	24° ♎ 45'
Mc	03° ♐ 33'
Asc	02° ♒ 41'
⊗	10° ♑ 12'

On 31 December 1861, there was a solar eclipse which fell upon this Part of Fortune in Rossetti's chart.

PART OF FORTUNE IN THE CHART OF ROSSETTI:	10.12 CAPRICORN
SOLAR ECLIPSE OF 31 DECEMBER, 1861:	09.57 CAPRICORN

Can we trace any event in the life of Rossetti, about this time, which might reflect this conjunction?

Less than six weeks after the eclipse, on 11 February 1862, tragedy struck. His wife, the beautiful model and poet, Elizabeth Siddal, committed suicide, shortly after giving birth to a stillborn child.[82]

Rossetti had painted Elizabeth Siddal, with that full head of red hair which he so much loved, in a picture called *Dantis Amor* (over). The true significance of this extraordinary picture has never been understood, simply because its meaning can only be grasped within an astrological context. It is actually a painting of a lunar eclipse.

Rossetti painted *Dantis Amor* in 1860. In the central vertical of the picture area a winged woman stands in long robes. She grasps a bow and arrow in her left hand. The pictorial frame is divided by two diagonals. The one which runs upwards from left to right divides the ground into two areas, the top one of which is occupied by a flag–like representation of solar rays: the bottom is occupied by a ground of eight-pointed stars. In the top left, centering on the solar rays is a roundel containing the head of a crowned Man, who is (on one level of symbolism) the Christ.

In the bottom right, set in stellar ground, is a roundel in the shape of a Moon, inset with a female head, below the chin of which is a five-pointed star. The solar head in the male roundel looks down towards the lunar-crescent roundel, and the female in turn gazes up at the male. They are caught in the cosmological equivalent of a lunar eclipse, in which the two are linked on the material plane by the bow and arrow in the hand of the central figure. As we shall see, Rossetti, consciously or unconsciously, used this bow and arrow as symbol of the zodiacal sign Sagittarius, the bow–man.

The direct symbolism of the 'Love of Dante' has many different shades of meaning. On the one hand, as a devout Christian, the chief love of the Italian poet Dante (Rossetti's namesake) was Christ. This explains why the head of Christ is painted in a roundel at the top left. On a more worldly, yet still spiritual, level, the love of Dante's life had been the Florentine beauty, Beatrice, whose head is shown in the roundel at the bottom right. On a more philosophical level, the love of Dante was the stars – which explains why he completed each of his three great poems in the *Commedia* with the Italian word '*stelle*', which means 'stars'.[83]

The picture is painted on a simple geometry of two diagonals. The

triangular half which frames the head of Beatrice is filled with stars, against a backdrop of blue night. That which frames the head of Christ is radiant, as though with a sunburst. In fact, it *is* a sunburst, for the head of Christ is represented in the form of a Sun, just as the head of Beatrice is represented in the form of a Moon. The two – the ideal man and the idealized woman – gaze across the zodiac at each other, in solar eclipse. We know it is an eclipse for the representative of the Earth (Elizabeth Siddal herself) stands between them, as the body of the Earth interposes itself between Sun and Moon in a lunar eclipse.

My suspicion is that Rossetti (who was widely read in occult literature) borrowed the composition from an engraving in an arcane work by the English Rosicrucian, Robert Fludd. This engraving is reproduced, to give some idea of what I mean. If he did borrow it, then there is a poignant symbolism in the relationship between the image of the lunar face in his picture and the Moon in the Fludd image: the latter has just left the shadow of the Earth, and is once again swinging in space in the full light of the Sun. This was exactly symbolic of what happened to Elizabeth Siddal.

Because Rossetti's painting was never finished, we cannot satisfy

71

ourselves about one detail of the symbolism. The body of the female is curiously formed, with none of the accustomed grace which Rossetti bestowed upon his women. It is as though Rossetti were suggesting that the figure were hermaphrodite. Could it be that the unfinished wings are intended to portray the form as angelic – perhaps as the angel Gabriel, thus merging the painter's own name with the physical appearance of the woman he loved?

The woman carries a bow and arrow, which might suggest that Rossetti portrayed her as a representative of Diana, the huntress and lunar goddess. However, it is equally possible to see this bow and arrow as the attribute of the bow-man, Sagittarius.[84] The importance of this symbolism is emphasized by Rossetti through the device of making it the visual link between the two heads – the arrow points at the lunar Beatrice, as though it represented the benign gaze of Christ, looking upon the face of the woman who became Dante's guide through Paradise.

Rossetti painted the picture in 1859, the year he married Elizabeth Siddal. It remains unfinished, yet it has proved to be profoundly and sadly prophetic.

The sequel to the tale of Rossetti and Siddal would be too tragic to tell, did it not reflect upon the power of eclipses. Realizing that he had contributed to the death of his wife through his dalliance with another woman, Rossetti was filled with remorse by her suicide. Alongside her body, in the coffin, he buried all his unpublished poems. A decade later, thinking better of this, he had the body exhumed, and retrieved his poems.

In 1872, Rossetti published the poems he had taken from the realms of the dead in this macabre way. In May of that year, there was a lunar eclipse very close to his zenith – that part of the horoscope which governs careers and public standing. The eclipse was in Sagittarius, whose symbol of the bow and arrow had figured in the painting of their marriage-year:

LUNAR ECLIPSE OF 22 MAY, 1872:   02.05 SAGITTARIUS
ZENITH IN THE CHART OF ROSSETTI: 03.33 SAGITTARIUS

When published, these poems were not well-received. Whether or not it was this which finally unhinged his mind, we shall probably never know, but as time passed, he lapsed into an eccentricity that bordered on madness – that ultimate state of lunar disorder which the ancients called lunacy.

Rules for Interpreting Eclipses

In the last chapter I said that any eclipse (including the eclipse of August 1999) is unlikely to affect in any way at all the lives of more than one in twelve people. Even in such a limited number of cases, the effect will be slight, and in some cases it might even be beneficial. I also said that only about one in 200 people would find their lives dramatically influenced by the eclipse of 1999. How did I arrive at these rough estimates? In order to understand we must look at astrological theory, at the seven laws governing eclipse interpretation.

Given the long history of eclipse interpretation, it is not surprising that a number of rules have been formulated to enable astrologers to interpret their effects on charts. In fact, so far as it is possible to determine, some of the methods of interpreting eclipses have not changed much in thousands of years.

The rules for interpretation are very simple, and are built around the idea that eclipses leave *sensitive points* in the zodiac, in the degrees where they occur.

Rule One

The first rule is based on the premise that a lunar eclipse always leaves two sensitive points in the skies, while the solar eclipse leaves one sensitive point in the skies. The two points for the lunar eclipse are (1) the degree in which the eclipse takes place, and (2) the degree directly opposite in the ecliptic. The crude woodcut on page 45 illustrates this principle very well, for the lunar eclipse is a consequence of the Sun being in Cancer and the Moon being in Capricorn.

In contrast, since the solar eclipse is caused by the meeting of Sun and Moon in a single degree, only one point in the horoscope should be affected.

These rules mean that in 1999, for example, when there are two solar eclipses and one lunar eclipse, there should be four sensitive points left in the skies:

1 – solar eclipse of 16 February 1999, in 28 degrees Aquarius.

2 – lunar eclipse of 28 July 1999 in 5 degrees Aquarius/Leo.
1 – solar eclipse of 11 August 1999 in 19 degrees Leo.

However, although the solar eclipse sensitizes a single degree, tradition insists that the degree diametrically opposite that degree *may* also become a sensitive point. My own researches have shown that this tradition is correct. Thus, in 1999 there will be six sensitive points 'burned' into the ecliptic.

THE FIRST RULE: Both lunar and solar eclipses each leave two sensitive degrees in the zodiacal belt, marking precisely that degree in which the eclipse took place, and the degree diametrically opposite.

Rule Two

The second rule says that the sensitive degree becomes operative (that is, it has an influence on the life and destiny of a person) only if that degree is occupied by a planet or a nodal point. In other words, for a sensitive degree left by an eclipse to work, it must find a matrix in the chart on another sensitive degree.

We already know what planets are, but we should consider the meaning of nodal points. A nodal point, in astrology, is the Dragon's Head and Dragon's Tail, or one of the four *angles*. I have already touched upon the significance of the first two, on page 50. The four angles are marked in the chart by the crossing of the horizontal line with the vertical line which marks the highest point of the heavens towards the top, and the lowest point of the heavens at the bottom.

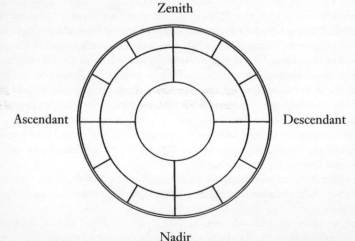

74

At the top is the *zenith* (this is often represented by the symbol MC, which is from the Latin *Medium Coeli*, 'the middle of the skies'). The zenith represents the highest point in any horoscope figure.

At the bottom is the *nadir*, the lowest point of the skies: this is often represented in astrology by the symbol IC, which is from the Latin, *Imum Coeli*, the lowest part of the skies.

To the left is the *Ascendant* – this marks the place of sunrise: the horizontal line represents the horizon, over which the Sun rises each morning. The Sun sets at the opposite point, at the *Descendant*. No matter where the Sun might be in a chart, there is always a degree of the zodiac arising over the Ascendant, and setting at the Descendant. This is because the outer circle represents the zodiac itself. In astrology, the most important angle is the Ascendant, and the second is the Zenith.

It might be useful to look at a basic horoscope with these four angles marked, just to see how this theory is set down in practice in an actual figure.

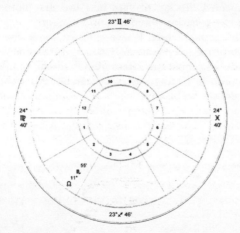

Here, by way of example, are the four angles abstracted from the horoscope of the film-maker, Walt Disney, whose horoscope we shall examine shortly.

You will see that:

His Ascendant is in 24.40 Virgo (♍).
His Zenith (MC) is in 23.46 Gemini (♊).
His Dragon's Head is in 11.55 Scorpio (♏).

In summary of this rule, then, we should recognize that the sensitive points which are, so to speak, burned by eclipses into the zodiac, only

75

become effective if they fall upon a point in the horoscope occupied by a planet, a nodal point, or one of the angles. The second rule of interpretation is:

THE SECOND RULE: The sensitive degrees left by eclipses become operative in a chart only when there is a corresponding degree occupied by a planet, an angle or a nodal point.

Rule Three
In very simple terms, we may visualize the meeting of a sensitive eclipse-degree with a planet, or nodal point, as the union of the Cosmos (the eclipse) with the personal human (the personal chart). It is the meeting of unlimited Space (the Cosmos) with the limitations of the time-bound (the human soul, as expressed through the horoscope). I could express this idea more clearly by saying that the meeting of the eclipse with a nodal point marks the opportunity which the spiritual world (the Cosmos) has to bring unexpected destiny or fate into the life (horoscope) of the individual, thereby releasing potential into actuality.

The two–rule method which I have outlined above can be applied to charts with extraordinary precision. Looking further at Walt Disney's chart, we see how an eclipse can affect an individual.

Disney was born in Chicago on 5 December 1901 at 12:30 am.[1] His chart and data are shown below:

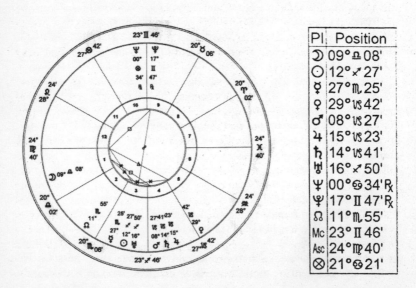

Pl	Position
☽	09° ♎ 08'
☉	12° ♐ 27'
☿	27° ♏ 25'
♀	29° ♑ 42'
♂	08° ♑ 27'
♃	15° ♑ 23'
♄	14° ♑ 41'
♅	16° ♐ 50'
♆	00° ♋ 34' ℞
♇	17° ♊ 47' ℞
☊	11° ♏ 55'
Mc	23° ♊ 46'
Asc	24° ♍ 40'
⊗	21° ♋ 21'

The horoscope is fascinating because of the considerable number of planets in Capricorn. You will observe that his Sun was in 13 degrees of Sagittarius. On 3 June 1928 there was an eclipse of the Moon in 13 degrees of this sign. The contact between the sensitive degree of the eclipse and that of the planet is therefore close:

SUN IN THE CHART OF WALT DISNEY: 12.27 SAGITTARIUS
LUNAR ECLIPSE OF 3 JUNE 1928:   12.37 SAGITTARIUS

Because the eclipse was involved with the Sun, which is a creative planet in any horoscope, we must presume that the eclipse had some influence on his creativity.

It was on 18 November 1928 that Walt Disney introduced his character Mickey Mouse to the world, through his cartoon *Steamboat Willy*, the first animated cartoon with sound.[2] Described as 'a riot of mirth' by a reviewer, the success of the film had not come easily to Disney, who had spent almost two years of desperate negotiations with film companies, who were reluctant to see the promise of the 'talkie-cartoon'.

The example shows how an eclipse can help in the dramatic unfolding of a creative potential with the chart of a native. As this eclipse demonstrates, one of the effects of eclipses can be to unlock creative potential, and to bring into the lives of individuals hitherto unexpected opportunities for success.

In passing, I should note that the astrologer Nelson Stewart worked out the horoscope for Mickey Mouse himself, taking the first public screening of 1928 as the birth date.[3] Although Stewart did not appear to be aware of the connection between the eclipse of this year, and the creation of the film, he was right in seeing Sagittarius as a 'sporting and happy-go-lucky sign'.

Perhaps, to emphasize that eclipses *can* often be fortunate, I should give another example of a Sagittarian success. Let us take the horoscope of Ludwig von Beethoven, who was born 16 December 1770 at 1:33:25 pm, in Bonn.[4] His chart is set out on the following page.

It would be very easy indeed to establish the astrological reasons why this chart is one of genius. However, my preliminary interest lies in a single eclipse which brought extraordinary benefits into his life.

Up to the age of thirty-eight, Beethoven had depended upon teaching as a means of earning a living, supplemented by the publication of his music and giving private concerts. This did not give him enough time to concentrate on composition. In 1809, however, three remarkable men – the Archduke Rudolph, Prince Kinsky and Prince Lobkowitz – decided to join together to offer him an income for life.[5]

In 1809 there was an eclipse in 11 degrees of Taurus, on his Ascendant,

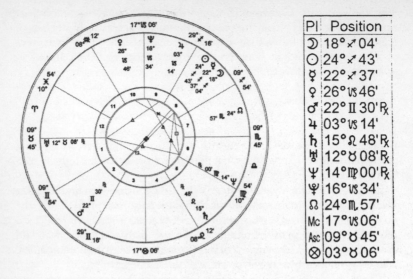

Pl	Position
☽	18° ♐ 04'
☉	24° ♐ 43'
☿	22° ♐ 37'
♀	26° ♑ 46'
♂	22° ♊ 30' ℞
♃	03° ♑ 14'
♄	15° ♌ 48' ℞
♅	12° ♉ 08' ℞
♆	14° ♍ 00' ℞
♇	16° ♑ 34'
☊	24° ♏ 57'
Mc	17° ♑ 06'
Asc	09° ♉ 45'
⊗	03° ♉ 06'

a place in the horoscope which is always concerned deeply with both self-image and self expression.

LUNAR ECLIPSE OF 30 APRIL 1809:   9.10 TAURUS-SCORPIO
ASCENDANT IN THE CHART OF BEETHOVEN: 9.45 TAURUS

The correspondence between the sensitive degree of the eclipse and the corresponding angle is not quite so close as in the case of the eclipse which influenced Disney's life, yet it is still well within the same degree, and therefore just as effective.

(A lunar eclipse, by its very nature, falls across two signs: in this case, the Sun was in Taurus and the Moon in Scorpio. Because of this, I have marked the two signs involved in the lunar eclipse: in future, however, I shall mark only the sign which corresponds to the sensitive degree of planet or nodal points.)

Through glancing at the charts of Disney and Beethoven, we have been introduced unwittingly to the third law of eclipse-interpretation. This law states that the nature of the event signalled by a sensitive-degree eclipse is determined mainly by the nature of the planet or nodal point involved. In both charts, the eclipses released benefits into the lives of the two natives. I have to say, however, that the two examples I have chosen can be read in a more complex way than I suggest here, for Beethoven's horoscope is essentially a tragic chart, while Disney's is a successful one in worldly terms. However, to understand these distinctions would require a knowledge of astrology which is not essential to this study of eclipse lore.[6]

The two examples are sufficient for me to set out the third rule, for when the Sun or Ascendant is touched by an eclipse, it is usually to the benefit of the person concerned. A further and most striking example of this is the chart of Pope John Paul II, who was born within two hours of an eclipse, which meant that his Sun was directly upon the eclipse point. It was this contact which helped lift him to the highest place of honour in the Catholic world (see page 185).

THE THIRD RULE: The influence of a sensitive degree left by eclipses exerts an influence which is determined by the intrinsic natures of the planet, angle or a nodal point on which that eclipse falls.

Rule Four

Now let us turn to a more sombre influence left by an eclipse. Let us look at the horoscope of the Emperor Franz Joseph of Austria, and see how fate can work into a horoscope of an individual who is protected by all the riches and security that the world may furnish. Franz Joseph was born on 18 August 1830 at 8:23 am, in Vienna.[7]

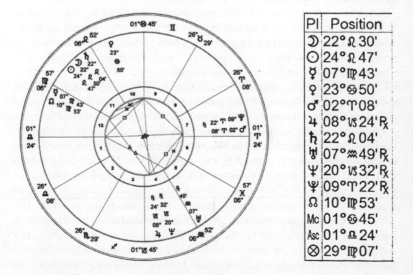

Pl	Position
☽	22° ♌ 30'
☉	24° ♌ 47'
☿	07° ♍ 43'
♀	23° ♋ 50'
♂	02° ♈ 08'
♃	08° ♑ 24' R
♄	22° ♌ 04'
♅	07° ♒ 49' R
♆	20° ♑ 32' R
♇	09° ♈ 22' R
☊	10° ♍ 53'
Mc	01° ♋ 45'
Asc	01° ♎ 24'
⊗	29° ♍ 07'

I have marked the position of Neptune (♆) in this chart: it is in 21 degrees of Capricorn. In this case, there is very little difference between the historical horoscope (which I have taken from the July 1910 edition of the magazine *Modern Astrology*) and the modern computer tabulation.

Did an eclipse ever fall on a sensitive degree in the chart of Franz Joseph?

On the 12 July 1889 there was a lunar eclipse in 21 degrees of Capricorn. According to the rules I have just outlined, this meant that the sensitive points left by the eclipse in both 21 Capricorn and the opposite degree, 21 Cancer, could be sparked off by the planet Neptune to produce an important event in Franz Joseph's life, during that year.

SOLAR ECLIPSE OF 12 JULY 1889:	20.36 CAPRICORN
NEPTUNE IN THE CHART OF FRANZ JOSEPH:	20.32 CAPRICORN

There are various rules for enabling an astrologer to determine the nature of events sparked off by the presence of a planet in a sensitive degree, linked with the intrinsic natures of the planets and of the nodal points involved in the eclipse degree. The same sensitive degree will manifest on the material plane in different ways according to the different planets which are located on it.

In the case of the chart of Franz Joseph, it is the planet Neptune which conducts the power of the 1889 eclipse into his life. This means that we must expect a Neptunian event to materialize in this year.

Sensitive points created by the meeting of an eclipse with a planet or nodal point tend to be coloured by the nature of the planets or nodal points involved. At its best, Neptune is dreamy, illuminated, inspired and poetic. At its worst (that is to say, when under pressure), Neptune is a dissolver of form, casting a veil over human perceptions, and inducing deceit, obscurations and guilt. It is a kind of lens, which makes everything appear distorted, disjointed and mad. Looking at the world through the lenses of Neptune is somewhat like peering through deep waters into the sunlit world above: nothing can be seen quite rightly, or in its truthful form, because of hidden currents and undulations in the water. The nature of the world is distorted, and made unreal by such lenses. It is significant that the planet should be named after the god of the Sea, rather than after a god of the Earth, or of the Heavens. The effect of Neptune in a human life is to plunge that person into the inner sea, which is the subconscious, a repository not only of memory and dreams, but also of guilt.

Of course, we do not have to learn all the associations of Neptune: for the sake of our example, we should merely observe that the meeting of the nebulous and confusing planet Neptune with the lunar eclipse can be charged with guilt, misunderstandings and recriminations on a huge scale.

How did this Neptunian charge explode (so to speak) in the life of Franz Joseph?

In 1889 his son was murdered.

As this murder was linked with an eclipse, we shall look at the astrological factors behind the death later (see page 210). The story has become famous in recent years, for a version of the events was told, within a somewhat romanticized setting, in the film *Mayerling*. Franz Joseph's son was Crown Prince Rudolph of Austria, an extremely talented and sensitive young man, deeply interested in literature, and well prepared in many ways to take over the Austrian empire from his father. Although married in 1881 to Stephanie, daughter of the king of the Belgians, Rudolph took mistresses, one of whom was the seventeen-year-old Baroness Mary Vetsera. The pair were murdered in Rudolph's hunting lodge, at Mayerling. What we shall find interesting as we study the case more closely later is that, just as the murder was reflected in the sensitive degree of the father's chart, so it was reflected in another eclipse-induced sensitive degree in the horoscope of Rudolph himself.

We have applied the two simple rules of eclipse-prediction to the chart of Franz Joseph, and seen how a sensitive degree can release an explosive charge of energy – in this case, energy connected with Neptune. Now, the eclipse took place on 12 July 1889, yet the double-murder had occurred some months earlier, in January 1889. Is there any explanation to account for this time-lapse between eclipse and event?

The question brings us to the fourth eclipse-prediction rule. According to tradition, the sensitive degree engendered by an eclipse is so powerful that it leaves, as it were, ripples in time. We can perhaps best visualize an eclipse degree as being a sort of vortex into the Cosmos. The actual channel is quite narrow (a degree's width, so to speak) while the surrounding turbulance is much wider. Astrologers have learned to interpret this breadth of turbulance in time. A sensitive degree formed by an eclipse can leave an effect for some months before the eclipse actually takes place, and some months afterwards.

The ancient astrologers recognized this gap in time very well, and insisted that the time differences depended entirely upon the *duration* of an eclipse. As we have seen, when we looked at what a seventeenth-century astrologer wrote on this subject, in the case of a slow-moving lunar eclipse, the scale of hours in the Cosmos would be equated to years on the human plane. If for example, an eclipse lasted for two hours, then it was believed that its effect would endure for two years around the sensitive degree it formed.

The lunar eclipse of 12 July 1889 lasted for well over an hour, which meant that in terms of this theory the murder of Rudolph was well within the time limits of the eclipse-prediction rule.

THE FOURTH RULE: The event to be read from a sensitive degree made by an eclipse falling on planets, angles or nodes in a chart will occur within the period determined by the duration of the eclipse. This duration is in the ratio of one year to each hour of eclipse. This duration is regarded as being extended over the centre of the time of the eclipse, and is operative both forwards and backwards in time.

The latter sentence really means that an eclipse of two hours will radiate its influence for approximately one year prior to the eclipse and one year afterwards.

Timing events through astrological means can be quite difficult, not because astrology is an inexact tool, but because the Cosmos seems to work creatively, rather than mechanically. This is not an issue to develop here, but it might be a good idea to look at its implications in a very interesting chart. This is the chart of the French film actress, Brigitte Bardot, who was born at 01:15 pm, on 28 September 1934, in Paris.[8]

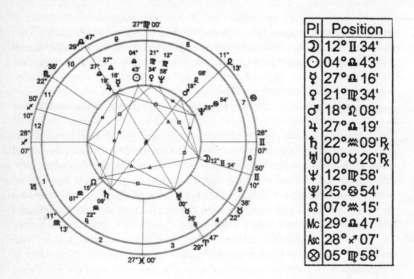

Pl	Position
☽	12° ♊ 34'
☉	04° ♎ 43'
☿	27° ♎ 16'
♀	21° ♍ 34'
♂	18° ♌ 08'
♃	27° ♎ 19'
♄	22° ♒ 09' ℞
♅	00° ♉ 26' ℞
♆	12° ♍ 58'
♇	25° ♋ 54'
☊	07° ♒ 15'
Mc	29° ♎ 47'
Asc	28° ♐ 07'
⊗	05° ♍ 58'

The physical beauty and sensuality for which she was famous is expressed through the exact contact between Mercury and Jupiter in Libra. However, it is not the chart itself which interests me here – it is the series of eclipses which influenced her career.

Brigitte's career is said to have taken off in 1952, when she was eighteen years old.

In fact, she had often been photographed for the press before this, but was by no means a star. Accordingly her first husband, Roger Vadim, was very surprised when their wedding photographs were published in a four-page spread in *Paris-Match*. This fame is what he later called 'part of the Bardot mystery', which was that she seemed to create an event through the magnetism of her presence. In fact, Bardot turned a film down in this year in order to get a part in Jean Anouilh's play *An Invitation to the Castle*. I think that the real importance of 1952 for the young actress was her relationship with Vadim, and her marriage.[9]

What was it (talent and contacts apart) which helped select Bardot from all the other thousands of aspiring actresses in that year, to lift her to stardom? In 1952 there were two eclipses which fell upon her chart:

LUNAR ECLIPSE OF 11 FEBRUARY 1952:	21.19 AQUARIUS
SATURN IN THE CHART OF BARDOT:	22.09 AQUARIUS
SOLAR ECLIPSE OF 25 FEBRUARY 1952:	05.43 PISCES
PART OF FORTUNE IN THE CHART OF BARDOT:	05.58 VIRGO

In 1955 a solar eclipse fell across the most sensitive of all points in a personal chart – the Ascendant-Descendant axis – in the sign associated with acting and the stage, Gemini:

SOLAR ECLIPSE OF 20 JUNE 1955:	28.05 GEMINI
ASCENDANT IN THE CHART OF BARDOT:	28.07 SAGITTARIUS

Now, it is this last eclipse which interests me in terms of timing. In this year she was making the film which was to reveal her as a great actress and create her fame as the 'sex-kitten' of French cinema, *And God Created Woman*. My question (which touches on the nature of the creative process itself) is, when is a film made? It takes a very long time to make a film, from the inception of the idea to the final release. This film was not released until 1956, but Brigitte was working on it when the eclipse took place upon her Ascendant. It would therefore be accurate to say that there was no time-gap between the eclipse and the success it promised. On the other hand, one had to wait almost a year for box-office success. These considerations – writ large in such a long-drawn-out thing as making a film, or some similar creative activity – point to one of the differences between the cosmic timing and the ordinary timing, which we call history. It is often difficult to establish a precise time-link between the two – especially as some eclipses seem to leave their creative mark after the event which is recognized in time on the earth plane.

As a matter of fact, from an astrological point of view, the zenith of

Bardot's career should have been 1958. In that year the extraordinary gathering of planets around her 'career centre' (the zenith) was touched by an eclipse which fell across her zenith-nadir axis:

MERCURY IN THE CHART OF BARDOT:	27.16 LIBRA
JUPITER IN THE CHART OF BARDOT:	27.19 LIBRA
ZENITH IN THE CHART OF BARDOT:	29.47 LIBRA
SOLAR ECLIPSE OF 19 APRIL 1958:	28.34 LIBRA

This cosmic promise is met in the films she made during this extraordinary period – films like, *The Devil is a Woman* and *Mam'zelle Pigalle*. Now, I have no wish to suggest that Bardot was an astounding actress: she herself famously said, 'I started out as a lousy actress and have remained one,'[10] but I am interested in how eclipses can lift someone of passable talent into the heights of fame. I doubt if the spiritual realms in which we live are too interested in talent – they seem rather to be interested in exploiting creative opportunity.

In view of this dating problem, let us look at another creative enterprise, whose date of formation has been recorded with considerable care. Officially, the Theosophical Society was founded in the City of New York, in 1875.[11]

Very precise details as to when it was founded have been recorded, and from these details we glean that it was first proposed, as an idea, on 7 September 1875, in 46 Irving Place, New York.[12]

Now, here we have a very exactly recorded time and place for the founding of an idea which spread through the world with extreme rapidity, and which still exists as an active force. Was there any eclipse connected with this foundation? The answer is, of course, yes. The leading force behind the foundation of the Theosophical Society was Madame H. P. Blavatsky, whose chart is given below.[13] She was present at the meeting of September 1875, when it was decided to found the society. Blavatsky was born on 12 August 1831 in Dnepropetrovsk, Russia, at 02:12 am.

In September, 1875 an eclipse fell upon her zenith:

LUNAR ECLIPSE OF 15 SEPTEMBER 1875:	22.23 PISCES
ZENITH IN THE CHART OF MADAME BLAVATSKY:	22.02 PISCES

We see from this that in the very month that the lunar eclipse fell, the idea of the Theosophical Society was being mooted.

There is a period of only eight days between this 'official' date and the time of the eclipse. Rarely is such exactitude possible when considering eclipse influences, if only because it is usually difficult to pin down exactly when an idea may be said to have begun.

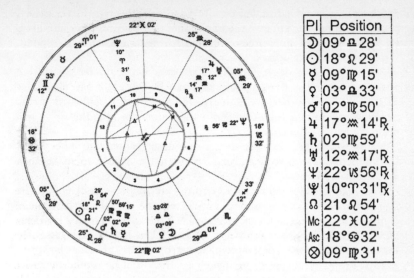

Pl	Position
☽	09° ♎ 28'
☉	18° ♌ 29'
☿	09° ♍ 15'
♀	03° ♎ 33'
♂	02° ♍ 50'
♃	17° ♒ 14' Rx
♄	02° ♍ 59'
♅	12° ♒ 17' Rx
♆	22° ♑ 56' Rx
♇	10° ♈ 31' Rx
☊	21° ♌ 54'
Mc	22° ♓ 02'
Asc	18° ♋ 32'
⊗	09° ♍ 31'

Why is it so difficult to say precisely when a creative activity begins and ends, or comes to fruition? Whatever we believe, creativity on the human plane is always involved with participation in the spiritual realm around – with the ideas and impulses which circulate around us, and which we regard as our spiritual and artistic heritage. In the spiritual realms within which all thinking and feeling people live there is not the same sense of time and space as in the more mundane world. The simple truth is that whether we like it or not, and whether we are educated or not, in our spiritual worlds the ideas of Aristotle, Dante and Einstein jostle with the same imperious demand for our attention as ideas in our daily newspapers. We must always bear this in mind when attempting to date future events from eclipses, for eclipses seem to deal more with the creative realm of timeless ideas than we are accustomed to. Indeed, we must regard eclipses only as indicators of events, rather than as timers of events, and rely on other astrological techniques for working out precise times.

The solar eclipse which took place on 16 September 1997 lasted for 1 hour and 6 minutes. This means that, were we contemplating the chart of someone born around this time, who had a planet upon the 25 degrees of Pisces, then (in terms of the fourth rule) we would expect some event to take place about six months before or after September. Such a considerable gap might lead us to ask, how do we time events from an eclipse? The answer, strictly speaking, is that we do not. The eclipse merely tells us that the Sun and Moon are working on a sensitive degree, and that within a year or so of the eclipse we should expect something in

85

the chart to respond to this degree. The words have been chosen carefully, because I do not wish to give the impression that eclipses *cause* anything: eclipses merely set up cosmic conditions to which a chart may respond, through its sensitive degrees.

An eclipse on a degree in the chart of a native merely alerts the astrologer to the fact that a major event may be expected. The astrologer will make use of other predictive techniques, well established in the astrological tradition, for working out approximately what this event will be, and when it will happen.[14]

Is it possible, then, to make accurate predictions merely from eclipses? Undoubtedly, the answer is, yes – though the ability to make such predictions is very rare.

The remarkable nineteenth-century astrologer, Zadkiel – the pseudonym of R.J. Morrison[15] – predicted the terrible earthquake at Cumana, in Venezuela, on 15 July 1853.[16] Like Lilly, he cast a chart for the moment of eclipse, to study its influence. Also like Lilly, he assumed that it would involve some sort of catastrophe. In this case, however, Zadkiel predicted the event with such accuracy that he named the exact place and date of the catastrophe, from the chart for the total eclipse of 6 June 1853.[17]

Rule Five

There are three more rules of eclipse-interpretation which we must examine. To understand them, we need to study something of the history of astrology, and to glance at one or two interesting horoscopes, through which eclipses worked.

The method of interpreting eclipses is deeply rooted in mediaeval astrology. As it happens, the mediaeval technique of eclipse-interpretation was extremely complicated, and hedged in by rules.[18] There are few things more bemusing to astrologers than the numerous – often contradictory – series of complex rules for eclipse interpretation recorded by the seventeenth-century English astrologer, William Lilly.[19] Fortunately for us, modern astrology has simplified this predictive technique by discarding many of the more complex methods. In consequence, it is now possible to set down a reliable method of eclipse interpretation in a few paragraphs, and formulate this in a few rules.

To return to the earlier eclipse of 1853. In that year, millions of people would have been born. As we have seen, these people would have been affected by the eclipse only if, at the moment of their births, they had planets or nodal points on the degree sensitized by it. In the case of such a contact, or conjunction, the life of the native would probably be coloured to some extent by the conditions pertaining to the eclipse. Let us look into this idea.

In fact there were three eclipses in 1853, taking place in Gemini and Sagittarius:

SOLAR ECLIPSE OF 6 JUNE 1853:	15.57 GEMINI
LUNAR ECLIPSE OF 21 JUNE 1853:	29.37 SAGITTARIUS
SOLAR ECLIPSE OF 30 NOVEMBER 1853:	08.34 SAGITTARIUS

I should also add that the previous year, 1852, had seen no fewer than six eclipses, three of which were solar. The last two occurred in December of that year, and (from an astrological point of view) might therefore be interpreted as throwing their influences into the year we are considering – 1853. These two eclipses, late in 1852, may be summarized as:

SOLAR ECLIPSE OF 11 DECEMBER 1852:	19.19 SAGITTARIUS
LUNAR ECLIPSE OF 26 DECEMBER 1852:	04.57 CANCER

Of the millions of people born in 1853, there is one in particular who is still remembered – the great Dutch artist, Vincent van Gogh.[20]

The exact moment and place of Vincent's birth are known.[21] He was born at Zundert, on 30 March 1853 at 11:20 am. The horoscope for this time and place is given below:

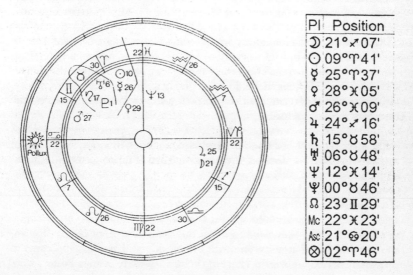

Is it possible that Vincent's horoscope reflects any sensitive degrees which link with the eclipses prior to, or shortly after, his birth? The answer is yes. The solar eclipse of 11 December, 1852 took place in a degree very close to the position of his own Moon:

SOLAR ECLIPSE OF 11 DECEMBER 1852:   19.20 SAGITTARIUS
MOON IN THE CHART OF VAN GOGH: 21.07 SAGITTARIUS

Now we see immediately that the contact is far from being exact. What the astrologers call an *orb* of 01.48 degrees is just too wide for the effect to be very dramatic. Under normal circumstances, it would not be regarded as being operative at all. However, this detail in Vincent's chart permits us to formulate another interesting rule of eclipse interpretation. Briefly, the rule states that if a part of the horoscope is marked by a number of planets or nodes in close conjunction, then these may together be taken as having a wider orb than usual.[22] In other words, a group of influences creates an arc, rather than a degree of sensitivity.

In Vincent's chart, the planets and nodes are so disposed as to offer a much wider orb than usual. As we can see from the data below, the distribution of planets and nodes in Vincent's chart is so close that they span an arc of almost 4 degrees:

MOON IN THE CHART OF VAN GOGH: 21.07 SAGITTARIUS
DRAGON'S TAIL IN THE CHART OF VAN GOGH: 23.29 SAGITTARIUS
JUPITER IN THE CHART OF VAN GOGH: 24.16 SAGITTARIUS

This trebly strong configuration of planets makes a powerful set of sensitive degrees – indeed, a sensitive *arc* – which was sufficient to lend an explosive intensity to the life of the painter, through the eclipse that fell at its edge. We shall look at his horoscope later, to see how this intensity manifested itself in terms of other eclipses, and to take note of more tragic trends in the artist's life.

THE FIFTH RULE: When a number of degrees in a chart are bound together in close conjunction, the permitted orb of influence is wider than usual.

Rule Six

How close do planets and eclipses need to be for them to become operative? Ideally, they need to be in the same degree, of course, but in practice we find that a few minutes either side still renders the contact operative. An example is the chart of the story-writer, Beatrix Potter, who was born on 28 July 1866, in London.[23]

Her Saturn is in Scorpio, very close to the eclipse of 31 October 1902:

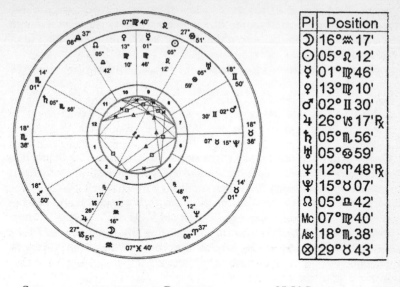

Pl	Position
☽	16°♒17'
☉	05°♌12'
☿	01°♍46'
♀	13°♍10'
♂	02°♊30'
♃	26°♑17'℞
♄	05°♏56'
♅	05°♋59'
♆	12°♈48'℞
♇	15°♉07'
☊	05°♎42'
Mc	07°♍40'
Asc	18°♏38'
⊗	29°♉43'

SATURN IN THE CHART OF POTTER: 05.56 SCORPIO

SOLAR ECLIPSE OF 31 OCTOBER, 1902:   06:58 SCORPIO

In this case we have an eclipse which is 2 minutes outside the degree permitted. In fact, this slight deviation from the permitted orb did not appear to make much difference to the chief event in the literary life of Beatrix Potter.

It was in 1902 that the first of her children's stories, *Peter Rabbit* was accepted for publication, by a firm which became bound up with her own destiny.

As a matter of fact, *The Tale of Peter Rabbit* had been rejected by Frederick Warne & Co., and by other publishers long before 1902. In despair, Beatrix published it herself with her own meagre savings. It came out in this form, with black and white illustrations by Beatrix, in December 1901, and was sold in small batches, mainly to friends. Late 1902 proved to be the magical time, however, for just as she was printing her own small second edition, she received word from Frederick Warne, that they would publish it, if she would be prepared to do coloured illustrations to replace the black and white ones. In consequence of this, the year saw more than the publication of her first book – she had an experience of a new and less lonely family life among the Warnes in London, where she often stayed as a guest.

In this household, Beatrix was attracted to Norman Warne, the youngest of the Warne family. In the summer of 1905, Norman Warne proposed to her, and Beatrix Potter – then almost forty years old – accepted. Unfortunately, domestic happiness was not to be hers. A month or so later, Norman discovered that he had leukaemia, and at the end of August he died.

This loss is reflected in an eclipse of February of that year, which fell on her Mercury.

MERCURY IN THE CHART OF POTTER:	01.46 VIRGO
LUNAR ECLIPSE OF 19 FEBRUARY 1905:	00.34 VIRGO

Once again, the contact is slightly wide of orb – this time, by as much as 12 minutes – yet the eclipse certainly reflected a major change in her life, influencing that literary life which is reflected by Mercury.

Beatrix sank back into her lonely life with her parents, and did not marry until 1913, when she was 47 years old.[24] On 31 August 1913, there was a solar eclipse on her zenith – suggesting that her marriage to the solicitor William Heelis was more of a career move – more involved with escaping loneliness – than a matter of pure love.[25]

ZENITH IN THE CHART OF POTTER:	07.40 VIRGO
SOLAR ECLIPSE OF 31 AUGUST, 1913:	07.49 VIRGO

Do eclipses continue to have a bearing on the lives of people after death? I cannot answer this question with any certainty, but it is clear that the destiny of works of art in literature, music and painting which are left behind after death are certainly linked with the artist by eclipses. One of the works which Beatrix Potter wrote in her lifetime – unknown to anyone who lived around her – was published exactly one century after her birth, and there is little doubt that this was overshadowed by an eclipse.

During her lifetime Beatrix had kept a secret diary in code. The word 'diary' does not do this justice, for it was over 200,000 words of cipher-writing in manuscript form. After her death, this remained hidden until Mrs Stephanie Duke, a first cousin once removed, found it in the attic of the house where Beatrix had lived. The diary was decoded over a period of five years by Leslie Linder, and published in 1966 as *The Journal of Beatrix Potter*.

In 1966 a lunar eclipse fell opposite the Pluto of Beatrix's chart, like a shadow from the grave.

PLUTO IN THE CHART OF POTTER:	15.07 TAURUS
LUNAR ECLIPSE OF 4 MAY 1966:	14.02 TAURUS

A more unpleasant example of the working of the fifth rule may be found in the chart of a famous murderer – Walter Shaw of Texas, who was born in Galveston, on 4 May 1856 at 11:30. His horoscope and data are given below: the records for his birth, crime and execution are of great value to astrologers because these appear to have been made with great care, and are within a minute or two of accuracy.[26]

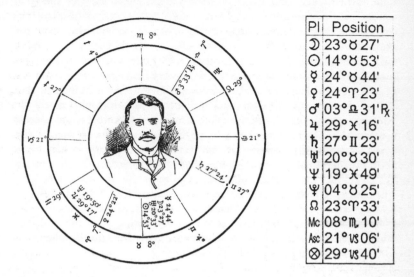

Pl	Position
☽	23°♉27'
☉	14°♉53'
☿	24°♉44'
♀	24°♈23'
♂	03°♎31'℞
♃	29°♓16'
♄	27°♊23'
♅	20°♉30'
♆	19°♓49'
♇	04°♉25'
☊	23°♈33'
Mc	08°♏10'
Asc	21°♑06'
⊗	29°♑40'

Round about 7:30, on 30 March 1892, Shaw murdered both his mother and sister cutting their throats. He was tried for the crime, found guilty, and hanged in Houston at 11:37 am, on 4 August 1893.

The series of horoscopes which can be derived from this data is of great interest, but I shall pay attention only to the birth chart, for this illustrates to perfection the idea of how an orb may be extended by conjunctions.

Before we do this, let us consider what the astrological background to the double murder might have been. This carries us almost naturally to a consideration of the next rule of eclipse-interpretation, for if we study these charts we encounter the interesting notion that *fixed stars* work through eclipses. (They were first called 'fixed stars' by the ancients who saw that a few stars moved across the sky in relation to the others, while the rest stayed still. We now know that the moving 'stars' are planets, but the term 'fixed stars' for the others has remained.)

Fixed stars are of profound importance to the study of eclipses. In the mechanism of their influences and effects, they work rather like eclipses, and with the same dramatic effect. They work into the lives of natives as *sensitive degrees* which are sparked off by planets, nodes and angles. This fact, which is of profound importance in astrology, takes us directly to the sixth rule of interpretation.

The astrological tradition that fixed stars can have a profound, and even dramatic effect on personal charts may be traced back to the earliest astrological literature.[27] The second–century astrologer Ptolemy recorded some of the ancient names for such stars, and gave what has been shown to be an excellent summary of their influences in terms of planetary equivalents. For example, the star which is now named Alpheratz (the prime star of the constellation Andromeda) was said by Ptolemy to be of the nature of Jupiter and Venus combined. By linking the star to these two stars, Ptolemy was intimating that it was a very beneficial star: Jupiter is a planet of spiritual and material expansiveness, while Venus is the planet of beauty. This explains why, in the astrological tradition, Alpheratz should be regarded as giving to natives honour, favours from others, and success in business, with a propensity to achieve the ambitions they set themselves.

In the astrological tradition, a fixed star becomes operative when it falls upon a planet, a node or an angle in a chart. In this respect, it works rather like an eclipse, save that its influence is far more specific than an eclipse. The natures of stellar influences have been studied for centuries, and have been described in considerable detail. As we shall see from many examples of horoscopes which follow, fixed stars work with extraordinary drama into the lives of men and women. They work most dramatically when they fall directly upon a planet, an angle or a node.

What happens if a fixed star is rendered operative in a chart, by virtue of its being on a planet, a node or an angle, and this combination is *also* overlaid by an eclipse? As one may imagine, the effect can be quite

ALGOL

extraordinary and explosive. This is why William Lilly reminded his readers: 'Be not unmindful of the images of the fixed Stars, wherein the Eclipses . . . doe happen.'[28] It is perhaps the best line of advice he gave in his entire book on eclipses.

The trouble with the mass-murderer, Walter Shaw, was the fixed star Algol – the most evil star in the heavens. Algol, called in some works of astronomy the 'demon star', is set in the severed head of the Gorgon Medusa (opposite).[29] It has a reputation for violence, and particularly with violence relating to the face. This stark tradition is encapsulated in an early tenth-century Persian drawing of the constellation of Perseus, showing an Arabic version of the classical hero holding the severed head of the Gorgon Medusa in his left hand. The star shown above the right eye of this demonic face whose look turned people to stone is the star Algol.

At the time of Shaw's birth, this star was upon his Mercury, in Taurus.

MERCURY IN THE CHART OF SHAW:	24.44 TAURUS
POSITION OF STAR ALGOL IN 1856:	24.09 TAURUS

In May 1892 – two months before the murder – there was a lunar eclipse which fell across Taurus–Scorpio, very close to this position of Mercury:

LUNAR ECLIPSE OF 11 MAY 1892:	21.37 TAURUS

It is clear that the orb of over three degrees is too much for us to expect there to be any influence at all between the eclipse and the position of Mercury. However, if we consider Shaw's horoscope again, we shall see that a number of planets are gathered around this area of Taurus:

MERCURY IN THE CHART OF SHAW:	24.44 TAURUS
MOON IN THE CHART OF SHAW:	23.27 TAURUS
URANUS IN THE CHART OF SHAW:	20.30 TAURUS

In effect, there is an entire arc of five degrees in Taurus which may be regarded as being sensitive to influences – a sensitive arc, rather than degree. In terms of the rule I have just set down, this means that the arc of sensitivity may be regarded as stretching from about 19 degrees to 26 degrees of Taurus.

Now, the lunar eclipse of 11 May 1892 fell between Shaw's Moon and his Uranus:

MOON IN THE CHART OF SHAW:	23.27 TAURUS
LUNAR ECLIPSE OF 11 MAY 1892:	21.37 TAURUS
URANUS IN THE CHART OF SHAW:	20.30 TAURUS

In this way, the influence was transmitted directly to Mercury, in the sensitized arc, thus sparking off the terrible power of what is sometimes called 'the beheading star', Algol.

In fact, the year in which he committed the murders must have been very difficult for Shaw for *two* eclipses fell upon sensitive degrees in his chart. On 26 April 1892, there was a solar eclipse upon his nadir – the 'House of the Mother':

NADIR IN THE CHART OF SHAW:	08.10 TAURUS
SOLAR ECLIPSE OF 26 APRIL 1892:	07.05 TAURUS

The dramatic example of Shaw's chart indicates that we have just touched upon something of profound importance to the study of eclipses. The truth, sometimes formulated in mediaeval astrological rules, is that fixed stars play a very important role in predictive astrology. Whenever a fixed star is on a sensitive degree in a chart, it can pour very powerful forces into the life of the individual concerned. Indeed, the influence of fixed stars can be so immensely powerful in charts that it is often quite impossible to understand a horoscope without reference to the fixed stars operative within it.

Men and women of genius almost always have fixed stars within their charts. This means that when eclipses fall upon the degrees sensitized by fixed stars, the effects can often by quite galvanic. In the course of this book I shall tend to deal with the charts of famous or infamous human beings. Almost by definition, therefore, I shall at times be dealing with fixed stars, studying how these are allowed to pour their energies on to the material plane by means of eclipses.

When dealing with fixed stars, the astrologer and astronomer have recourse to a somewhat specialist terminology. In order to make things simple for the non-specialist reader, I shall restrict this terminology. Even so, there are one or two terms I should comment upon, because I shall use them.

Almost since the beginning of astronomy, the heavens have been divided into loosely defined pictorial areas, called constellations. For example, one part of the skies has been linked with the picture of the classical hero Perseus, who rescued Andromeda (a woman in the skies nearby), and also killed the dreadful Medusa (picture on page 92). On his return home, after these adventures, he accidentally killed his own grandfather, and died of grief. In pity, and to mark his heroic exploits, Jupiter raised him to the skies, as a constellation.[30] In astrology, most of the stars of this constellation are benign, in that they promote courage, intelligence and the same kind of adventurous spirit as drove Perseus in his exploits. Algol is the very notable exception.

Of course, what we have here is the development of a Greek vision of the stars, linked with that ancient Greek notion that the gods and goddesses mixed on friendly and even amorous terms with mankind.

It is perhaps difficult to trace in this pattern of stars the image of the Arabic hero – the later version of Perseus – on page 92. The pattern of the stars we still call Perseus (alongside) does not look even remotely like a giant or hero. This probably explains why other cultures have called the constellation by other names.[31]

The constellations that have come down to us from a distant past are specific gatherings of stars. Astrologers are less interested in the constellations than they are in the individual stars themselves. However, the stars are identified by the constellation in which they are located – that is why I might describe the star Algol as being *set* in the constellation of Perseus. In some cases (and this is certainly dramatically true of Algol) the location of the star throws some light on the astrological tradition concerning its power: even the name we use for the star, Algol, is derived from an Arabic word meaning 'the head of the spectre'.

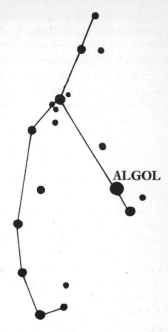

ALGOL

Mediaeval astrologers selected fifteen powerful stars for especial consideration, linking each star with a special magical stone, or gem, and a plant. For example, the powerful star which they called Cor Leonis and which we tend to call Regulus was linked with the stone granitos, and the plant mugwort.[32] In establishing these links, the astrologers were recognizing that the distant stars had an influence upon the Earth and that there is a delicate interconnection between all things.

The thing which has to be constantly born in mind by astrologers dealing with fixed stars in chart interpretation is the phenomenon of *precession*. The effect of precession is that the stars appear to move against the position of the vernal equinox in the ecliptic. This movement is steady, and is measured at the rate of about one degree in every seventy-two years. This means that if we wish to locate whether a fixed star falls on a particular planet in a given horoscope, we must establish the year to which that horoscope refers. In 1856, when the murderer Shaw was born,

Algol was in 24.09 degrees of Taurus, which is why I could describe it as being upon his Mercury.

POSITION OF STAR ALGOL IN 1856:	24.09 TAURUS
MERCURY IN THE CHART OF SHAW:	24.44 TAURUS

In 1928 – seventy-two years after Shaw's birth – the star would be in 25.09 Taurus. In AD 2000 it will be in 26.09 Taurus.

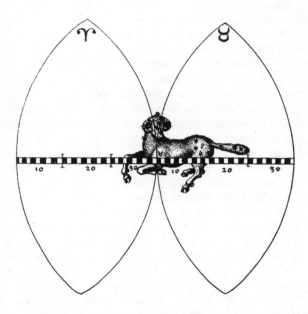

The seventeenth-century Rosicrucian, Robert Fludd, illustrated the principle of precession very beautifully in an engraving which shows an image of the constellation Aries, marked with the two great arcs which delineate the positions of the two adjacent signs of the zodiac Aries and Taurus. Fludd is graphically illustrating that the constellation Aries is not in the same position as the sign Aries. Due to precession, the stars of Aries – like all other stars – are drifting along the zodiacal path, at the rate of one degree every seventy-two years.

The star which Fludd shows just above the head of the Ram in his engraving is Hamal.[33] In 1574 – the year in which Fludd was born – this star had just moved into Taurus, and was in 01.42 degrees of the sign. This is probably why he has shown the star between the great arcs of Aries (♈) and Taurus (♉). Following the imperatives of precession, Hamal moved further along the zodiacal belt. By the year 1800, it was in 04.52 Taurus – the degree upon which the solar eclipse of 24 April 1800 fell. This eclipse participated in bringing about a profound effect on the life of Beethoven (see page 78), and hence it was a combination of eclipse and fixed star that changed Beethoven's life for the better.

If Fludd had published his work at the end of the twentieth century, then he would have shown his ram of Aries several degrees further along the zodiacal band, with Hamal in 07.39 of Taurus (see below).

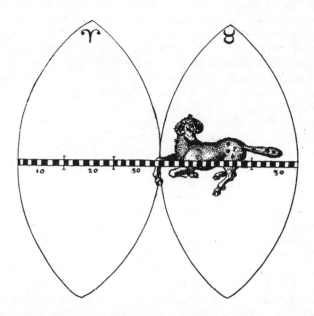

You do not need to make your own calculations as to which part of the ecliptic, or zodiacal belt, a fixed star would be in any given year, as I will provide such information at the appropriate places. I simply wish to explain why, when I deal with the positions of fixed stars, I must also place them in time. For this reason, when I give the position of a fixed star in the zodiac I also stipulate the year in question.

Although the emphasis in mediaeval astrology was upon the fifteen stars, astrological tradition has provided us with a list of well over 100 fixed stars whose influences have been carefully studied and recorded. These stars form the basic material for the study of star-lore in astrology even today.

The one thing which seems to dominate the application of this fixed-star lore to personal horoscopy is the idea that most stars work dramatically in life. Some stars are beneficial, others evil, but there is not a single star which does not work in a dramatic way when it is located on the sensitive degree of a horoscope. This dramatic outflow – almost an explosion of power – is particularly evident when this sensitive degree is touched by an eclipse. The more one studies astrology, the more one comes to the conclusion that the power of the fixed stars is awaiting release through the spiritual mechanism of eclipses.

Let us look at some chart data relating to fixed stars that have been touched by eclipses, to learn more about what such contacts can mean. Fixed stars tend to be prominent in the charts of famous or important people because the reputation of the more powerful stars hinges upon their ability to lift people into greatness. These same stars are also often known to dash these same people down – to bring about an unfortunate end. An example is given in the chart of a person who was more than usually troubled by fixed stars, and who (after his death) achieved an extraordinary fame.

Suppose that someone born in 1853 had the Mars of their chart in 27 degrees of Pisces. In that year, the fixed star Scheat was in this same degree. From this we might assume that the power of the star would deeply influence the personality of the native. Scheat is one of the so-called 'violent' stars, which has the reputation for bringing into the life of the native misfortunes, mental instability and even a violent suicide.

Now, let us suppose further that the person was born in 1853 when 22 degrees of Cancer was on their Ascendant. Since the Ascendant degree is so very sensitive this contact with a fixed star could be very explosive. Now, as it happens, in 1853 the powerful fixed star Procyon was very close to the same degree. From this fall of the star on a sensitive degree, we would know that it would reflect in some way in the life of the native. Procyon is the *alpha* of the constellation Canis Minoris, the Lesser Dog. In the mediaeval tradition, the nature of the star is the equivalent of Mercury and Mars – which is to say that it is prone to being changeable and moody (Mercury), yet forcefully direct, and active (Mars). In the astrological tradition, the star is supposed to make the native careless and violent. Like the constellation of which the star is part, the influence tends to induce a dog-like nature – the person tends to bite unexpectedly, and to be quarrelsome. The person also tends to be 'dogged' in their approach to things: once he or she has taken hold of an idea, they simply will not let go. Of course, in some situations this can be a failing, and in others a virtue.

Now, let us make a third supposition. Let us suppose that someone born in 1853 had the planet Mars of their horoscope in 26 degrees of Aries. In that year, it happened that the fixed star Al Pherg was within a degree of this position. This would mean that the planet Mars would react with the sensitive degree of the fixed star, and manifest in a particularly strong way. The star Al Pherg is well known in the astrological tradition for bestowing an almost indomitable drive and determination to achieve specific aims.

It is evident from this line up of fixed stars that a person born at that time would have a fairly tempestuous life, in which will–power and determination would be the main driving force.

Each of these sensitive degrees, involving the fixed stars Sheat, Procyon and Al Pherg, are in the chart of Vincent van Gogh. The precise alignments for these three stars in his chart are:

POSITION OF STAR SCHEAT IN 1853:	26.54 PISCES
MARS IN THE CHART OF VAN GOGH:	26.09 PISCES
POSITION OF STAR PROCYON IN 1853:	23.45 CANCER
ASCENDANT IN THE CHART OF VAN GOGH:	21.20 CANCER
POSITION OF STAR AL PHERG IN 1853:	24.46 ARIES
MERCURY IN THE CHART OF VAN GOGH:	25.37 ARIES

It will be evident from these powerful stars that Vincent van Gogh lived under tremendous psychological pressure, and that he was extremely unstable.

We need not find it surprising that so many stars are involved in this chart: it is one of the characteristics of geniuses and major figures of history, that their lives should be dominated by powerful fixed stars in such a way. The traditional reading of the stars is that they will pluck individuals out of the general mass of people into a particular historical, political, military or artistic role. We shall examine van Gogh's chart in more detail later (see page 168), but at the moment we should note that it is the sensitive degrees of the fixed stars which contributed to both his genius as a painter, and to his erratic and violent disposition.

Now I would like to glance at the fixed star and eclipse which seem to have reflected his suicide, for this combination offers a most instructive example of how eclipses can work.

Before we can fully appreciate the next detail of van Gogh's life, we should note that his Ascendant degree was on the same degree as the fixed star Pollux:

ASCENDANT OF THE CHART OF VAN GOGH:	21.20 CANCER
POSITION OF STAR POLLUX IN 1853:	21.12 CANCER

In 1990, a Japanese businessman, Ryoei Saito, paid 82.5 million dollars for van Gogh's portrait of Dr Gachet – the same doctor who had tended the artist during the last weeks of his life. This just happens to have been the highest price ever paid for a painting, and the purchase stunned the art world.

I have mentioned before that it is sometimes possible to trace eclipses which have taken place long after the death of an artist with his or her products, and this painting of Dr Gachet is no exception. A few months after Ryoei Saito purchased the picture, there was an eclipse of the Sun near to the Ascendant of van Gogh's horoscope, which had a wider orb due to its connection with the fixed star Pollux:

SOLAR ECLIPSE OF 11 JULY 1991:	18.59 CANCER
ASCENDANT IN THE CHART OF VAN GOGH:	21.20 CANCER
POSITION OF STAR POLLUX IN 1853:	21.12 CANCER

In 1890, Vincent was not only unknown, but he was also suffering with greater frequency from mental breakdowns, and had become something of a liability to his friends and doctors. In mid-June, when the solar eclipse took place, he was actually under medical supervision, and suffering from periods of intense depression. Typically, in spite of these difficulties, he was still doggedly painting.

If a proficient astrologer had happened to have access to Vincent's chart at the time, then he or she would have observed – probably with some concern – that the eclipse of 12 December 1890 would fall exactly upon the Moon in this horoscope:

MOON IN THE CHART OF VAN GOGH:	21.07 SAGITTARIUS
SOLAR ECLIPSE OF 12 DECEMBER 1890:	20.05 SAGITTARIUS

The astrologer would scent a whiff of danger from this conjunction of eclipse with the erratic Moon. He or she would probably estimate that an eclipse on a Moon in a chart as sensitive and overloaded as that of Vincent van Gogh, could be fairly explosive. If he or she were really proficient in the art of astrology, they would observe something else of profound importance. They would have noted that the Moon in van Gogh's chart was on a fixed star, in Sagittarius.

This star, the alpha of Pegasus, is called Rasalhague. In the astrological tradition it has the reputation of being an extremely difficult star, the bringer of misfortunes, hallucinatory experiences and alcoholism: it is recognized as the bringer of sudden death. On seeing such a triple combination of star, planet and eclipse, the astrologer would have been very worried indeed about Vincent's survival: the three-fold pressure would be very difficult for anyone to bear.

POSITION OF STAR RASALHAGUE IN 1853:   20.24 SAGITTARIUS
MOON IN THE CHART OF VAN GOGH: 21.07 SAGITTARIUS
SOLAR ECLIPSE OF 12 DECEMBER 1890:   20.05 SAGITTARIUS

The astrologer would have been right to harbour such fears. In that year, the pressure became too much for van Gogh. He shot himself in the chest, and died from the wounds, on 29 July.

The weak eclipse effect which overshadowed Vincent's birth carries into a most interesting and little-explored area of astrology. The fact is that exactly one year earlier, to the very day – on 30 March 1852 – his mother had given birth to another child. This baby was born dead, yet before burial it was named Vincent. The Vincent who was born a year later lived in the shadow of the stillborn child, even to the extent of being aware of its tombstone, marked with the name 'Vincent'. Just as the darkness of the eclipse seemed to hover in the spiritual life of Vincent van Gogh, so the darkness of the tomb seemed to remain displayed in his youthful everyday consciousness.

From an astrological point of view, this still-birth is interesting. If we examine the horoscope for this strange birth we see that it has exactly the same solar position as that in the horoscope of the painter. However – and this is the significant point – in comparison with Vincent's, it is a fairly mediocre chart.

Now, by astrological standards, the chart of Vincent II can never be described as mediocre. It is a chart of genius, with its connection with eclipses and fixed stars. In contrast, the chart of the first Vincent *does not exhibit a single trace of the fixed stars under which the artist was born* in the following year.

We shall look at the chart of van Gogh in more detail later (see page 168), and study it from a slightly different point of view. For the moment, I shall state the sixth rule of eclipse-interpretation.

THE SIXTH RULE: The most powerful way in which an eclipse can work in a horoscope is when the degree occupied by a planet, angle or node is also on a fixed star.

Rule Seven
Since we know from the writings of William Lilly that he used eclipse charts to predict events, we might ask if we know of any similar techniques of eclipse-prediction used in more recent times?

Although certain forms of eclipse-prediction are still practised in the United States,[34] the most remarkable of 'modern' astrologers to make extensive use of the eclipses for predictive purposes was scarcely modern, for he was publishing his best work over a hundred years ago. Even so, this work has left a powerful influence upon modern astrology, and his methods are worth looking into.

The nineteenth-century astro-meteorologist, inventor and retired naval lieutenant R.J. Morrison was a brilliant astrologer who, like many of his calling, was not treated fairly by the popular press of his day. Morrison has been described, with some justification, as 'the central figure on the early Victorian astrological stage'.[35] He certainly had a most extraordinary facility for making accurate astrological predictions. For example, so precise was his running commentary on the futurity of the royal family – and especially of Queen Victoria and the Consort, Prince Albert – that he was eventually persuaded to silence, as a matter of social propriety. However, although he toned down his royal predictions, he never fell entirely silent, for he resorted to obscure language to make his predictions known.

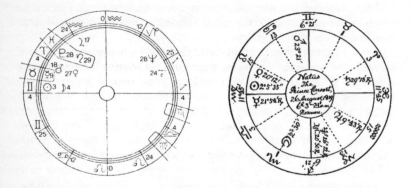

A considerable number of Morrison's astrological predictions were based on his study of eclipses. Some of these were published in his almanacs, and occasionally reviewed in later works by followers. Fortunately for us, Morrison was generally careful to record the bases for his predictions. From the observations he made when publishing these, it has proved possible to establish in detail his method of working, which was, in some respects, remarkably simple.

In order to establish a crisis period for a native, he would normally construct a 'progressed' chart as a preliminary. A progressed chart is one which is developed, or unfolded, by a clearly formulated symbolism from the original horoscope (the natal chart), to enable the astrologer to study the effects of this original chart on specific years in the life of the native.[36]

The progressed chart reveals the subsequent interactions of planets and nodal points that are contained, as it were as seeds, or *potentia*, in the original horoscope.

If, from this preliminary examination, Morrison observed that the progressed chart indicated a crisis were looming in a particular year, he would then look at the solar or lunar eclipse in that year to study its effects. He would note (for example) the longitude of the solar eclipse in the crisis year, and relate this to any equivalent degree in the natal chart.

As we have seen, this emphasis would be established by either a close conjunction of planet or nodal point to the eclipse degree, or by a close opposition to it. The effect, or outcome, of this congruity of degree-with-eclipse would depend upon the nature of the planet or node involved.[37]

If the eclipse fell on (or within a degree of) either the Sun or the Moon, then it would be possible for Morrison to date the expected crisis with considerable accuracy. Morrison was especially adroit at dating by such means the crisis of death, or very serious illness.

Among the many accurate predictions he made in his popular annual, *Zadkiel's Almanac*, perhaps the most famous were those relating to the deaths of the prime minister of Great Britain, and the Prince Consort, Albert.

Writing in 1864, Morrison observed that the eclipse of the Sun on 19 October 1865 would fall very near the degree held by the natal Sun in the horoscope of the then prime minister, Lord Palmerston.[38]

☉	☽	☿	♀	♂	♃	♄	♅	♆
° ′	° ′	° ′	° ′	° ′	° ′	° ′	° ′	° ′
27♎44	12♑27	11♎40	16♏57	20♎34	28♒ 6	18♑10	16♋21	14♎10

Palmerston had been born at Broadlands, near Romsey, on 20 October 1784. At noon on that day the Sun was in 28 degrees of Libra. The eclipse of the Sun on 19 October 1865 fell in 27 degrees of Libra.[39]

SUN IN THE CHART OF PALMERSTON: 27.44 LIBRA
SOLAR ECLIPSE OF 19 OCTOBER, 1865:   26.18 LIBRA

From consideration of this proximity of the eclipse to the solar position (marked above), Morrison came to the conclusion that it would 'put an end to his power, and endanger his life'. Palmerston died at Brocket Hall, after a short illness, on 18 October 1865, just as the eclipse was forming.[40]

Morrison had designated 1861 as evil for those born on the 26 August, mentioning by name 'the worthy Prince Consort of these realms'. Of course, as most of Morrison's readers would have known, Prince Albert, the beloved husband of Queen Victoria, had been born on 26 August 1819.[41] The date (26 August) was probably intended merely to enable his readers to identify the Prince Consort, who by that time seems to have lost his enthusiasm for Morrison's astrology, despite having previously been sufficiently interested to furnish the astrologer with data for the birth of his eldest child. Interestingly enough, the Prince admitted that he did not know his own birth data, yet he undertook to have it researched. It is possible that his researchers found it, for later horoscope-lists note a birth of 6:00 am, at Coburg.[42]

When the youthful Albert died on 14 December 1861, Morrison's prophecy seemed justified, but this did not bring the recognition it deserved. In the following month, after an outcry in the press about the humbug of predictive astrology (which actually contravened the law, in those days) Morrison became involved in a libel action against Rear-Admiral Sir Edward Belcher, who had criticized him, anonymously, in the *Daily Telegraph*.[43] Although the astrologer eventually won the case, the judiciary were biased against him, and the damages he obtained were derisory. This unpleasant brush with the law dampened his former enthusiasm for making forthright predictions in public. In this way, the most brilliant of Victorian astrologers was silenced by the Establishment.

Morrison left a sufficiently well-argued body of eclipse-prediction work for us to reconstruct and admire both his technique and the insight which lay behind it.

In addition to using eclipse-prediction in personal horoscopes,

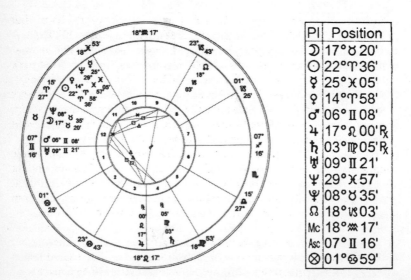

Pl	Position
☽	17° ♉ 20'
☉	22° ♈ 36'
☿	25° ♓ 05'
♀	14° ♈ 58'
♂	06° ♊ 08'
♃	17° ♌ 00' ℞
♄	03° ♍ 05' ℞
♅	09° ♊ 21'
♆	29° ♓ 57'
♇	08° ♉ 35'
☊	18° ♑ 03'
Mc	18° ♒ 17'
Asc	07° ♊ 16'
⊗	01° ♋ 59'

Morrison was also adroit in applying the lore of eclipses to interpreting the destiny of countries, through what is often called Mundane Astrology. For example, he had predicted the terrible potato famine in Ireland (a country traditionally ruled by the sign Taurus) by the eclipse of the Sun in Taurus (6 degrees) on 25 April 1846.[44]

More dramatically, Morrison had also predicted accurately the end of the Civil War in America: this he did from the position of Jupiter at the partial eclipse of the Moon on 11 April 1865. In making this prophecy, Morrison had applied the classical rules of eclipse-reading by observing that the eclipse had taken place on the degree opposite the Sun at the outbreak of hostilities on 12 April 1861 (opposite). At the moment of eclipse, the planet Jupiter had been in 29 degrees of Sagittarius. This was the degree exactly on the overhead angle (the mid-heaven) at the outbreak of the war. The confluence of eclipse-degree and this happy union of Jupiter with the angle could only mean that formal hostilities would come to an end.[45]

This brings me to the seventh and final rule of eclipse-interpretation, which recognizes that eclipses exert influences not merely through the personal horoscopes of individuals, but also through the horoscopes for places.

THE SEVENTH RULE: Eclipses may be interpreted as having the same effect in charts cast in a valid form for places and things (such as cities, towns, ships and buildings) as for personal charts.

An outstanding example of this kind of chart is that cast for the launching of the *Titanic* at Belfast, on 31 May 1911, at 12:14:30 pm (overleaf).[46]

One can only presume that the management of the White Star line did not have a horoscope cast for this launching, for no astrologer could have allowed a ship to begin a maiden voyage under such cosmic conditions.

The launching did not go entirely without incident: one of the workers with the responsibility of knocking away shoring timbers on the slip-way, James Dobbins, was pinned down in such a way that his left leg was crushed. He died in hospital on the next day.

The astrologer, Sepharial, on casting the chart, wrote, 'the whole amphitheatre of the heavens was witness to the indications of the impending danger'.[47] The chart was threatened with no fewer than six difficult fixed stars.[48] Undoubtedly, the worst combination of stars are those arising from the gathering of the Moon, Venus and Neptune in Cancer:

MOON IN THE CHART OF *TITANIC* LAUNCHING: 24.53 CANCER
VENUS IN THE CHART OF *TITANIC* LAUNCHING: 20.51 CANCER
NEPTUNE IN THE CHART OF *TITANIC* LAUNCHING: 19.45 CANCER

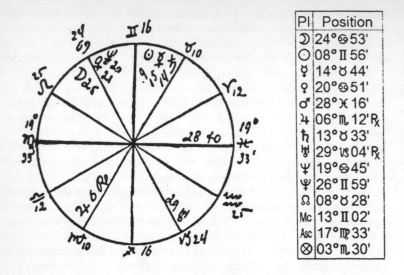

Pl	Position
☽	24°♋53'
☉	08°♊56'
☿	14°♉44'
♀	20°♋51'
♂	28°♓16'
♃	06°♏12'℞
♄	13°♉33'
♅	29°♑04'℞
♆	19°♋45'
♇	26°♊59'
☊	08°♉28'
Mc	13°♊02'
Asc	17°♍33'
⊗	03°♏30'

Unbelievable as it may be, each of these three planets was upon a fixed star which threatened the safety of the ship. These stars were the powerful Procyon, Pollux and Castor:

MOON IN THE CHART OF *TITANIC* LAUNCHING:	24.53 CANCER
POSITION OF FIXED STAR PROCYON IN 1911:	24.33 CANCER
VENUS IN THE CHART OF *TITANIC* LAUNCHING:	20.51 CANCER
POSITION OF FIXED STAR POLLUX IN 1911:	21.59 CANCER
NEPTUNE IN THE CHART OF *TITANIC* LAUNCHING:	19.45 CANCER
POSITION OF FIXED STAR CASTOR IN 1911:	19.03 CANCER

Given the closeness of these planetary contacts, the effects of the stars would comingle: however, the one thing they have in common is a reputation for loss – especially loss through water and drowning.

It is evident even from a brief consideration of these stars that the *Titanic* should not have been launched at this time. However, even more extraordinary than these threatening stars is the danger which the position of Saturn represented to the launching of the ship. At the launching, Saturn was on the fixed star Menkar, one of the stars infamous for bringing danger, ruin and loss of fortune. It has in particular a bad reputation for shipping, as it is located in the gaping jaw of the sea-monster Whale, Cetus.

SATURN IN THE CHART OF *TITANIC* LAUNCHING:	13.33 TAURUS
POSITION OF FIXED STAR MENKAR IN 1911:	13.04 TAURUS

The lunar eclipse in November of that fatal year fell upon Saturn in the launching chart.

SATURN IN THE CHART OF *TITANIC* LAUNCHING:	13.33 TAURUS
LUNAR ECLIPSE OF 6 NOVEMBER 1911:	13.00 TAURUS

No ship – even the 'unsinkable' *Titanic* – could have survived such a cosmic onslaught. When it collided with an iceberg on the 14 April 1912, 1,502 passengers and crew were drowned.[49]

One of the interesting pieces of flotsam and jetsam which washed up in astrological circles from the *Titanic* sinking was the horoscope of the courageous band-leader, Wallace Hartley, who famously played as the ship went down. As an aside, I should point out that Hartley's own destiny seems to have been tied up with the ship, as his Neptune (the 'watery' planet) was exactly upon the Dragon's head of the *Titanic* launching chart.[50]

The eclipse of 17 April fell upon Venus in Hartley's chart.

SOLAR ECLIPSE OF 17 APRIL 1912:	27.05 ARIES
VENUS IN THE CHART OF HARTLEY:	27.57 ARIES

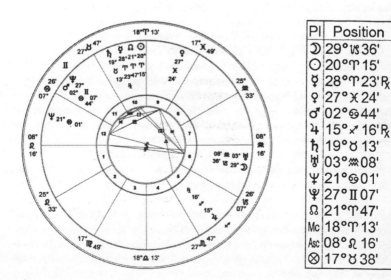

Pl	Position
☽	29° ♑ 36'
☉	20° ♈ 15'
☿	28° ♈ 23' R
♀	27° ♓ 24'
♂	02° ♋ 44'
♃	15° ♐ 16' R
♄	19° ♉ 13'
♅	03° ♒ 08'
♆	21° ♋ 01'
♇	27° ♊ 07'
☊	21° ♈ 47'
Mc	18° ♈ 13'
Asc	08° ♌ 16'
⊗	17° ♉ 38'

The chart is valuable in itself, if only for its human interest, yet the data it reveals regarding the solar eclipse that took place during the journey of the fated ship reveals the great secret of its sinking. The eclipse of April 1912 fell exactly upon the planet Venus of the chart cast for the sailing of the *Titanic* for America, from Southampton, on 10 April, 1912 at noon. The chart and data are given on the previous page.

The solar eclipse of 17 April fell within the orb of Mercury – the planet of communications – in this chart.

SOLAR ECLIPSE OF 17 APRIL 1912:	27.05 ARIES
MERCURY IN THE CHART *TITANIC* SAILING FOR USA:	28.23 ARIES

Just in case it is argued that this is a wide orb to allow for a sensitive degree, I should point out that Mercury in this case is permitted a wider orb because it is on the fixed star Mirach.[51]

Among the extraordinary conditions surrounding the fate of this doomed ship was that it was originally scheduled to begin its maiden voyage in February 1912, but was thwarted when the White Star vessel *Olympic* had to go in for repairs after a collision with a Royal Navy cruiser, and the *Titanic* workmen were pulled off that ship to carry out repairs. Had the *Titanic* sailed in February, then the eclipse of 17 April would not have been operative in her chart.

An equally interesting example of fixed stars may be seen in the unlikely-seeming context of the dropping of the Atomic Bomb on Nagasaki, in Japan, in 1945. This carries us into a fascinating realm of astrology, which traces chains of events in history through eclipses.

A chart for the first controlled release of atomic energy was cast by an American astrologer for 2 December 1942, at 3:01 pm local time, in Chicago University.[52] The chart is given opposite:

It has been recognized for some considerable time that atomic energy, which is involved with atomic fission, falls under the domain of the planet Pluto. On the day the experiment with atomic fission was conducted, 2 December 1942, Pluto was in 7.08 Leo. There was a solar eclipse within this degree eight months later.

PLUTO AT RELEASE OF ATOMIC ENERGY:	07.08 LEO
SOLAR ECLIPSE ON 1 AUGUST 1943:	08.03 LEO

Pluto has not been studied for a sufficiently long period for us to know precisely what contacts with certain stars imply, but astrologers know that Uranus and Neptune on fixed stars tend to bring out their worse sides. We must presume that Pluto, which is so intimately linked with the Underworld, and with the untamed magmatic powers within the Earth,

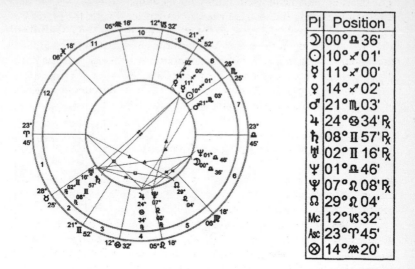

Pl	Position
☽	00°♎36'
☉	10°♐01'
☿	11°♐00'
♀	14°♐02'
♂	21°♏03'
♃	24°♋34'℞
♄	08°♊57'℞
♅	02°♊16'℞
♆	01°♎46'
♇	07°♌08'℞
☊	29°♌04'
Mc	12°♑32'
Asc	23°♈45'
⊗	14°♒20'

must be even more disposed towards violence when it is connected with a star such as South Asellus.

PLUTO AT RELEASE OF ATOMIC ENERGY:	07.08 LEO
SOLAR ECLIPSE ON 1 AUGUST 1943:	08.03 LEO
POSITION OF SOUTH ASELLUS IN 1943:	07.54 LEO

The first atomic bomb was dropped on Hiroshima, on 6 August 1945, shortly after 8:00 am (see chart overleaf). On 9 July 1945, a month before the bomb was dropped, there was an eclipse of the Sun on the position the Moon would occupy at the time of the dropping:

MOON AT DROPPING OF BOMB, 6 AUGUST 1945:	17.54 CANCER
SOLAR ECLIPSE ON 9 JULY 1945:	16.57 CANCER

What is remarkable is that this degree of Moon and eclipse in 1945 was on either side of the fixed star Wasat, one of the most violent and evil stars in the skies – second only in destructiveness to Algol.

MOON AT DROPPING OF BOMB, 6 AUGUST 1945:	17.54 CANCER
SOLAR ECLIPSE ON 9 JULY 1945:	16.57 CANCER
POSITION OF STAR WASAT IN 1945:	17.44 CANCER

109

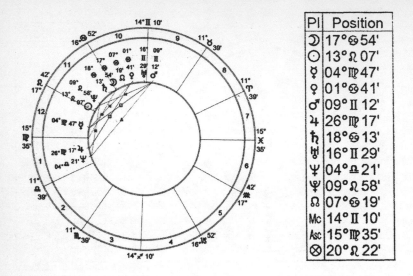

Pl	Position
☽	17°♋54'
☉	13°♌07'
☿	04°♍47'
♀	01°♋41'
♂	09°♊12'
♃	26°♍17'
♄	18°♋13'
♅	16°♊29'
♆	04°♎21'
♇	09°♌58'
☊	07°♋19'
Mc	14°♊10'
Asc	15°♍35'
⊗	20°♌22'

What becomes even more remarkable is that the arc established by this triple contact was opposite Saturn in the birthchart of the Japanese Emperor Hirohito (whose chart is given on page 180).

SATURN IN THE CHART OF EMPEROR HIROHITO: 16.23 CAPRICORN
The chart for the dropping of the atomic bomb has interesting connections with the chart for the first controlled explosion. For example:

SATURN AT EXPLOSION OF DECEMBER 1942:   08.57 GEMINI
MARS AT DROPPING OF BOMB, 6 AUGUST 1945: 09.12 GEMINI

As a direct consequence of the dropping of the atomic bomb and Japan's subsequent surrender, the Emperor Hirohito renounced his divine status, and a new constitution was adopted in the country, based on democratic principles. This was ratified in November 1946. While these complex negotiations were being conducted, there was a solar eclipse on the atomic bomb Saturn-Mars contact in Gemini:

SOLAR ECLIPSE OF 30 MAY 1946:   08.49 GEMINI
SATURN AT EXPLOSION OF DECEMBER 1942:   08.57 GEMINI
MARS AT DROPPING OF BOMB, 6 AUGUST 1945: 09.12 GEMINI

This triple arrangement also falls on the star Aldebaran, which, in the astrological tradition, threatens a violent death:

POSITION OF STAR ALDEBARAN IN 1945:	09.01 GEMINI
SOLAR ECLIPSE OF 30 MAY 1946:	08.49 GEMINI
SATURN AT EXPLOSION OF DECEMBER 1942:	08.57 GEMINI
MARS AT DROPPING OF BOMB, 6 AUGUST 1945:	09.12 GEMINI

This glance at the way the Cosmos seems to interweave in even the darkest deeds of mankind brings us to the end of our account of the seven rules of eclipse-reading. Before I illustrate how these rules may be applied to a number of famous charts, here they are again, for ease of reference.

Summary of Rules
THE FIRST RULE: Both lunar and solar eclipses each leave two sensitive degrees in the zodiacal belt, marking precisely that degree in which the eclipse took place, and the degree diametrically opposite.

THE SECOND RULE: The sensitive degrees left by eclipses become operative in a chart only when there is a corresponding degree occupied by a planet, an angle or a nodal point.

THE THIRD RULE: The influence of a sensitive degree left by eclipses exerts an influence which is determined by the intrinsic natures of the planet, angle or a nodal point on which that eclipse falls.

THE FOURTH RULE: The event to be read from a sensitive degree made by an eclipse falling on planets, angles or nodes in a chart will occur within the period determined by the duration of the eclipse. This duration is in the ratio of one year to each hour of eclipse. This duration is regarded as being extended over the centre of the time of the eclipse, and is operative both forwards and backwards in time.

THE FIFTH RULE: When a number of degrees in a chart are bound together in close conjunctions, the permitted orb of influence is wider than usual.

THE SIXTH RULE: The most powerful way in which an eclipse can work in a horoscope is when the degree occupied by a planet, angle or node is also on a fixed star.

THE SEVENTH RULE: Eclipses may be interpreted as having the same effect in charts cast in a valid form for places and things (such as cities, towns, ships and buildings) as for personal charts.

The Rules Applied

Having studied these rules, we are in a better position to understand the more subtle effects of eclipses in personal horoscopes. With this in mind, we shall look at a number of interesting charts, in the hope that these will throw some light upon how these rules work in practice.

First, we shall study the effect of eclipses and fixed stars upon the lives of two artists who suffered greatly from physical disabilities, yet persisted in their art – Renoir and Toulouse-Lautrec. I shall then turn to the influence of a single star on the destinies of three men who came to very different ends – Oliver Cromwell, Lord Protector of England, Otto von Bismarck, who wielded together and strengthened the German Empire in the nineteenth century, and Joachim von Ribbentrop, the Nazi war criminal. We shall see the effect of eclipses on the explorer Richard Burton who had river-stars in his chart when he followed his destiny in search of the source of the Nile. We shall end by glancing at the remarkable chart of Albert Einstein, whose complex theories about gravity were proved with the help of eclipses, and whose life was also directed by eclipses.

It is really a shame that eclipse lore is not so widely studied by astrologers as was the case in the past. In an interesting article on a mass murder which took place in Chicago, in 1966, a modern astrologer admitted that he could not see from the nativity of the murderer anything to account for the crime. However, if he had used eclipse lore, he would have had all the

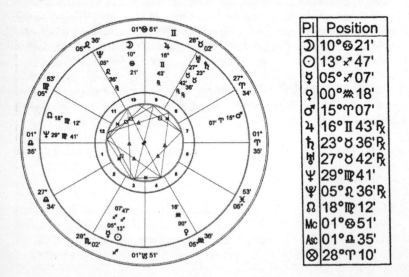

112

information he required.[53]

On 16 July 1966, Richard Speck ran amok in a Chicago apartment and killed eight nurses. At the time, much was made of the fact that Speck had the words 'Born to raise Hell' tattooed on his left arm. He was born at 1 am, on 6 December 1941: his chart is given opposite.[54]

I do not wish to comment upon the chart as a whole, but I should point out that one indication alone is sufficient to tie Richard Speck down to a crime of violence in 1966. His Uranus (a planet to which violence comes naturally) is not only on the fixed star Alcyone (a notoriously violent star), but it was darkened by an eclipse of the Moon in the year of the mass murder, less than two months before the crime was committed.

URANUS IN THE CHART OF SPECK:	27.42 TAURUS
POSITION OF STAR ALCYONE IN 1941:	28.01 TAURUS
SOLAR ECLIPSE OF 20 MAY 1966:	28.55 TAURUS

Here we have a good example of how a familiarity with eclipse lore could enable an astrologer to predict a fairly unpleasant event in the life of a native sufficiently to look more closely into the chart.

Van Gogh's chart (page 169), peppered as it is with some fairly difficult fixed stars, makes an interesting comparison with another painter of approximately the same period who had a very different life. The French artist, Pierre Auguste Renoir, was born on 25 February, 1841 in Limoges, at 6:00 am.[55] His horoscope data is given below:

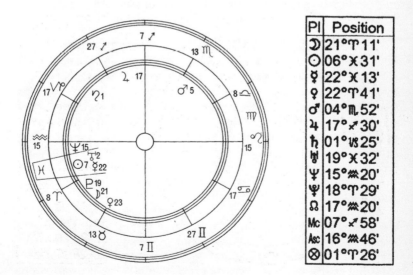

Pl	Position
☽	21°♈11'
☉	06°♓31'
☿	22°♓13'
♀	22°♈41'
♂	04°♏52'
♃	17°♐30'
♄	01°♑25'
♅	19°♓32'
♆	15°♒20'
♇	18°♈29'
☊	17°♒20'
Mc	07°♐58'
Asc	16°♒46'
⊗	01°♈26'

Now Renoir, like van Gogh, was an extraordinary man – a genius, indeed – and we should not be surprised to find that he had just as many fixed stars in his chart as Vincent.[56] However, few of these stars threatened Renoir's well-being.

In fact, the star Skat, which is upon his Sun, in 7 degrees of Pisces, is one of the best stars for ensuring lasting good fortune.

SUN IN THE CHART OF RENOIR:	06.31 PISCES
POSITION OF FIXED STAR SKAT IN 1841:	06.46 PISCES

Again, the triple star Polis, set in the bow of Sagittarius, in 3 degrees of Capricorn, confers ambition and success. This is on the Saturn of Renoir's chart, in 2 degrees of the sign.

SATURN IN THE CHART OF RENOIR:	01.25 CAPRICORN
POSITION OF FIXED STAR POLIS IN 1841:	01.05 CAPRICORN

However, there is one star in Renoir's chart which did not augur well, and this was placed on the important angle at the top of his chart – the zenith, or mid-heaven. This was the star Antares, which was on the MC in 8 degrees of Sagittarius. It is a very powerful star, the *alpha* of Scorpius, and has a mixed reputation among astrologers. While, like many other stars, it can lift the native to high honours in a chosen career, it can also bring difficulties or even downfall through various bodily ailments.

Now, in 1853 – the same year that Van Gogh was born – there was an eclipse of the Sun very close to this sensitive degree in Renoir's chart:

ZENITH IN THE CHART OF RENOIR:	07.58 SAGITTARIUS
POSITION OF FIXED STAR ANTARES IN 1841:	07.40 SAGITTARIUS
SOLAR ECLIPSE OF 30 NOVEMBER 1853:	08.34 SAGITTARIUS

In 1853, Renoir was paralysed by congenital rheumatic arthritis, which stayed with him for the rest of his life. Eventually, the illness confined him to a wheelchair. This incapacity did not prevent him from travelling extensively, or from painting over 6,000 pictures, for (in astrological terms) he was supported by Skat and Polis. So dedicated was he to his art that towards the end of his life, when his hands became useless, he painted with brushes tied to his twisted fingers.[57]

Another French painter, who knew both Vincent van Gogh and Renoir, was Toulouse-Lautrec. I do not wish to discuss his chart in depth, because in astrological terms it is quite complicated.[58] However, in view of what we have seen about the influence of fixed stars and eclipses, it is interesting that his Jupiter, in Sagittarius, was on a fixed star and was eventually affected by an eclipse.

He was born at Albi, in France, on 24 November, 1864, time unknown.[59] His data is:

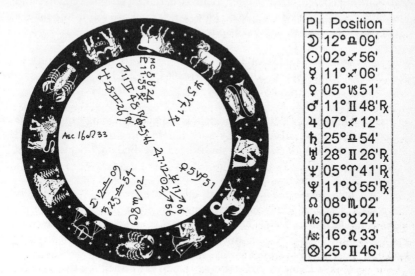

Pl	Position
☽	12° ♎ 09'
☉	02° ♐ 56'
☿	11° ♐ 06'
♀	05° ♑ 51'
♂	11° ♊ 48' ℞
♃	07° ♐ 12'
♄	25° ♎ 54'
♅	28° ♊ 26' ℞
♆	05° ♈ 41' ℞
♇	11° ♉ 55' ℞
☊	08° ♏ 02'
Mc	05° ♉ 24'
Asc	16° ♌ 33'
⊗	25° ♊ 46'

There are three planets in Sagittarius in Lautrec's chart, and it is not without significance that this sign should rule the thighs in the human body. Between 1878 and 1879 Lautrec had two separate falls, in which he broke the thigh-bones of each leg. The bones never healed properly, and he was left a stunted cripple. Here is the conjunction which affected his life in this terrible way:

JUPITER IN THE CHART OF LAUTREC: 07.12 SAGITTARIUS
POSITION OF THE FIXED STAR HAN IN 1864:   07.11 SAGITTARIUS

The small star Han is set in the knee of the constellation Ophiuchus, and has a reputation for ruining those with whom it forms a contact. It is especially renowned for affecting the thighs.

This contact between Jupiter and Han was eventually occulted by an eclipse.

Lautrec's first accident took place on 30 May 1878; his second, when he fell in the dry bed of a stream, fourteen months later, in October 1879.[60] The period in which these accidents occurred was terminated by an eclipse which fell on the Venus of his chart:

115

LUNAR ECLIPSE OF 28 DECEMBER 1879:	06.30 CAPRICORN
VENUS IN CHART OF LAUTREC:	05.51 CAPRICORN

In spite of his success as a painter, Lautrec became a serious alcoholic, and this hastened his death. In May 1900, a solar eclipse fell in the degree opposite Lautrec's star-struck Jupiter:

JUPITER IN THE CHART OF LAUTREC:	07.12 SAGITTARIUS
POSITION OF THE FIXED STAR HAN IN 1864:	07.11 SAGITTARIUS
SOLAR ECLIPSE OF 28 MAY 1900:	06:47 GEMINI

By the middle of 1899 he had been hospitalized, suffering from *delirium tremens*. He recovered sufficiently to complete a few more drawings and paintings, but his illness was very advanced. He died on 9 September, at 2:15 am.[61]

As we have seen, the seventeenth-century astrologer William Lilly recognized the importance of fixed stars in chart interpretation. Like some modern astrologers, he saw that the energies of fixed stars can transmit powerfully through the sensitive degrees of eclipses with quite extraordinary consequences. [62]

If we look back at his predictions (page 57), we shall see that he took fixed stars into account, not only in his general horoscopic work, but also in regard to his eclipse predictions. In fact, during the late mediaeval period and the Renaissance, fixed stars were held to be so important in chart interpretation that astrologers often took the trouble to mark them in their horoscope charts.

For example, the personal chart of the seventeenth-century astrologer and author, John Gadbury – an old enemy of William Lilly[63] – has three fixed stars marked. These are Cor Scorpii, Cor Leonis and Oculus Tauri, the names used at that time for Antares, Regulus and Aldebaran (opposite).

We shall look at these three stars later, for they are each found in the horoscopes of famous individuals. Regulus (Cor Leonis) is an interesting star, for among its many influences is one that gives a lively interest in astrology: this is probably why John Gadbury recorded it as being on his zenith.[64]

The Gadbury chart is fairly typical of the period, for it demonstrates the lively interest taken at that time in the lore of fixed stars. Given this awareness of the importance of fixed stars, it must have been quite clear to William Lilly that the horoscope of Oliver Cromwell was intimately linked with the chart he had cast for the solar eclipse of 1652.[65]

Cromwell's Mars fell almost exactly upon the Dragon's Head of the 1652 eclipse. Cromwell's chart, cast for the early morning of 25 April 1599 (OS) is given in figure 7, but here is a digest of the interesting correspondence between planet and eclipse:

MARS IN THE CHART OF CROMWELL:	10.25 ARIES
DRAGON'S HEAD ECLIPSE OF 1652:	10.23 ARIES

In 1653, Cromwell was invested with the unique title of Lord Protector of England, Scotland and Ireland. Three years later, Parliament actually offered him the Crown of England, which he wisely refused. He died on 3 September 1658, after being in power for five years. The watershed of his life was 1653, and his later years – after the eclipse of 1652 – were markedly different from those prior to that time. It was as though he had been lifted to great eminence by some superior power.

Modern astrologers would probably have little difficulty recognizing something of the nature of this strange elevation of a commoner to a position where he controlled the political life of Britain. They will see behind such events far more than merely an eclipse, or even a conjunction of an eclipse with the planet of action, Mars. *They would, of course, see the influence of a fixed star.*

I italicize this important idea because, as I have already said, the whole theory of eclipses is bound up with the lore of fixed stars. As I hope you will discover, long before you finish this book, it is quite impossible to understand the major events in the lives of powerful men and women – and especially of geniuses and those of historical importance – without considering the effects in their lives of eclipses and fixed stars.

The star Alpheratz, which is sometimes called Sirrah, happens to have the reputation of being one of the most powerful stars in the heavens for

117

bestowing high political standing. Its reputation may have derived from its original position in the body of the flying horse, the constellation Pegasus.[66] In astrology, the star is renowned for lifting the native upwards – as though he were borne on wings. It lifts to high position of fame and popularity – even if this elevated position must at times be held in the face of considerable opposition. Alpheratz sometimes proves to be a delicate position, and this fame may easily be withdrawn or eclipsed – sometimes with disastrous results.

A good example of the working of this star in a political area is in the personal chart of the German 'Iron Chancellor', Otto, Prince von Bismarck, who had his Sun on Alpheratz.[67] Just in case you question whether it was at all remarkable that a German aristocrat should rise to the chancellorship of Germany, or even be instrumental in unifying the many princeling states of Germany into a nation, I should point out that he was born into an impoverished, if ancient, family, and though he was well connected, his achievements were essentially a result of his own activity and will.

The year of Bismarck's greatest power was in 1871, when under his personal guidance Prussia had weakened France by war, in consequence of which the emergent Germany became (along with Britain) the most powerful nation in Europe. It was in this same year that Bismarck was made Chancellor.

This rise to the pinnacle of success was of course reflected in his chart. In that year, there was a solar eclipse in 20 degrees of Sagittarius, on his Neptune:

SOLAR ECLIPSE OF 12 DECEMBER 1871:	19.44 SAGITTARIUS
NEPTUNE IN THE CHART OF BISMARCK:	19.54 SAGITTARIUS

The Nazi, Joachim von Ribbentrop, who also achieved one of the highest positions possible in Germany under the dictator Adolf Hitler, had his Mercury on Alpheratz, but ended on the gallows.[68]

In fact, it is worth examining the chart of the notorious Ribbentrop, not only because this was dramatically activated towards the end of his life by an eclipse, but also because we can see again how planets work with fixed stars and eclipses.

Joachim von Ribbentrop had the planet Pluto (♇) on the fixed star Aldebaran, in 9 degrees of Gemini (see opposite). Pluto is generally a difficult planet in any chart, for it points to the hidden, unresolved issues in the native's psyche. Since this personal side is also reflected in society, the darker realm of Pluto's workings have often been linked with fascism. In Ribbentrop's horoscope, this dark nature was mingled with the influence of a fixed star which had a reputation for bringing both 'military preferment' and a violent death.

118

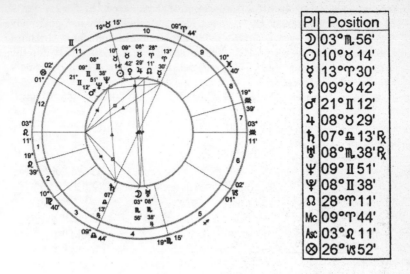

Pl	Position
☽	03° ♏ 56'
☉	10° ♉ 14'
☿	13° ♈ 30'
♀	09° ♉ 42'
♂	21° ♊ 12'
♃	08° ♉ 29'
♄	07° ♎ 13' ℞
♅	08° ♏ 38' ℞
♆	09° ♊ 51'
♇	08° ♊ 38'
☊	28° ♈ 11'
Mc	09° ♈ 44'
Asc	03° ♌ 11'
⊗	26° ♑ 52'

In the case of Ribbentrop, this violent death was reflected in the heavens by an eclipse on the sensitive degree of the star and planet. After the Second World War, Ribbentrop was tried by the Allies at Nuremburg (November 1945–October 1946) and was hanged for his war crimes. On 30 May 1946, during this trial, there was an eclipse of the Sun in 9 degrees of Gemini, upon his Pluto. The correspondences in this triple data are quite remarkable:

PLUTO IN THE CHART OF VON RIBBENTROP:	08.38 GEMINI
POSITION OF THE STAR ALDEBARAN IN 1893:	08.17 GEMINI
SOLAR ECLIPSE OF 30 MAY 1946:	08.49 GEMINI

When I looked at the horoscope of Vincent van Gogh I observed that his chart (and consequently his life) was coloured by an eclipse which had taken place prior to his birth. It may seem strange to those who have not studied astrology that an eclipse which takes place prior to a birth can affect the life of a child (and hence the adult), but this is the case. This should not surprise us, as the astrological tradition insists that eclipses work backwards and forwards in time. This fact does suggest that eclipses can have an influence of some kind on the embryo, and perhaps explains why the ancients would sometimes cast conception charts when studying the lives of individuals.

A most interesting example of an influential pre-birth eclipse is found in one of the most powerful horoscopes of the nineteenth century, parts of which were called by the astrologer Isabelle Pagan 'positively uncanny'.[69] This is the chart of the explorer and translator, Richard Burton. His chart is particularly relevant to us, because Burton died in the same year as Vincent van Gogh, and because his chart was also strongly influenced by an eclipse.[70]

Richard Burton was born on 19 March 1821, in Torquay at 9:30 pm.[71]

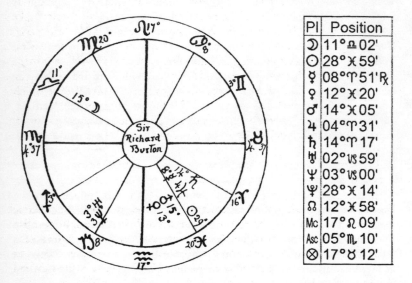

Pl	Position
☽	11°♎02'
☉	28°♓59'
☿	08°♈51'℞
♀	12°♓20'
♂	14°♓05'
♃	04°♈31'
♄	14°♈17'
♅	02°♑59'
♆	03°♑00'
♇	28°♓14'
☊	12°♓58'
Mc	17°♌09'
Asc	05°♏10'
⊗	17°♉12'

The chart is remarkable for several reasons, not least because it had two especially sensitive degrees in Pisces, due to conjunctions of planets. These were:

SUN IN THE CHART OF BURTON:	28.59 PISCES
PLUTO IN THE CHART OF BURTON:	28.14 PISCES
VENUS IN THE CHART OF BURTON:	12.20 PISCES
DRAGON'S HEAD IN THE CHART OF BURTON:	12.58 PISCES
MARS IN THE CHART OF BURTON:	14.05 PISCES

On 4 March 1821, fifteen days before Burton was born, there was a solar eclipse in 13.23 degrees of Pisces. This fell on the two planets and nodes near the centre of Pisces, technically activating both the planet Mars and the Dragon's Head. In its most positive action, Mars is the planet of exploration, and Burton was one of the greatest explorers of all time, aided

by his prowess as a brilliant linguist (he mastered thirty-five languages).

The solar eclipse of 1858 offers me an opportunity to show the working of a rule I set down earlier. The second rule states that in eclipse-prediction, it is not only the sensitive degree on which the eclipse takes place that becomes operative in a chart, but the degree diametrically opposite is also sensitive. In Burton's chart we have an example of this 'opposite degree' effect.

In February 1858, travelling with John Hanning Speke on their famous search for the source of the Nile, Burton discovered the freshwater Lake Tanganyika. Shortly afterwards, while Burton was blind due to malaria, Speke discovered the Victoria Nyanza, the source of the Nile. This was an important year for exploration, as indeed for the two heroes, who were fêted on their return to England. It is not at all surprising that the achievement should have been reflected in the heavens on a degree which was already touched by the eclipse of 1821, the year of Burton's birth.

On 7 September 1858, there was a solar eclipse in 15 degrees of Virgo, exactly opposite Burton's Mars:

MARS IN THE CHART OF BURTON:	14.05 PISCES
SOLAR ECLIPSE OF 7 SEPTEMBER, 1858:	14.37 VIRGO

Burton's relationship with the fixed star Achernar, the alpha of Eridanus, is a curious one. In 1821, when Burton was born, Achernar was not exactly upon his Mars: the star was actually 1.18 degrees from Mars, which means that it was outside the permitted orb. However, as we have seen, in Burton's horoscope Venus and the Dragon's Head were very close indeed to Mars, mingling their influences with it. As a matter of fact, in 1821 Achernar was in the same degree as both Burton's Venus and his Dragon's Head. This close contact of all four sensitive points pulled Mars into contact with the star, which has the effect of linking Burton's planet of exploration with the cosmic river. This is a summary of the contacts:

POSITION OF THE STAR ACHERNAR IN 1821:	12.47 PISCES
VENUS IN THE CHART OF BURTON:	12.20 PISCES
DRAGON'S HEAD IN THE CHART OF BURTON:	12.58 PISCES
MARS IN THE CHART OF BURTON:	14.05 PISCES

The constellation Eridanus is the longest star-group in the skies: in ancient times it was called by the Greeks simply Potamos, and by the Romans Flumen, meaning in both cases simply 'river'. The many variant names which appear in the eighteenth century star lists of European astrologers (such as Guad, or Guagi) are all derived from the Arabic Wadi, meaning river.[72] Perhaps it is poetic accident, but the fixed star with which Richard Burton's Mars was involved during this courageous search for the origins of the Nile was called 'The End of the River'. Fortunately for Burton, the brightest star in this constellation – Achernar, in the mouth of the river – which was emphatic in his natal chart, promises success, with the attainment of high office.[73]

In her fascinating book on Burton, Fawn M. Brodie wrote of the last chapter in his life as being a 'sad eclipse'.[74] There is probably more significance in this phrase than Brodie realized, for Burton's death was involved with the eclipse-point of the lunar nodes in his chart.

Three days before he died, a bird had been tapping at his window during the morning – a curious event which Burton read as a bad omen. On 19 October 1890, he rescued a robin which he had found drowning, and wrapped it in his fur coat until he was certain that it would live.[75] He died at approximately five o'clock on the following morning.

The chart cast for his death (which took place in Trieste, then in Austria) reveals that on that same day the planet Saturn was hovering over the Dragon's Tail of his natal horoscope:

DRAGON'S TAIL IN BURTON'S NATAL CHART: 12.58 VIRGO
POSITION OF SATURN ON 20 OCTOBER 1890: 13.17 VIRGO

I started out with the chart of Prince Charles, which showed an eclipse that seemed to mark a special event on the very day the eclipse occurred. I have just finished a brief account of the seven rules of eclipse-interpretation with another chart which was accurate to the day. The first chart was involved with a birth, the second with a death, which shows that eclipses are themselves no great respecters of persons. Eclipses seem to mark cosmic situations, to which individuals apply their individualistic charts, to receive the karmic benefits or tribulations, as their destiny requires.

In most of the other charts I have examined so far, there has not been the same precision of timing. I have tended to follow the astrological tradition, and have assumed that an eclipse will radiate its influences as a sensitive degree for approximately six to eight months, depending upon the length of the eclipse. However, we might ask if this is a reasonable time to permit for a sensitive degree engendered by an eclipse?

We have seen that it is not possible to date events from eclipses, and that one of the rules of eclipse interpretation is that one regards the eclipse as casting a sort of shadow forwards and backwards in time in a way which makes the dating of events quite difficult. Even so, astrologers do manage at times to date events with remarkable accuracy – even when using eclipses as the basis for their predictions.

How is it possible to time such eclipse events, then, and relate these to personal horoscopes? The answer is that we time events by means of somewhat specialist astrological techniques called *progressions* and *transits* (see glossary, page 260). Briefly, progressions and transits are methods for studying how the planetary and nodal placings in a chart unfold influences in the life of the individual, with the passage of time. During this unfoldment, the planets move – usually in the direction of the zodiac itself. In the course of this movement, they may pass (that is, transit, or progress) sensitive degrees. It is at these moments that the conditions then dormant in the eclipse degrees will find a correspondence in the life of the person.

If this is true, we might ask how long an eclipse degree will remain 'sensitive', even though dormant? In mediaeval astrology, it was believed that an eclipse degree was so powerful that it could retain its energies unexploded for two or even three years. Modern astrologers tend to see the degree as retaining its sensitivity for just a little over a year. None of the examples of the 'explosion of eclipse degrees' I give in this book have had a duration of as much as a year.

One of the twentieth-century specialists in astrological techniques, Ronald Davison, suggests that the average length of time elapsing before an eclipse takes effect may be five to six months, though in some cases this can be extended to twelve months.[76] He also points out something which I have touched upon – namely, that the effect of an eclipse can be felt before the eclipse itself falls due.

This last idea does sound extraordinary, yet what Davison claims proves to be absolutely true in practice. The sensitive eclipse degree works with just the same ease backwards as it does forwards. In many ways, Davison's opinions coincide with those formulated in the late mediaeval astrological tradition, save that the mediaeval astrologers were inclined to see the forward effects of eclipses lasting for much longer. They too had no doubt that an eclipse *could* manifest its effects some time (even months) before falling due, provided the correspondence with the sensitive point was within the prescribed degree.

Like Davison, I have come to the conclusion that when eclipses fall on sensitive points in a horoscope, they may be interpreted as having the force of a double transit of the Sun and Moon. This may need some explanation for non-specialists. One of the important theories underlying predictive astrology is that a birth chart is a series of sensitive points, marked in degrees by such things as planets, angles and nodal points. This birth chart is regarded as being a *radical* or 'root' chart, which may be affected by the later disposition of planetary movements. These 'effects' are created when, in a future time, a planet moves over, or transits, a sensitive point in a horoscope.

In order to explain this theory, let us take the chart of the mathematical genius Einstein, who was born in Ulm, Germany, on 14 March, 1879 at 11:36 am.[77]

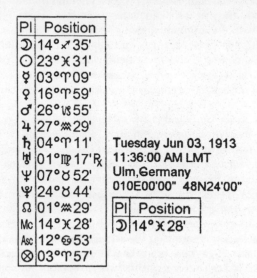

Pl	Position
☽	14° ♐ 35'
☉	23° ♓ 31'
☿	03° ♈ 09'
♀	16° ♈ 59'
♂	26° ♑ 55'
♃	27° ♒ 29'
♄	04° ♈ 11'
♅	01° ♍ 17' ℞
♆	07° ♉ 52'
♇	24° ♉ 44'
☊	01° ♒ 29'
Mc	14° ♓ 28'
Asc	12° ♋ 53'
⊗	03° ♈ 57'

Tuesday Jun 03, 1913
11:36:00 AM LMT
Ulm, Germany
010E00'00" 48N24'00"

Pl	Position
☽	14° ♓ 28'

Alongside the planetary tables I have reproduced the effect of a single 'progression' – which is to say the movement of a planet by the symbolical method used by astrologers, to a single point in the original chart.

In 1913, the Moon had progressed to Einstein's zenith (see diagram). As we have seen, the zenith is one of the four Angles of the chart, and represents that place in the heavens where ambitions are achieved, or not achieved, as the case may be. It is the point at which the world views (and often records with pleasure or dismay what it sees) the achievements of the person represented in the horoscope.

By the time the Moon had moved to, or progressed to, the mid-heaven in Einstein's chart in 1913, the Sun had entered exactly in conjunction with Mercury, suggesting that Einstein's creative source of energy (Sun) had united harmoniously with his brilliant intellect (Mercury).

In astrological terms, it was inevitable that these two factors should be reflected in Einstein's life and career.

It was in this year that Einstein's genius was recognized by authorities in Berlin and a special post was created to allow him to work unimpeded: he was made director of the prestigious Kaiser-Wilhelm Physical Institute, and provided with both a sufficient salary and freedom to devote all his time to research. This recognition is typical of what can happen when the Moon passes a beneficially strong mid-heaven in a chart.

However, with this particular chart we are dealing with genius, and genius does not always follow the normal rules. In order to understand what happened in Einstein's life in 1913 we must recognize that there was something rather special about his mid-heaven. The fact is that Einstein's mid-heaven was on a powerful fixed star.

When Einstein was born, on 14 March 1879, the fixed star Achernar was within the same degree as his mid-heaven.

POSITION OF MID-HEAVEN IN EINSTEIN'S CHART: 14.28 PISCES
POSITION OF FIXED STAR ACHERNAR IN 1879:   13.36 PISCES

If we wish to understand what this means, we must visualize the star pouring its influence into Einstein's career on a more or less continuous basis throughout the duration of his life. This means that the mid-heaven in his chart (a sensitive point in any chart) had been rendered additionally sensitive. In turn, this also means that the mid-heaven would become especially powerful whenever one of the planets (such as the Moon, in 1913) passed over it.

Achernar is one of the more beneficial of the fixed stars. It is a white star set in the mouth of the river of Eridanus, a constellation which was famous among mediaeval astrologers as radiating a love of science and knowledge.[78] The mediaeval astrologers realized that the star Achernar expressed the beneficent power of Jupiter. When emphasized in a chart it always gives great public success and benefits. It also deepens the religious life of the person, reminding us, in this instance, of Einstein's deep spirituality as a philosopher. The German philosopher and poet, J.W. Goethe, also had this star emphatic in his chart.[79]

Einstein's chart leads us to what was probably the most famous eclipse in modern history. One of the theories implicit in Einstein's formulation of the theory of relativity was that a body as powerful as the Sun could deflect light by its gravitational force. Astronomers recognized that one way to test this – and thus to prove or disprove Einstein's theory – was to wait until a total eclipse of the Sun occurred and measure the light coming from stars adjacent to the Sun's disk at the moment of total occultation.

There were to be two solar eclipses in 1919. The one that was to take place on 29 May would be in 7.06 Gemini. Its total occultation would be visible from the tropics, and two expeditions went to study it from extreme vantage points: one group went to northern Brazil, the other to the island of Principe, in West Africa. Both groups took photographs to see what effect the Sun's gravitational force had on light waves. The images showed that the light from the stars had been deflected, just as Einstein predicted would happen. The observations displaced Newton's theory of gravity, and replaced it with Einstein's.[80]

Charts of Some Famous Individuals

I have selected the following horoscopes, illustrating the effects of eclipses on famous personalities, mainly because of the teaching points they contain.

The cases are set out in alphabetical order, and range from the sixteenth to the twentieth century. The notes, numbered by each named section, begin on page 240.

A list of all eclipses mentioned, ranged in zodiacal order, appears on page 225. To these I have added all the eclipses mentioned in the preceding two chapters.

Alexander II, Tsar of Russia

The Russian Tsar, Alexander II was one of the great reformers, who helped lead Russia into the modern world. Not only did he develop the first railway system throughout Russia, but he also oversaw the emancipation of serfs. He was born on 29 April 1818, at 10:02 am.[1]

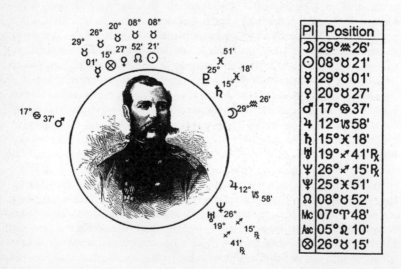

Pl	Position
☽	29° ♒ 26'
☉	08° ♉ 21'
☿	29° ♉ 01'
♀	20° ♉ 27'
♂	17° ♋ 37'
♃	12° ♑ 58'
♄	15° ♓ 18'
♅	19° ♐ 41' ℞
♆	26° ♐ 15' ℞
♇	25° ♓ 51'
☊	08° ♉ 52'
Mc	07° ♈ 48'
Asc	05° ♌ 10'
⊗	26° ♉ 15'

126

At the moment of birth, the powerful fixed star Rasalhague was in 20 degrees of Sagittarius, exactly upon his Uranus.

URANUS IN CHART OF TSAR ALEXANDER: 19.41 SAGITTARIUS
FIXED STAR RASALHAGUE IN 1818:   19.55 SAGITTARIUS

The contact between the destructive planet Uranus, and the sapphire star Rasalhague, has been recognized as bestowing strong passions and bringing a sudden death. The Tsar was killed by an assassin's bomb in St Petersburg, on 13 March 1881.

This death was presaged by the lunar eclipse which occurred on 12 June 1881, in 22 degrees Sagittarius, extremely close to the Uranus of his horoscope.

URANUS IN CHART OF TSAR ALEXANDER: 19.41 SAGITTARIUS
LUNAR ECLIPSE OF 12 JUNE 1881:   21.22 SAGITTARIUS

The contact between eclipse and planet is not exact. Under normal circumstances, this would exclude it from being an influence in the chart. However, it is clear that the sensitive degree was more emphatic than usual because of the double strength of the original Uranus/Rasalhague contact (see Rule Five, p. 86). My suspicions are confirmed by other factors in the birth chart and the eclipse chart.[2]

Hans Christian Andersen

Our study of eclipses may at times have given the impression that all eclipse-driven events lead to blood and thunder. It is certainly true that eclipses do tend to work dramatically, and explode the darker events in the lives of certain individuals. However, this is not always the case. An interesting example of how an eclipse seems to have bestowed meaning to the life of someone who was, until that time, almost entirely without direction in life, may be seen in the chart of the famous Danish poet and fairy-tale writer, Hans Christian Andersen.

He was born at 42 minutes after midnight, at Odense, on 2 April 1805. His chart is given overleaf.

Andersen's horoscope reflects the dreamy and impractical nature of a person in whom the imaginative and sensitive planet Neptune is strongly placed.[1] The early death of his father, a poor shoemaker, left the boy with little education, and surprisingly little wish to be educated in ordinary worldly knowledge. He was more interested in dreaming. In fact, Hans Christian Andersen was what would nowadays be called a 'slow developer': indeed, so far as the ordinary world was concerned, he seemed scarcely to develop at all. When as a young boy he went on impulse to

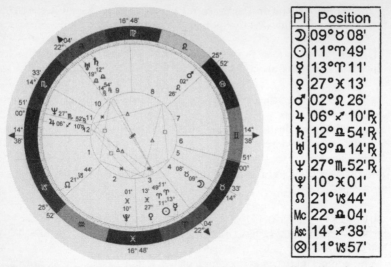

Pl	Position
☽	09°♉08'
☉	11°♈49'
☿	13°♈11'
♀	27°♓13'
♂	02°♌26'
♃	06°♐10'℞
♄	12°♎54'℞
♅	19°♎14'℞
♆	27°♏52'℞
♇	10°♓01'
☊	21°♑44'
Mc	22°♎04'
Asc	14°♐38'
⊗	11°♑57'

Copenhagen to become an opera singer, he was quite literally taken for a lunatic. He lived in a realm of imagination which seems to have been unique, yet the isolation which this brought allowed his sensitive and romantic faculties of mental picture-making to develop almost without the distortions to which formal education usually lead.

Perhaps the most significant event in his life was the unexpected success of the first published collection of his *Fairy Tales*, which came out in 1835. He continued to write his fairystories in instalments for almost the rest of his life, and the last collection was not published until the Christmas of 1872. Such a major event in the life of an author could not go unrecognized in the horoscope, and in this case the beginning of this unique contribution to literature was marked by an eclipse. In November, 1835 there was an eclipse in 28 degrees of Scorpio, which fell on Anderson's Neptune, in 28 degrees of the same sign.

SOLAR ECLIPSE OF 20 NOVEMBER, 1835:   27.26 SCORPIO
NEPTUNE IN THE CHART OF ANDERSEN: 27.52 SCORPIO

Marie Antoinette

The entire life of Marie Antoinette, the Queen of France and wife of Louis XVI, seems to have been dominated by the power of fixed stars.[1] Her horoscope has always been something of a puzzle, for there are no fewer than four fixed stars operative within it (a rare phenomenon), yet while each star contributes to her somewhat unfortunate reputation, only one threatened her death by the guillotine.[2]

The astrologer Ebenezer Sibly, who was alive at the time of her execution in 1793, was among the first to cast and publish alongside her birth chart the death chart (figure 4). His data shows that Marie was born 2 November 1755, at 7:23 pm, in Vienna, Austria.[3] The data for the chart (which varies slightly against that given by Sibly, in figure 4) are:

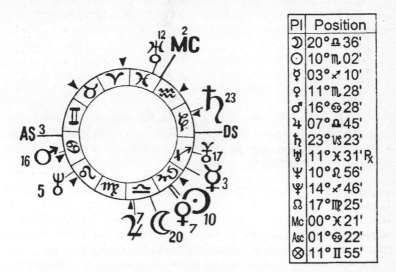

Pl	Position
☽	20°♎36'
☉	10°♏02'
☿	03°♐10'
♀	11°♏28'
♂	16°♋28'
♃	07°♎45'
♄	23°♑23'
♅	11°♓31'℞
♆	10°♌56'
♇	14°♐46'
☊	17°♍25'
Mc	00°♓21'
Asc	01°♋22'
⊗	11°♊55'

Not only did Sibly have Marie Antoinette's horoscope engraved for his book, but he also included in the same plate the chart for her husband, Louis XVI, and the time of his execution. Pressed between these charts is the somewhat pathetic (as it seems in retrospect) figure for the King's coronation (figure 4).

Sibly did his best to analyse these figures, but for some reason he missed the most important contact, which was the position of Venus.[4] Marie Antoinette's chart shows that Venus was in 12 degrees of Scorpio, exactly on the double fixed star Southern Scales.

VENUS IN THE CHART OF MARIE ANTOINETTE: 11.28 SCORPIO
POSITION OF SOUTHERN SCALES IN 1755:   11.40 SCORPIO

These stars have a reputation for ruination and disgrace in the astrological tradition. The modern astrologer Elsbeth Ebertin has thrown some further light on the operation of the star by indicating that when the Southern Scales are on a sensitive degree they bestow an immortal name through tragic circumstances. There may be no doubt that the Southern Scales leads to untimely deaths of a particularly violent nature. In addition, the star is reputed to bring false accusations along with general disgrace and imprisonment – an interesting set of influences in view of the long and cruel rigged trial which Marie Antoinette had to suffer during her incarceration in the Temple prison in Paris, before her execution by guillotine.

There was no eclipse on the sensitive degree of 12 Scorpio in 1793 but on 3 November 1793, only eighteen days after she was guillotined, *there was a conjunction of the Sun and Moon* in that degree!

VENUS IN THE CHART OF MARIE ANTOINETTE:	11.28 SCORPIO
POSITION OF SOUTHERN SCALES IN 1755:	11.40 SCORPIO
CONJUNCTION OF 3 NOVEMBER 1793:	11.54 SCORPIO

This is an important confirmation of the astrological tradition which maintains that the conjunction of Sun and Moon has the same effect as an eclipse. On reflection, such an idea is not too difficult to accept, for after all, a solar-lunar conjunction is merely the equivalent of an eclipse which does not cast a shadow on the Earth. From this point of view, the non-ecliptic conjunction of Sun and Moon may be regarded as an invisible eclipse.

Benjamin Banneker

I first became intrigued by the life and work of Benjamin Banneker when I was researching the astrological background to the founding of the federal city of the United States, which was later named Washington DC.[1] My interest was directed towards him not merely because he was a genius of a very special kind, but because he was deeply interested in eclipses.

Banneker was a free African American of mixed blood, living at a time when slavery had degraded both the image and life-style of his race to appalling levels. His grandmother had been an indentured servant, deported from England in the last decades of the seventeenth century. Once freed of her term of indenture, she purchased, freed and married a native African from Guinea. One of their daughters, Mary (born about 1700), had repeated the pattern by purchasing a slave of African origin and marrying him. From this union a small family developed, among which was Benjamin, born in 1731. In spite of the obstacles which such humble origins put in his way, Banneker became a self-taught mathematician and astronomer, with some knowledge of astrology: indeed, in 1791 (a significant year, as we shall soon see) he published the first of several annual almanacs, containing useful tables of planetary and stellar positions and observations on lunar and solar eclipses for the year to come.

The date, but not the time, of Banneker's birth has been preserved.[2] By means of a special astrological technique known as rectification, I have attempted to work out his birth time. The resultant horoscope and data, cast for 2:37 in the afternoon, are given below:

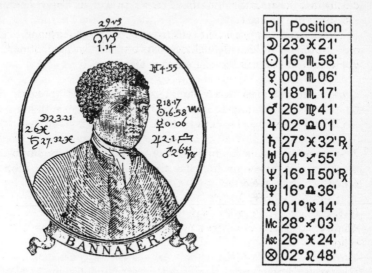

Pl	Position
☽	23° ♓ 21'
☉	16° ♏ 58'
☿	00° ♏ 06'
♀	18° ♏ 17'
♂	26° ♍ 41'
♃	02° ♎ 01'
♄	27° ♓ 32' ℞
♅	04° ♐ 55'
♆	16° ♊ 50' ℞
♇	16° ♎ 36'
☊	01° ♑ 14'
Mc	28° ♐ 03'
Asc	26° ♓ 24'
⊗	02° ♌ 48'

His almanacs aside, Banneker's main claim to fame was the short period he spent working alongside Andrew Ellicott in the survey of the land set aside for the federal city. This survey began officially in the early months of 1791.

Records suggest that on the morning of 3 April 1791, Banneker had observed the eclipse of the Sun over what was then called Jenkins Heights, but which would later be called Capitol Hill.[3] This solar eclipse took place in 14 degrees of Aries.

Banneker's personal chart did not reflect this eclipse of 3 April, but it certainly did reflect one which had occurred six months earlier. The earlier eclipse took place in the October in the previous year, when the opposition of Sun and Moon had fallen within 16 minutes of Banneker's Mercury. Perhaps I should remind the reader that the sign Scorpio follows immediately the sign Libra:

LUNAR ECLIPSE OF 23 OCTOBER 1790:   29.50 LIBRA
MERCURY IN THE CHART OF BANNEKER: 00.06 SCORPIO

This date is very significant, for it was at this time – round about October 1790 – that Ellicott invited Banneker to work with him on the survey of the city.[4]

131

Banneker was keenly interested in eclipses, which he used to calculate personally. For example, in his almanac for 1793 he notes that the lunar eclipse of 25 February would be visible in 8 degrees of Virgo (it was actually in 7.56 of that sign). Alongside this eclipse data, he gives positions of such stars as Arcturus, Spica and the asterism of the Pleiades.

Such information was usually offered in almanacs at that time, yet it is evident from his surviving notebooks that Banneker had a deep interest in the theory of eclipses and stars. Like most almanac makers of that time, he gave in his published works the 'seven-star risings' – that is, the rising, setting, and sometimes the 'southing' (or culmination) of the seven main stars.[5] This external interest in the stars is reflected in his own horoscope which is involved with no fewer than six important stellar contacts, three of which support the idea of a keen intellect and probing mind.[6] The only star I am interested in exploring in this context of eclipses, however, is Princeps which was on his Mercury, the planet involved in the eclipse of 1790 which I mentioned above.

MERCURY IN THE CHART OF BANNEKER:	00.06 SCORPIO
POSITION OF THE STAR PRINCEPS IN 1731:	29.24 LIBRA

Princeps is a pale yellow star in the spear-shaft of the constellation Bootes. In the astrological tradition, it gives a keen and studious mind, and is well known for bestowing an ability to do research. At the beginning of our era, Ptolemy saw the influence of the star as being the equivalent of Saturn and Mercury combined, though the seventeenth-century Rosicrucian-astrologer, Robert Fludd, saw it as reflecting the nature of Saturn and Mars.[7] Both positions increase the depth of intellect, and the ability to work alone in abstruse fields of research.

Banneker died on 9 October 1806. Two months later, there was a solar eclipse in the degree opposite the Neptune of his chart:

SOLAR ECLIPSE OF 10 DECEMBER 1806:	17.25 SAGITTARIUS
NEPTUNE IN THE CHART OF BANNEKER:	16.50 GEMINI

Ludwig van Beethoven

The chart and data for Beethoven's birth are given opposite.[1] One notes almost immediately the gathering of the first three planets in Sagittarius, and the opposition thrown against these by Mars: it is almost as though Beethoven stood astride the Cosmos, resting one foot on the planet of Mercury, in the fire-sign Sagittarius, and the other on the energetic Mars in the air-sign Gemini.

I have already touched on the more fortunate events in the life of Beethoven's horoscope in relation to eclipses. In a slightly different

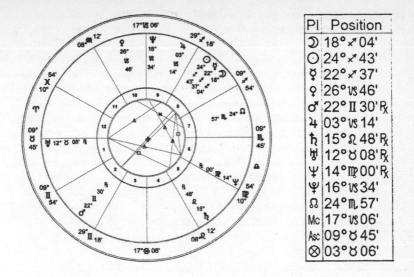

Pl	Position
☽	18° ♐ 04'
☉	24° ♐ 43'
☿	22° ♐ 37'
♀	26° ♑ 46'
♂	22° ♊ 30' ℞
♃	03° ♑ 14'
♄	15° ♌ 48' ℞
♅	12° ♉ 08' ℞
♆	14° ♍ 00' ℞
♇	16° ♑ 34'
☊	24° ♏ 57'
Mc	17° ♑ 06'
Asc	09° ♉ 45'
⊗	03° ♉ 06'

context, I should point out that Beethoven's famous deafness was recognized as being serious in the year that an eclipse fell upon the composer's Part of Fortune. This solar eclipse occurred in April 1800, in 4 degrees of Taurus:

SOLAR ECLIPSE OF 24 APRIL 1800:   3.33 TAURUS
PART OF FORTUNE IN THE CHART OF BEETHOVEN: 3.06 TAURUS

Strangely enough, the developing deafness seemed to parallel his own musical development: for example, it is interesting that his first Symphony was first performed in 1800.

By 1822, his isolation in deafness was so complete that an attempt he made to conduct in a public performance proved to be quite disastrous. His most ambitious choral work, the 'Mass in D' – among the most magnificent choral pieces ever composed – was begun in 1820, and was intended for the enthronement of his friend, the Archduke Rudolph as Archbishop of Olmutz, but was not completed until 1823. This was a year of six eclipses. That, and the previous year, had been incredibly productive for Beethoven. Even while working on the *Missa Solemnis*, he was already composing the Symphony No. 9 in D minor. While this was not completed until February 1824, the year 1822 was of profound importance to his artistic development. In that year there was an eclipse on Saturn – the representative of depth and structure (as well as with the isolation connected with deafness) in his chart:

| LUNAR ECLIPSE OF 6 FEBRUARY 1822: | 16.59 LEO |
| SATURN IN THE CHART OF BEETHOVEN: | 15.48 LEO |

It is quite intriguing to link other details in Beethoven's creative life with eclipses, yet this can be very misleading, as Beethoven is unique. Few men and women ever experience more than one major contribution to their lives through more than one eclipse. Beethoven was exceptional – one of those individuals who seemed to be so intimately linked with the heavens that several eclipses poured their influences into his life and work. As a matter of fact, it was a lunar eclipse that paralleled his death, which took place in Vienna on 26 March 1827, in a fierce thunderstorm that seemed almost to echo the might of his own music.[2]

| LUNAR ECLIPSE OF 3 NOVEMBER 1827: | 10.29 TAURUS |
| ASCENDANT IN CHART OF BEETHOVEN: | 09.45 TAURUS |

William Blake

William Blake's horoscope, cast by his friend John Varley, is given below. Blake's achievements, both as poet and painter, were prodigious: he was undoubtedly a man of genius, possessed of quite extraordinary vision. Like Beethoven, Blake seemed to live in the effects of eclipses in a way that lesser men do not. For example, there was an eclipse on his 'revolutionary' planet Uranus in 1792 – the year he wrote his revolutionary poem, *America*, which was published in the following year.

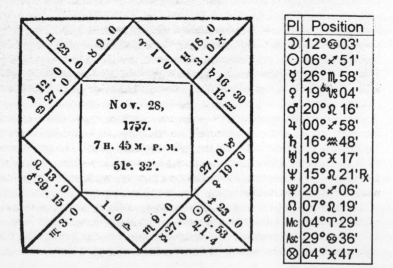

Pl	Position
☽	12°♋03'
☉	06°♐51'
☿	26°♏58'
♀	19°♑04'
♂	20°♌16'
♃	00°♐58'
♄	16°♒48'
♅	19°♓17'
♆	15°♌21'℞
♇	20°♐06'
☊	07°♌19'
Mc	04°♈29'
Asc	29°♋36'
⊗	04°♓47'

LUNAR ECLIPSE ON 8 MARCH 1792:	19.05 PISCES
URANUS IN THE CHART OF BLAKE:	19.17 PISCES

Blake was an extremely complicated writer, while his paintings incorporated arcane symbols which have not yet been fully appreciated. In his later years he seems to have learned astrology from his friend John Varley, who published Blake's horoscope in the astrological magazine *Urania*:[1]

The lore of astrological symbolism (and the lore of eclipse symbolism) seems to have played an important role in his later poetry and painting. Even these major developments were, so to speak, overlooked by eclipses. For example, in 1804 Blake published the remarkable poem *Milton*. In that year, there was an eclipse of the Moon across his Ascendant and Descendant, in 30 degrees Cancer:

LUNAR ECLIPSE OF 22 JULY 1804:	29.38 CAPRICORN
DESCENDANT IN THE CHART OF BLAKE:	29.36 CAPRICORN

Blake, being a Romantic poet, was deeply interested in eclipses, and even introduced pictures of them in his poems. In one poem – *Jerusalem*, which he wrote and illustrated over a period of almost sixteen years – he drew illustrations which included both a lunar and a solar eclipse.[2]

The lunar eclipse (figure 14 – but see detail above) shows the dark Spectre, 'insane and most deform'd' in the shape of a bat-like creature, hovering over female body. To the right of the figure is a radiant Sun, to its left an eclipsed Moon. In this complex image, Blake seems to be linking the eclipse in the heavens with the equivalent experience in mankind, when an inner darkness falls over the soul.

The solar eclipse from the same poem (figure 15, but see detail over) is portrayed as seen through the gateway of one of the massive trilithons of Stonehenge. The poem is not clear about what this stone doorway represents, yet in the arcane tradition which interested Blake, the sign

135

Cancer was often called 'the gate of Birth' while the opposite sign, Capricorn, was called 'the gate of Death'.

In fact, in 1805, the year after which Blake first started to write and illustrate *Jerusalem*, there was an eclipse of the Sun in both Cancer and Capricorn:[3]

SOLAR ECLIPSE OF 1 JANUARY 1805:	10.16 CAPRICORN
SOLAR ECLIPSE OF 26 JUNE 1805:	04.48 CANCER

In the section of the poem just above the massive lintel of the stones, Blake identifies the three figures which stand at the entrance to the 'gate', and, therefore, below the eclipse. These are 'Bacon & Newton & Locke'. The presence of these great thinkers in the picture suggests that Blake had in mind the Gate of Cancer, for this was the gate of the new-born, the place where (according to Blake) imagination comes into the world.

The three men portrayed in the picture were, in Blake's view, the great enemies of Imagination, which Blake valued so highly: they had introduced materialistic science into human thinking. Francis Bacon, the founder of experimental science, emphasized that knowledge should be bounded upon material facts (as Blake saw it, to the detriment of imagination). John Locke had denied that a person was born into the world with an innate knowledge, or instinct – this was almost the opposite of what Blake believed. Blake saw the new-born soul new-descended from the stellar realms, as a repository of spiritual wisdom and knowledge, which could often be lost, as the physical body grew old. Sir Isaac Newton laid the foundations for the mechanistic vision of the Cosmos, which swept away the highly mystical (and often misunderstood) spiritual view. This materialistic vision possibly explains why, close to the drawing, Blake could write: 'The Starry Heavens all were fled from the mighty limbs of Albion.'

Albion was one of the names used by Blake for Britain, and perhaps explains the reference to Stonehenge, a type and scale of structure unique to this country. The three figures standing below the eclipse were representatives of this 'mighty race', who had driven away the stars – symbols of imagination. In view of this, we may interpret the illustration as relating to the eclipse of the lunar Imagination, through the gate of birth.

Blake knew enough about astrology to be aware that this eclipse of 1805, in 10.16 Capricorn, was almost opposite to his own birth-chart Moon, in 11.57 Cancer.[4]

In March 1819, there was an eclipse in 5 degrees of Aries, on Blake's own zenith, which paralleled a complete change in Blake's life and art.

ZENITH ON THE HOROSCOPE OF BLAKE:	04.29 ARIES
SOLAR ECLIPSE ON 25 MARCH 1819:	04.30 ARIES

It was in this year that William Blake's life suddenly changed for the better. He met the portrait painter, John Linnell, who introduced him to a wide circle of friends, many of them artists or poets. Linnell also introduced him to John Varley, an astrologer who was making a special study of the newly discovered planet, Uranus.[5] Until this time, Blake had been a somewhat lonely individual (though happily married) with few friends, and even fewer people who could understand either his painting or his poetry. Suddenly, he was surrounded by a group of people who understood his art, and among these were some younger men who became virtually his disciples.[6]

Encouraged by this new lease of life, and supported financially by Linnell, Blake began one of his most creative works – a series of copperplate illustrations to the *Book of Job*, in the Bible. This would prove to be the last of his prophetic books: he worked on it during 1824, completing it the following year. During that time, there was a lunar eclipse on his Venus, in 19 degrees Capricorn.

LUNAR ECLIPSE ON 11 JULY 1824:	18.38 CAPRICORN
VENUS IN THE CHART OF BLAKE:	19.04 CAPRICORN

Having completed this undertaking, Blake published the book of twenty-one prints in March 1826. Unlike many of Blake's other mystical pictures, he now had a circle of friends who appreciated them. The year of publication saw a solar eclipse on his own Sun, in 7 degrees of Sagittarius:

SOLAR ECLIPSE ON 29 NOVEMBER 1826:	06.46 SAGITTARIUS
SUN IN THE HOROSCOPE OF BLAKE:	06.51 SAGITTARIUS

Sometimes, when the Sun is touched by an eclipse, the outcome can be overwhelming or serious for the native. By this time, Blake was sixty-seven years old, and suffering very badly from gallstones. In spite of this, and once again supported financially by Linnell, he threw himself into a supreme effort by beginning a vast cycle of illustrations for Dante's *Divine Comedy*. He had completed 100 watercolour designs, and made seven engravings, when he died on 12 August 1827, singing the praise of the Lord.

Charlotte Brontë

Sometimes an eclipse will have the effect of raising an unknown writer from obscurity into almost instant fame.

The three Brontë sisters had written secret stories, and what they called 'novels', for years before they felt it appropriate to submit their material for publication. They lived in an obscure yet delightful parsonage in Haworth, on the edge of the Yorkshire Moors, and they each, in their different ways, allowed the cold isolation of the place to blow through their works.

In 1847, the first novel that Charlotte Brontë submitted to a publishing house was rejected, yet the publisher expressed an interest in another work she had mentioned, called 'Jane Eyre'. When he read this work, he was delighted with it, and published it in August of the same year. It was an instant success.

Charlotte Brontë was born on 21 April 1816, at 2:41 pm, in Thornton, Yorkshire.[1]

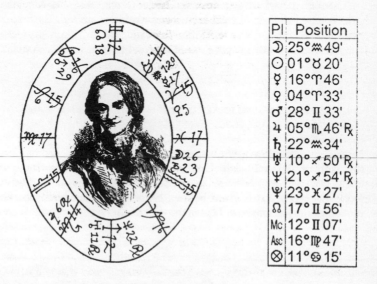

Pl	Position
☽	25° ♒ 49'
☉	01° ♉ 20'
☿	16° ♈ 46'
♀	04° ♈ 33'
♂	28° ♊ 33'
♃	05° ♏ 46' ℞
♄	22° ♒ 34'
♅	10° ♐ 50' ℞
♆	21° ♐ 54' ℞
♇	23° ♓ 27'
☊	17° ♊ 56'
Mc	12° ♊ 07'
Asc	16° ♍ 47'
⊗	11° ♋ 15'

Although there are *some* factors in the horoscope which point to a satisfaction of her ambition to become a published writer, during 1847 these were certainly supported by the weak orb from an eclipse which helped so radically to change her life.[2]

This was the eclipse of the Sun on 9 October 1847, which was directly opposite Charlotte's Mercury, in 17 degrees Aries.

MERCURY IN CHARLOTTE BRONTË'S CHART: 16.46 ARIES
SOLAR ECLIPSE OF 9 OCTOBER 1847:   15.28 LIBRA

As one might imagine, the chart of such a talented woman as Charlotte Brontë was marked with a fixed star: this was Bellatrix (Female Warrior), a yellow star in the left shoulder of the constellation Orion. This star was within a few minutes of her Dragon's Head. In the astrological tradition, Bellatrix brings honours and wealth, usually through some courageous or outstanding activities. The star also usually threatens blindness, but

139

Charlotte was not afflicted in this way.[3] However, it is worthy of note that, towards the end of her novel, *Jane Eyre*, the hero, Rochester, becomes blind.

DRAGON'S HEAD IN CHARLOTTE BRONTË'S CHART: 17.56 GEMINI
POSITION OF BELLATRIX IN 1816: 18.23 GEMINI

Although Charlotte's fame was assured after 1847, her life was not emotionally fulfilled. She married relatively late in life, on 29 July 1854, and died in childbirth in the following year, on 31 March. In October, 1855 there was a lunar eclipse exactly upon her Sun, in the 1st degree of Taurus.

SUN IN THE CHART OF CHARLOTTE BRONTË: 01.20 TAURUS
LUNAR ECLIPSE OF 25 OCTOBER 1855: 01.21 TAURUS

Emily Brontë

Life went very differently for Charlotte's younger sister, Emily. Perhaps this is to be expected, as her horoscope is so very different from that of Charlotte. She was born 30 July 1818 at 2:49 pm, also in Thornton, Yorkshire: the chart is given below.[1] Shortly after her birth, the family moved to the parsonage in Haworth, which is now the Brontë Museum.

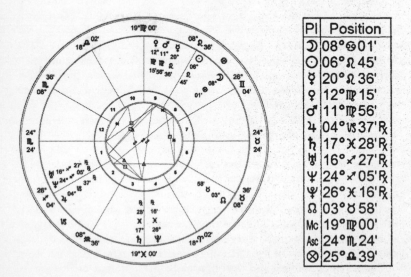

Pl	Position
☽	08°♋01'
☉	06°♌45'
☿	20°♌36'
♀	12°♍15'
♂	11°♍56'
♃	04°♑37'℞
♄	17°♓28'℞
♅	16°♐27'℞
♆	24°♐05'℞
♇	26°♓16'℞
☊	03°♉58'
Mc	19°♍00'
Asc	24°♏24'
⊗	25°♎39'

It is almost as though this young woman came to earth just to leave behind what must be among the most brooding, sombre and passionate novels in the English language. This novel, *Wuthering Heights*, was published in 1847, the same year as Charlotte's *Jane Eyre*, yet it did not receive the same acclamation. In fact, it took some decades for the brilliance of this dark and moving tale of the self-destructive Heathcliffe to be fully appreciated. Just as the publication of Charlotte's book was signalled by an eclipse, so was the one book which Emily published. In April 1847 there was a solar eclipse opposite to her Part of Fortune:

SOLAR ECLIPSE OF 15 APRIL 1847:	24.39 ARIES
PART OF FORTUNE IN EMILY'S CHART:	25.39 LIBRA

The genius of this young woman is reflected in the two fixed stars which dominated her chart, the most powerful being Facies. The other was Scheat.

POSITION OF FIXED STAR SCHEAT IN 1818:	26.50 PISCES
PLUTO IN THE CHART OF EMILY BRONTË:	26.16 PISCES

Scheat is set in the left leg of the flying horse Pegasus. In the ancient tradition expounded by the second-century astronomer and geographer Claudius Ptolemy, the star represents the nature of Mars and Mercury combined, so we must visualize this degree in Emily's chart as representing all the pent-up energies of the need to express (Mercury) the dark and brooding inner world (Pluto) working through an aggressive and untamed man (Mars). *Wuthering Heights* is almost Plutonic in its exploration of the underworld soul of an unhappy creature.

In general, Scheat is bad for the health, and often gives an unsatisfactory environment – though Emily does appear to have been almost obsessive about the power of the Yorkshire Moors, in spite of the unsanitary condition of Haworth, at that time.

I have already discussed something of the way the star Facies brings serious illnesses to the native: this was not mitigated in the case of Emily's chart, even though the contact between star and planet was at the widest permissible orb. While Jupiter always tends to soften and spiritualize everything it touches, even this influence cannot soften entirely the stellar threat of sickness, or, in this case, an early death.

POSITION OF FIXED STAR FACIES IN 1818:	5.47 CAPRICORN
JUPITER IN THE CHART OF EMILY BRONTË:	4.37 CAPRICORN

Emily died in the year following publication of her masterpiece, on 19

December 1848, from an illness brought about partly by the unexpected death of her brother Branwell in the September of the same year. Emily's early death at the age of thirty-one, was overshadowed by an eclipse in 19 degrees Pisces on 9 March 1849, within a degree of her Saturn, and very close to her nadir, at the bottom of the chart.

LUNAR ECLIPSE OF 9 MARCH 1849:	18.19 PISCES
SATURN IN THE CHART OF EMILY BRONTË:	17.28 PISCES
NADIR IN THE CHART OF EMILY BRONTË:	19.00 PISCES

An eclipse on the degree of Saturn is a classical indication of serious ill-health, a loss, and, in extreme, even of death. Poor Emily (emotionally hypersensitive, with her Moon in Cancer) experienced all three of these effects. The astrology of eclipses permits us a privileged insight into the forces behind her early death, but Emily's biographer, Virginia Moore, was inclined to see this death in a very different light. It was, in her opinion, nothing short of welcomed – a 'virtual suicide'.[2]

Lord Byron

I have mentioned more than once that genius seems to attract eclipses. Perhaps the galvanic power behind eclipses is essential to allow genius to pour its spiritual energy into creative endeavour. An example of this is the life of the Romantic poet, Lord Byron, who seems to have been dominated by the power of eclipses and fixed stars. The following account is based only on three[1] eclipses which occurred at important milestones in his life.[2]

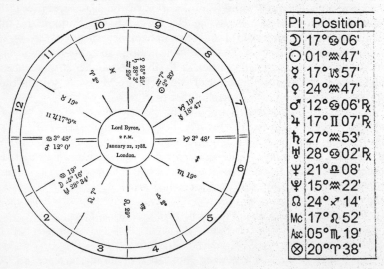

Pl	Position
☽	17°♋06'
☉	01°♒47'
☿	17°♑57'
♀	24°♒47'
♂	12°♋06'℞
♃	17°♊07'℞
♄	27°♒53'
♅	28°♋02'℞
♆	21°♎08'
♇	15°♒22'
☊	24°♐14'
Mc	17°♌52'
Asc	05°♏19'
⊗	20°♈38'

Byron's chart is a particularly complex figure to interpret, but one of the outstanding things in it is the fixed star Algenubi which dominates the zenith.

Leo on the zenith is usually a sign of a somewhat flamboyant nature, but when it is with such a strongly unpleasant star as Algenubi, the flamboyance would be so tempered at times as to suggest an almost dual personality in which the light of the Leonine impulse would fight with the darkness of the star.

Algenubi is a yellow star in the lion's mouth. In the figure above, which was influenced by the Arabic tradition, the star is the left-hand of the three in the hair-line of the lion, but in the later maps it is represented lower down the image, in the mouth of the creature. The position explains the epithet attached to the star – 'The one who rends'.[3] The position of the star in the mouth of a beast explains the traditional reading of the star as giving a cruel, heartless and destructive nature, tempered by an artistic power of linguistic expression.

ZENITH IN THE CHART OF LORD BYRON: 17.52 LEO
POSITION OF STAR ALGENUBI IN 1788:   17.44 LEO

Byron's marriage to the beautiful and precocious heiress, Anne Isabella Milbanke, is best described as a marriage from Hell – Byron's immaturity, petulance, cruelty and violence in this relationship ensured that it came to a quick end.

The couple were married on 2 January 1815. On 10 January a solar eclipse fell *close* to Byron's Mercury. It was an effective eclipse, however, because this degree was exactly opposite to Byron's Moon, which increased the permitted orb.

SOLAR ECLIPSE OF 10 JANUARY 1815:	19.32 CAPRICORN
MERCURY IN THE CHART OF LORD BYRON:	17.57 CAPRICORN
MOON IN THE CHART OF LORD BYRON:	17.06 CANCER

On 10 December 1815, Byron's wife gave birth to a girl, Augusta Ada. As Byron recorded the exact moment of birth, the horoscope for the child has entered the mainstream of nineteenth-century horoscope collections.[4]

On 16 December of that year, there was an eclipse on the Dragon's Head in Byron's chart.

DRAGON'S HEAD IN THE CHART OF LORD BYRON:	24.14 GEMINI
LUNAR ECLIPSE OF 16 DECEMBER 1815:	23.47 GEMINI

Shortly after Ada was born, Isabella, realizing that she would never be able to reform Byron, decided that she would have to leave him. On 15 January 1816, unable to stand his behaviour any longer, she left their home, and never saw him again. I suspect that it was this loss of both child and wife (rather than the birth of the child, which seems to have delighted Byron) that was reflected in the ominous contact of eclipse with the Dragon's Tail.

As a matter of fact, this contact with the Dragon's Tail was repeated later at an even more crucial moment in Byron's life.

In December 1823, Byron travelled to Missolonghi (Greece), to support the cause of the Greeks, who were struggling against Turkey for independence. In April 1824 Byron became feverish. Although the fever did not at first appear to be serious, Byron was apprehensive. While lying on his sofa, talking with his friend Dr Millingen, Byron recalled a prediction made in his youth by a fortune-teller in Scotland – that he should beware his thirty-seventh year. The warning had left a deep impression on his mind, and he had now reached that fateful year.[5]

Byron died at 6:00 pm on 19 April 1824. The lunar eclipse which followed in July was threatening a particularly strong influence on his horoscope, for it fell across the opposition of Mercury and Moon which was one of the keys to Byron's personal life, if not also to his poetry. It was precisely the same eclipse which overshadowed the death of William Blake (see page 138).

LUNAR ECLIPSE OF 11 JULY 1824:	18.38 CAPRICORN
MOON IN THE CHART OF LORD BYRON:	17.06 CANCER
MERCURY IN THE CHART OF LORD BYRON:	17.57 CAPRICORN

Dr William Parry, who was present at Byron's deathbed, wrote later, 'At the very time Lord Byron died, there was one of the most awful thunderstorms I ever witnessed. The lightning was terrific. The Greeks . . . believe that such an event occurs whenever a . . . supreme man dies.'[6]

King Charles I

I suppose that no king in history has had such a welter of predictions about his impending death as Charles I of England.[1] Perhaps this excess of prophetic material is due to the fact that he lived through what was probably the heyday of predictive astrology in England, and because he and his subjects experienced the kind of troubled times – a Civil War and the deposing of a king – which seem always to call for prophets. The predictions of the King's death began early – indeed, if we wish, we may trace at least one back to the quatrains published in 1557 by Nostradamus. Among these was a prophetic description of the King's execution – almost a hundred years before it happened.[2]

The horoscope for the king, alongside a modern tabulation, is given below. According to the astrologer Ebenezer Sibly, Charles was born 19 November 1600, at the very precisely formulated time of 10:2:35 pm.[3]

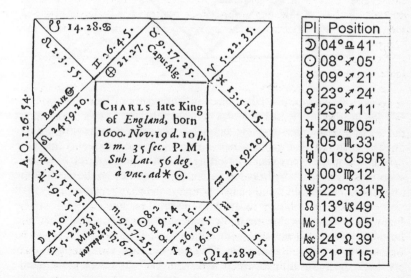

Pl	Position
☽	04° ♎ 41'
☉	08° ♐ 05'
☿	09° ♐ 21'
♀	23° ♐ 24'
♂	25° ♐ 11'
♃	20° ♍ 05'
♄	05° ♏ 33'
♅	01° ♉ 59' R
♆	00° ♍ 12'
♇	22° ♈ 31' R
☊	13° ♑ 49'
Mc	12° ♉ 05'
Asc	24° ♌ 39'
⊕	21° ♊ 15'

The seventeenth-century English astrologer, William Lilly, was in the forefront of those who made several lightly veiled predictions concerning the death of the King. Some of these were based on the readings of eclipses. Among the most dire of these predictions was one which he read

145

into the eclipse of 11 August, 1645 (OS). Since this formed Lilly's most explicit prediction of the King's death by the astrologer, the woodcut horoscope which accompanied it is worth some study.[4]

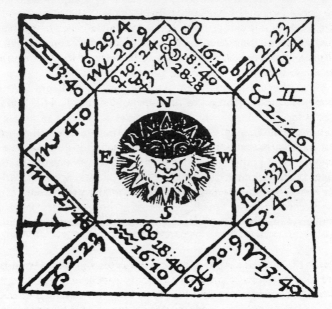

This solar eclipse had taken place in 29 degrees of Leo. Having been visible in England, it had caused a considerable stir. Lilly's own interest in the eclipse is understandable, because in the seventeenth century it was widely believed that eclipses had a more profound influence in those places where they were visible (whether as total or penumbric). No doubt, this was one reason why Lilly felt authorized to relate it to the death of the King. In addition, the eclipse had taken place in the royal sign, Leo, which further encouraged him to link it with the royal person.

In actual fact, there was no planet in Leo in the natal chart of Charles I, and his Ascendant was far too wide of the eclipse to allow Lilly to read into it a connection with the life of the King himself. Lilly avoided this thorny problem by interpreting the figure as though it referred to kings in general – to 'some famous King or Prince' who could (among other things) be slaughtered. Lilly was quite aware that traditional astrology regarded the Ascendant (the Eastern Angle) as a nodal point receptive to eclipses, and he would have been keen to use this as a means of linking the dire eclipse prophecy with the King's own horoscope.

In fact (as is usually the case), the prediction based on the idea that an eclipse would bring about the end of the King became clear only after the event. In a pamphlet of 1652, Lilly wrote:

> In the Eclips of 19 November 1648, you see the Sun was in the 8 degree 44 minutes of Gemini. If the Astrologian known any man, who had in (his chart) either the Sun or Moon in that degree, or in the degree opposite . . . the native did suffer more or less by the influence of this Eclips.[5]

As every educated person of the time knew, Charles I had his Sun in that degree of Gemini.

The question remains, did the King die in accordance with an eclipse? The answer is quite emphatically, yes. A lunar eclipse took place on 30 November 1648. Since this date is given in accordance with the old calendrical system, it means that the eclipse fell directly upon the Sun of Charles's horoscope, when this is adjusted to the new calendar:

ECLIPSE OF 30 NOVEMBER 1648:	8.44 SAGITTARIUS
SUN IN THE HOROSCOPE OF CHARLES I:	8.05 SAGITTARIUS

One wonders why Lilly did not latch on to this significant eclipse, long before Charles had been imprisoned and beheaded, in 1649?

The regicide leads us to ask whether there was anything in his chart which would suggest such a fate? The answer is yes. At his birth, his lunar node, the Dragon's Tail, was on 14 degrees of Cancer. This was within orb of the same degree occupied by the fixed star Castor.

FIXED STAR CASTOR IN 1600:	14.57 CANCER
DRAGON'S TAIL IN THE CHART OF CHARLES I:	13.49 CANCER

The orb may seem to be just a little wide, until one realizes that in Charles's birth chart the Dragon's Tail was also on the beneficial fixed star Propus:

DRAGON'S TAIL IN THE CHART OF CHARLES I:	13.49 CANCER
POSITION OF STAR PROPUS IN 1600:	13.19 CANCER

It is little surprise that when the astrologer John Gadbury wrote an astrological commentary on the death of Charles, he quoted the doggerell:

> The Dragons Tail's no Planet, yet it is
> In mischief worser then the worst (I wis).[6]

The fact that the Dragon's Tail fell between the two stars increased the orb for both. Castor, a binary, is in the northern head of the mortal Twin (the constellation Gemini) and has a most unfortunate reputation. When with the Sun (or Mars), it threatens imprisonment and decapitation. When with the Moon, it threatens imprisonment, disgrace and injuries to the face and head. As the node marks the symbolic union of Sun and Moon, we may apply both these readings to the destiny of Charles I.

William Jefferson Clinton

William Jefferson Clinton, who was to become President of the United States in 1992, was born by Caesarian operation at Hope, Arkansas, on 19 August 1946, an hour after dawn.[1] His horoscope is given below:[2]

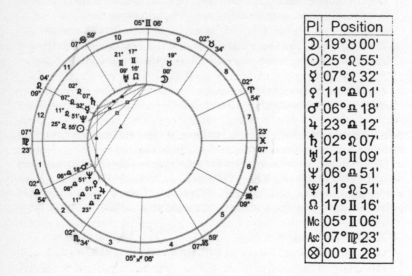

Pl	Position
☽	19° ♉ 00'
☉	25° ♌ 55'
☿	07° ♌ 32'
♀	11° ♎ 01'
♂	06° ♎ 18'
♃	23° ♎ 12'
♄	02° ♌ 07'
♅	21° ♊ 09'
♆	06° ♎ 51'
♇	11° ♌ 51'
☊	17° ♊ 16'
Mc	05° ♊ 06'
Asc	07° ♍ 23'
⊗	00° ♊ 28'

The most obvious thing that strikes any astrologer who examines this chart is the close conjunction between the planet of the libido – Mars – and the planet of confusion and nebulousness – Neptune. Both are in 7 degrees of Libra. These planets alone may be taken as a guide to the darker side of Clinton's life.

Clinton's undeniably magnetic personality seems to be connected with the fixed stars in his chart, which point to a genius rare in politicians. These stars are so interesting that I am listing the main five below:

SUN IN THE CHART OF CLINTON:	25.55 LEO
FIXED STAR AL JABHAH IN 1946:	27.06 LEO

MERCURY IN THE CHART OF CLINTON:	07.32 LEO
STAR SOUTH ASELLI IN 1946:	07.55 LEO
JUPITER IN THE CHART OF CLINTON:	23.12 LIBRA
FIXED STAR SPICA IN 1946:	23.02 LIBRA
URANUS IN THE CHART OF CLINTON:	21.09 GEMINI
FIXED STAR PHACT IN 1946:	21.22 GEMINI
PLUTO IN THE CHART OF CLINTON:	11.51 LEO
FIXED STAR ACUBENS IN 1946:	12.50 LEO
ZENITH IN THE CHART OF CLINTON:	05.06 GEMINI
STAR PRIMA HYADUM IN 1946:	04.59 GEMINI

Of these, the more obvious astrological connection is that which Jupiter holds to Spica, which is a star of tremendous importance to the well-being of the United States, and which is, indeed, the original star which appears as the five-pointed star on the Stars and Stripes. This suggests that Clinton, for all the difficulties to which his personal life-style has given rise, will represent an era in the United States that will later be considered beneficial: perhaps some political innovation that stems from Clinton's administration will prove to be very advantageous to the United States? Even in the chart of a non-politician, the contact between Jupiter and Spica is supposed to bring great popularity and success. Not all the other stars are quite so beneficial however: for example, Acubens on Pluto is one which tends to induce a lack of regard for truth in personal matters. The position of Prima Hyadum on the zenith suggests that Clinton will eventually be disgraced.

As with all important individuals, Clinton's life has been overshadowed by a number of eclipses. For example, there was an eclipse which marked his election to the presidency, in November 1992:

DRAGON'S HEAD IN THE CHART OF CLINTON:	17.16 GEMINI
LUNAR ECLIPSE OF 9 DECEMBER 1992:	18.12 GEMINI

It is usual for an eclipse falling on the Dragon's Head to advance the career of the native, for the node is connected with the outflowing of beneficial events. In contrast, a lunar eclipse on the zenith can sometimes lift up, and at other times thrust down – depending upon the past actions of the individual concerned, as the zenith is often affected by karma. On 25 May 1994 a solar eclipse fell almost across the axis of Clinton's zenith and nadir:

NADIR OF THE CHART OF CLINTON:	05.06 SAGITTARIUS
LUNAR ECLIPSE OF 25 MAY 1994:	03.37 SAGITTARIUS

This, relatively wide in orb, might not have led to too many difficulties, but (unfortunately for Clinton) in the same month, further promise of trouble was expressed when a solar eclipse fell on Clinton's own Moon:

MOON IN THE CHART OF CLINTON:	18.59 TAURUS
SOLAR ECLIPSE OF 10 MAY 1994:	19.49 TAURUS

As one might imagine, *two* eclipses upon sensitive points in a chart would inevitably prove catastrophic for any human being. In May 1994, Paula Jones filed her lawsuit against Clinton, thereby (unwittingly) unleashing a chain of difficulties for the President.

In many respects, 1998 – the year when the President testified before the Grand Jury (on 17 August), concerning his sexual relations with Monica Lewinsky – will have proved the most humiliating and embarrassing year in the whole of Clinton's political career.[3] Early in this year, a solar eclipse fell on Clinton's Descendant – in other words, on that angle which deals with relationships:

DESCENDANT IN THE CHART OF CLINTON:	07.11 PISCES
SOLAR ECLIPSE OF 26 FEBRUARY 1998:	07.55 PISCES

Nicolas Copernicus

The great Polish astronomer Nicolas Copernicus was born in Torun, Poland, on 19 February 1473 at 5:00 pm. We are fortunate to have his birth time because his horoscope was published by the Florentine astrologer, Junctinus, in 1583.[1] Our own tabulations, given below alongside the chart published by Junctinus, are not only more accurate, but also include the planets that were unknown in the sixteenth century.

Copernicus was a man of genius, and of very wide accomplishments – a sort of Leonardo da Vinci of Poland. He had, for example, studied mathematics at the University of Cracow. He took his studies in this area so far that in 1522 he was able (at the command of Sigismund I, the energetic King of Poland) to present to the Diet of Graudenz a brilliant scheme for the reform of the Polish currency.[2] Copernicus had also studied painting, and was widely admired in his day for his skill as an artist. He had studied medicine at Padua, and was much sought out as a doctor during his life, acquiring an enviable reputation for treating the poor without demanding a fee. However, it was his study of astronomy and astrology under Domenico Maria Novara[3] – who taught in the University of Bologna at the end of the fifteenth century – that led

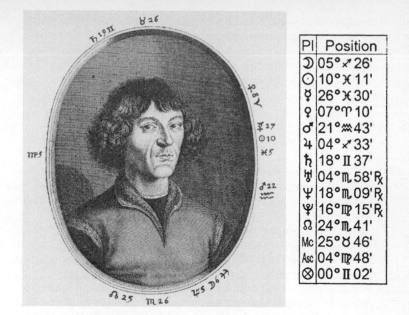

Pl	Position
☽	05° ♐ 26'
☉	10° ♓ 11'
☿	26° ♓ 30'
♀	07° ♈ 10'
♂	21° ♒ 43'
♃	04° ♐ 33'
♄	18° ♊ 37'
♅	04° ♏ 58' ℞
♆	18° ♏ 09' ℞
♇	16° ♍ 15' ℞
☊	24° ♏ 41'
Mc	25° ♉ 46'
Asc	04° ♍ 48'
⊗	00° ♊ 02'

Copernicus to the science of astronomy for which he is now world-famous.

Even in his student days, Copernicus had found himself unhappy with the ancient Ptolemaic system of astronomy, which gave an exceedingly complicated model of the Cosmos. One of the things that worried him was that the calculations of planetary positions by means of this system did not always measure up to the observable positions, and he began to wonder if it would be possible to construct a working model of the planetary system with the Sun, rather than the Earth, at the centre. By 1530, he had set down his ideas concerning the heliocentric (or solar-centred) theory in manuscript form, and this circulated among the intellectuals of Poland, Italy and Germany. The story of the publication of this work has helped it become one of the best known books in the history of the sixteenth century – even though it is a story which is not always told correctly.

Formal requests for the publication of the book were made by the Church in Rome, and under the direction of Copernicus' devoted disciple, George Joachim Rheticus, it was finally printed under the title of *De Revolutionibus*, in 1543.[4] The printed copy did not reach Copernicus (who was then in Frauenburg) until almost too late: it was presented to him on his sickbed, shortly after he had been paralysed by a stroke. He was unable to read his masterpiece, and he died the following year, on 24 May 1543.

It would be surprising if such an important event – important both for Copernicus and for the development of astronomy – was not recorded by an eclipse. Six days before his death, there was a lunar eclipse upon an important arc in his chart. The arc was marked by two planets – the Moon and Jupiter – upon which the eclipse fell:

MOON IN THE CHART OF COPERNICUS:	05.26 SAGITTARIUS
JUPITER IN THE CHART OF COPERNICUS:	04.33 SAGITTARIUS
LUNAR ECLIPSE OF 18 MAY 1543:	06.02 SAGITTARIUS

I have indicated that the works an artist, writer or musician leave behind are sometimes subject to the mutations of eclipses. The writings of Copernicus were no exception – save that in his case, the later influences of eclipses were manipulated by an astrologer.

It has been recorded in more than one history of astrology that it was the rare conjunction of Saturn and Jupiter in the final degree of Cancer, on 25 August 1563, which led Rheticus to begin his commentary on the writings of his master, Copernicus.[5] Certainly, Rheticus wrote from Cracow to say that he had begun this work, but we do not know if it was ever finished. The interesting thing is that the historians who record this astrological story do not really understand it. The indications are that Rheticus did not begin the work on Copernicus merely because of the rare conjunction of Saturn and Jupiter. He had begun the work because the eclipse preceding the conjunction had fallen exactly upon the Ascendant of the great man:

SOLAR ECLIPSE OF 18 AUGUST 1563:	04.38 VIRGO
ASCENDANT IN THE CHART OF COPERNICUS:	04.48 VIRGO

In those days, astrologers were far more interested in the power of fixed stars than in modern times, and I think that Rheticus would have been aware that the great man's Ascendant was also involved with a fixed star. This was Zosma:

POSITION OF STAR ZOSMA IN 1473:	04.37 VIRGO
SOLAR ECLIPSE OF 18 AUGUST 1563:	04.38 VIRGO
ASCENDANT IN THE CHART OF COPERNICUS:	04.48 VIRGO

Although I am not sure what conclusions to draw from this connection, the fact is that the degree is close to one that has proved to be important to modern Poland. In the horoscope cast in the twentieth century for the country, by the Polish astrologer Rafal Prinke,[6] the planet Mars is close to this same degree that was so important to Copernicus. The contact between the two is emphasized by the fixed star.

An important financial reform of Polish currency which began under Wladyslaw Grabski in the 1920s was painful to the economy, but eventually it did lead to financial stability. The concordat reached by Grabski with the Holy See, in Rome, also had considerable influence upon the future of the spiritual life of Poland, if only because the ecclesiastical divisions organized under this concordat were in future in the hands of Polish appointments, leaving Polish Catholicism beyond the control of politics.

These reforms were marked by an eclipse in the important degree of Virgo. Through its connection with Mercury, this sign has rule over the handling of finance. In addition, through the well-established and ancient connection Virgo holds with the Virgin Mary, it has dominion over Christian spiritual life:

Solar eclipse of 30 August 1924:   06.40 Virgo
Mars in the chart for Poland: 06.20 Virgo

The election of Karol Wojtyla, the Archbishop of Cracow, as Pope John Paul II in October 1978 seems to have been one consequence of these reforms. The significance of this appointment lies in the fact that he was the first non-Italian pope for over four centuries. The election of John Paul II was marked by a solar eclipse opposite the 'Polish degree', in 07:30 Pisces.

Perhaps more extraordinary is the fact that the position of Saturn in John-Paul's own natal chart is on that highly significant degree in Virgo which we noted in Copernicus' horoscope:

Ascendant in the chart of Copernicus: 04.48 Virgo
Saturn in the chart of Pope John Paul: 04.56 Virgo

Not surprisingly, John Paul's chart involves eclipses, so I have dealt with this horoscope in a separate section (see page 185).

Princess Diana

I have already commented upon the chart of Princess Diana, yet it is such an interesting one, in so far as eclipses are concerned, that I would like to examine it in a different light. She was born at Sandringham on 1 July 1961 at 07:45 pm.[1] The importance of this chart (overleaf) lies in a sequence of three solar eclipses which were on sensitive points in her chart, and deeply influenced the course of her life.

153

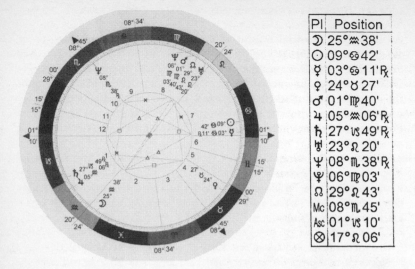

Pl	Position
☽	25° ♒ 38'
☉	09° ♋ 42'
☿	03° ♋ 11' Rx
♀	24° ♉ 27'
♂	01° ♍ 40'
♃	05° ♒ 06' Rx
♄	27° ♑ 49' Rx
♅	23° ♌ 20'
♆	08° ♏ 38' Rx
♇	06° ♍ 03'
☊	29° ♌ 43'
Mc	08° ♏ 45'
Asc	01° ♑ 10'
⊗	17° ♌ 06'

In a book written about Diana, and published shortly after her death, Anthony Holden wrote of a period when Diana's life was 'going into eclipse'.[2] I wonder if Anthony Holden knew just how apposite his choice of imagery was? At the time in question, Diana was six years old, and the year in question was 1967. Her mother left the family, and after a divorce, became Mrs Shand-Kydd. This disaster weighed heavily on the young girl, and she would say that for years later the memory of that day kept her awake at nights.

On 2 November 1967 there was a solar eclipse in Scorpio, exactly upon Diana's zenith – the point which determines how one relates to the external world. This zenith was already in close contact with the planet Neptune.

ZENITH IN THE CHART OF PRINCESS DIANA: 08.45 SCORPIO
NEPTUNE IN THE CHART OF PRINCESS DIANA: 08.38 SCORPIO
SOLAR ECLIPSE OF 2 NOVEMBER 1967:   09.07 SCORPIO

In August 1979, when Diana was eighteen years old, there was an eclipse in 30 degrees of Leo. According to astrological theory, we should expect there to be some major event in her life within the few months preceding or following the eclipse.

SOLAR ECLIPSE OF 22 AUGUST 1979:   29.01 LEO
DRAGON'S HEAD IN CHART OF PRINCESS DIANA: 29.43 LEO

The event that took place in 1979 was her first meeting since childhood with Prince Charles, and the subsequent development of a relationship with him: they were married in July 1981.

In 1982 there was a solar eclipse which created another sensitive point in Diana's chart. This was the eclipse of 20 July, in 28 degrees of Cancer, which was opposite Diana's Saturn, in 28 degrees Capricorn.

SOLAR ECLIPSE OF 20 JULY 1982:   27.42 CANCER
SATURN IN THE CHART OF PRINCESS DIANA: 27.49 CAPRICORN

On 21 June 1982 Diana gave birth to a boy – Prince William.[3]

Now, almost everyone is aware that the marriage to Charles did not work out as planned, and we are aware that Diana died in a terrible car accident – but looking back at these events of 1979 and 1982 we cannot help but see it as a release of great happiness into Diana's life at the time. These events fundamentally changed her status in the world, after 1979. This is an example of how eclipses may signal explosive changes which work for the immediate benefit of the individual. Such benefits contrast with the tragic circumstances surrounding her death.

I cannot imagine that anyone is certain about precisely what conspired to cause the death of Princess Diana. However, the fact of Diana's death is reflected with extraordinary lucidity in her natal chart, and its occurrence is linked with an eclipse of the Sun which took place on the day she died, in Paris.

I should observe at the outset that there are two patently obvious indications in this chart that Diana would meet a violent death. Her Venus, in 25 degrees of Taurus was just within orb of the most evil star in the heavens – Algol.[4]

VENUS IN THE CHART OF PRINCESS DIANA: 24.27 TAURUS
POSITION OF FIXED STAR ALGOL IN 1961:   25.37 TAURUS

Since Venus is a symbol of the love that one can give and receive, the implication is that Diana would involve herself in liaisons dangerous to her own spiritual welfare.

A proficient astrologer who was aware of the contact between her Venus and Algol would be inclined to presume from this contact with Algol that Diana would die in an accident, or be murdered. The astrologer would certainly look to the chart to see if there were any other confirmations of such a destiny.

In mediaeval astrology, Algol had such a reputation that even the contact with so soft a planet as Venus was regarded as a sign that the person would be liable to a violent death, or to public execution. The word

155

Algol is a corruption of the Arabic *Ras al ghoul* ('Head of the Demon' – see picture on page 92) and was given to the severed head of the Gorgon Medusa, held by the constellation Perseus in the skies. Before the Arabs gave mediaeval astrologers this word, the star was often called in Latin Caput Larvae ('Head of the Spectre').

Most of these names could be traced back to stories from Greek mythology. The Medusa had been a beautiful maiden whose hair was transformed into a mass of hissing serpents by Minerva, who was jealous of Medusa's sexual involvement with her own lover, Neptune. So fearful was this serpentine face that it transformed into stone anyone who looked upon it. In the most popular form of the myth, Medusa was slain by the prince Perseus, who had been fathered upon the princess Danae by Zeus, the King of the gods, when he appeared to her in the form of a shower of gold.[5] There is probably some arcane significance in this detail of the myth, as told by Ovid. In order to hide the petrifying stare of the Medusa, Perseus spread seaweed over the severed head, and was astonished to see the seaweed turn into coral. Now, the pink and golden corals reach skywards from the bottom of the waters, towards the heaven where once Zeus himself came down as a shower of gold.[6]

The second clear indication of an unfortunate and untimely end in Diana's chart is also indicated by a fixed star. In her natal chart, Diana's own Moon node (the Dragon's Head) was on the fixed star Regulus, in the last degree of Leo.[7]

DRAGON'S HEAD IN THE CHART OF PRINCESS DIANA: 29.43 LEO
POSITION OF FIXED STAR REGULUS IN 1961:   29.17 LEO

In the light of its connection with the chart of the Princess, the name of this star seems to be especially significant, for it is linked with royalty and a certain magnificence of style: the Latin regulus means 'king of a small country'. It is really quite extraordinary how often this royal star is found emphasized in the horoscopes of the more beneficent of European rulers. For example the Renaissance astrologers who cast the horoscope of Lorenzo de' Medici (called 'il Magnifico') were at pains to show that Regulus was strongly placed in his chart.[8]

In fact, these Italian astrologers called it Cor Leonis (heart of the lion), for it was not named Regulus until the sixteenth century. However, long before that time it was still linked with royalty: in Babylonian astrology it was Sharru (the King), in ancient Greek, Basilikos aster (the King star) and so on. In the astrological tradition, this proves to be a most curious star, for in spite of its undeniable association with royalty, it is also linked with a violent death.

Prior to their death, Regulus is said to lift individuals to very high honours, and to bestow a royal grace. In the astrological textbooks, the star is said to make the native generous, ambitious, high-spirited and fond of power. The early nineteenth-century astrologer, Vivian Robson, wrote of the star's influence that, when with the Moon, it makes women 'high-spirited and independent' and when with the Dragon's Head (as is the case in Diana's chart) it brings great preferment even from the lowest sphere to the highest rank. The star also brings dangers from enemies and false friends, public prominence, great power, honour and wealth – but still with that violent death.[9]

Diana died, in Paris, in the early hours of 1 September 1997.[10]

On 2 September there was a solar eclipse in 10 degrees of Virgo. This was close to the position of Pluto in Diana's natal horoscope, but the orb was probably too wide for it to be effective. However, there is a great deal to be learned from this eclipse, since it had an influence upon Diana's chart for very profound reasons. There were some quite remarkable correspondences between planetary positions at the moment of the eclipse and planetary positions in Diana's birth chart. The main ones are given below:

SOLAR ECLIPSE OF 2 SEPTEMBER 1997:	09.34 VIRGO
MERCURY AT SOLAR ECLIPSE OF 2 SEPTEMBER 1997:	06.52 VIRGO
PLUTO IN THE CHART OF PRINCESS DIANA:	06.03 VIRGO
URANUS AT SOLAR ECLIPSE OF 2 SEPTEMBER 1997:	05.26 AQUARIUS
JUPITER IN THE CHART OF PRINCESS DIANA:	05.06 AQUARIUS
NEPTUNE AT SOLAR ECLIPSE OF 2 SEPTEMBER 1997:	27.32 CAPRICORN
SATURN IN THE CHART OF PRINCESS DIANA:	27.49 CAPRICORN

Isadora Duncan

The influence of the demon-star Algol in the death of Princess Diana calls to mind another accidental death of a beautiful woman under the influence of this star. The innovative female dancer, Isadora Duncan, who was born in San Francisco, 27 May 1878 at 2:25 am, died in an accident under the influence of the same star. Isadora's Pluto was on Algol – just one unfortunate fixed-star among many in her chart.[1] The horoscope is given overleaf.[2]

Modern astrologers who have familiarized themselves with the working of Pluto, since its discovery in 1930, are inclined to read the contact of Algol with Pluto as involving strangulation.[3]

Isadora died on 14 September 1927, in Nice (France) when the long red woollen shawl she was wearing around her neck was caught in the moving wheel of a two-seater car, and strangled her. Her friend, Mary Desti, who

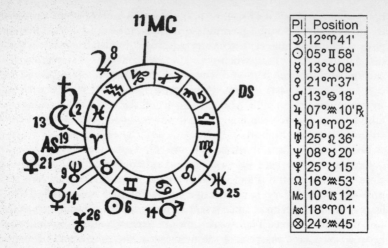

Pl	Position
☽	12° ♈ 41'
☉	05° ♊ 58'
☿	13° ♉ 08'
♀	21° ♈ 37'
♂	13° ♋ 18'
♃	07° ♒ 10' ℞
♄	01° ♈ 02'
♅	25° ♌ 36'
♆	08° ♉ 20'
♇	25° ♉ 15'
☊	16° ♒ 53'
Mc	10° ♑ 12'
Asc	18° ♈ 01'
⊗	24° ♒ 45'

was present at the accident, reported that the fast revolution of the wheels pulled in the scarf tightly, and both broke her neck and severed her jugular vein, killing her instantly.[4]

The accident was marked by an eclipse, which fell directly opposite Isadora's Mars, which was itself on the evil fixed star Canopus.

SOLAR ECLIPSE OF 3 JANUARY 1927:	12.29 CAPRICORN
MARS IN THE CHART OF DUNCAN:	13.18 CANCER
POSITION OF STAR CANOPUS IN 1878:	13.16 CANCER

Isadora Duncan did not have an easy life – indeed it was marred by terrible tragedies. Among these, the most difficult for her to bear was the drowning of both her children, Patrick and Deidre, when the car they were in ran into the river Seine (Paris), in 1913.

In that year, there was a lunar eclipse on Isadora's Saturn.

LUNAR ECLIPSE OF 22 MARCH 1913:	01.17 ARIES
SATURN IN THE CHART OF ISADORA DUNCAN:	01.02 ARIES

This contact would have been bad enough to ensure that some event of a dark Saturnine nature would take place around this time in Isadora's life, but her chart was even more difficult, as Saturn was on the evil fixed star, Difda.

SATURN IN THE CHART OF ISADORA DUNCAN:	01.02 ARIES
POSITION OF STAR DIFDA IN 1878:	00.53 ARIES

158

Difda causes destruction, misfortune and accidents. Its placing (in the tail of the constellation Cetus, the Whale or Sea-monster) links its influence with accidents at sea, and with drownings.

Ralph Waldo Emerson

In some ways, the American writer Ralph Waldo Emerson reflected perfectly the spiritual life of his times. He was a deeply religious man, closely in contact with the spiritual world, in a period when the older sense of faith was being eroded. His view of the world is perhaps summed up in two entries from his diary, which could almost be from the pen of an astrologer: 'All good and evil that can befall him (Mankind) must be from himself . . . There is a correspondence between the human soul and everything that exists in the world.'[1]

In reading his essays, one forms the impression of a man who was somehow insulated by his spiritual strength from all disturbances that life might offer. Yet, the fact is that his life, first as a religious minister and later as a writer and teacher, was disturbed by several tragedies, the severity of which was sufficient for them to be reflected in eclipses.

Emerson was born in Boston, 25 May 1803, at 1:18 pm. His horoscope data is given below.[2]

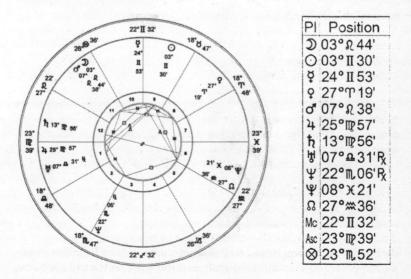

Pl	Position
☽	03° ♌ 44'
☉	03° ♊ 30'
☿	24° ♊ 53'
♀	27° ♈ 19'
♂	07° ♌ 38'
♃	25° ♍ 57'
♄	13° ♍ 56'
♅	07° ♎ 31' ℞
♆	22° ♏ 06' ℞
♇	08° ♓ 21'
☊	27° ♒ 36'
Mc	22° ♊ 32'
Asc	23° ♍ 39'
⊗	23° ♏ 52'

His Ascendant was on the fixed star Labrum, set in the bottom of the bowl of the celestial cup, Crater, which has been linked with the chalice of the Holy Grail.[3]

159

It is this entirely beneficial star which accounts for Emerson's idealism and intelligence, and for the success of his career in both ecclesiastical and scholarly circles. The star is well known in astrological circles for promoting success in religious and spiritual undertakings.

The star Labrum is a curious one, for it is only faintly visible to the unaided eye, yet is recognized in astrology as bestowing the spiritual benefice of the sacred Cup (Crater) with more directness than any of the other eight stars in the constellation. The Arabs recognized the cup in the pattern of the stars, and it is from their *al kas* (shallow basin) that we have our name Alkes for the prime star which is set in the bottom of the figure. The spiritual significance of Labrum seems to arise from the fact that it stands half way between the top of the bowl and the base. To the left (below) is part of the constellation image of the Crater, from an eighteenth-century star map. To the right, is a modern representation of how this constellation is drawn, with lines joining together the nine chief stars of the asterism. The star Alkes is that to the extreme right – in the modern image, it therefore represents the base of the cup.

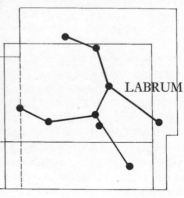

In view of the importance of this star, so firmly set on Emerson's Ascendant angle, we would imagine that it would throw a radiance over his whole life. If an eclipse were to fall upon it during his lifetime, it would almost certainly influence his career and life in a most powerful way.

As a matter of fact, an eclipse did fall on the Ascendant and star in his twenty-seventh year:

ASCENDANT IN THE CHART OF EMERSON:	23.39 VIRGO
POSITION OF STAR LABRUM IN 1803:	23.57 VIRGO
SOLAR ECLIPSE OF 17 SEPTEMBER 1830:	23.39 VIRGO

The eclipse was to overshadow a fundamental change in his life. In 1829 he had married the beautiful Ellen Tucker, and became the associated minister of the Second Unitarian Church, in Boston. He looked forward to a useful life in the ministry, living within a close-knit community. His cup seemed to be full of joy.

Within three years this was to change. On 27 July 1832, there was a solar eclipse on his Moon:

MOON IN THE CHART OF EMERSON:	03.44 LEO
SOLAR ECLIPSE OF 27 JULY 1832:	04.27 LEO

The year 1832 was to see fundamental changes in Emerson's life, which would completely redirect his interests and thought – even his way of living. It was as though this eclipse worked as a fulcrum in the balance of darkness and light in that momentous year.

Early in 1832 his wife died. On Christmas Day 1832, he left America for England, where he was to meet and befriend the leading literary figures of the day, such as Coleridge, Wordsworth and Carlyle. On his return to America, he changed his direction, and never took charge of a parish again. He became a public lecturer, and settled down to writing his wonderful books and essays.

On the whole, his life was untouched by evil contacts in the skies, with the exception of a brush he had with the evil star Algol, in 1872. The star Algol (figure on page 92) has a reputation for being the most evil star in the heavens: having pointed this out, I must say immediately that the star was not operative in Emerson's horoscope.

In 1803 Algol was in 23.25 degrees of Taurus. This meant that it was directly opposite his Part of Fortune. However, fixed stars work only from the degree they occupy – they do not throw their influences to other parts of the zodiac.[4] In this context, therefore, Algol did not throw its influence to the far side of the Cosmos, to touch Emerson's Part of Fortune. Just so, the Part of Fortune also works purely as a degree influence. Thus, there was no operative opposition between the Part of Fortune and the Star. However, this influence was galvanized for a short time when the lunar eclipse of 1872 fell across the pair, and bridged them.

On 15 November 1872, there was a lunar eclipse in 24 degrees of Taurus – this eclipse fell on the position of Algol in his birth chart forming a bridge between the evil star and the Part of Fortune.

PART OF FORTUNE IN THE CHART OF EMERSON:	23.52 SCORPIO
SUN IN LUNAR ECLIPSE OF 15 NOVEMBER 1872:	23.17 SCORPIO
POSITION OF ALGOL IN THE CHART OF EMERSON:	23.25 TAURUS
MOON IN LUNAR ECLIPSE OF 15 NOVEMBER 1872:	23.17 TAURUS

In 1872, Emerson's house burned down. Terrible as this loss was to Emerson, he bore it with equanimity. The house was eventually rebuilt by public subscription.

Emerson died on 27 April 1882, under the presage of an eclipse, which fell on the place of his Sun.

LUNAR ECLIPSE OF 25 NOVEMBER 1882:	02.38 GEMINI
SUN IN THE CHART OF EMERSON:	03.30 GEMINI

A wood-engraving of this eclipse, illustrating its dramatic corona, has survived.[5] 'Astrology interested us,' wrote Emerson, 'for it tied man down to the system. Instead of an isolated beggar, the farthest star felt him and he felt the star . . . a right and perfect man would be felt to the centre of the Copernican system.'[6]

Max Ernst
The horoscope of the artist Max Ernst (below) is fascinating for very many reasons, but my own personal interest in it lies in the fact that Ernst was fond of painting eclipses and curious cosmic phenomena.

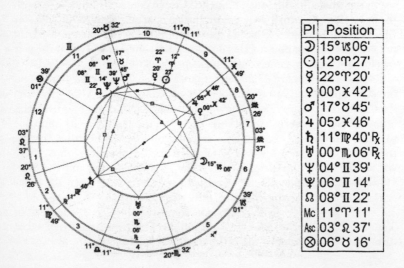

Pl	Position
☽	15° ♑ 06'
☉	12° ♈ 27'
☿	22° ♈ 20'
♀	00° ♓ 42'
♂	17° ♉ 45'
♃	05° ♓ 46'
♄	11° ♍ 40' ℞
♅	00° ♏ 06' ℞
♆	04° ♊ 39'
♇	06° ♊ 14'
☊	08° ♊ 22'
Mc	11° ♈ 11'
Asc	03° ♌ 37'
⊗	06° ♉ 16'

Ernst was born at Bruhl, near Cologne, on 2 April 1891. His horoscope is cast for midday.[1]

Before becoming a painter, Ernst studied philosophy. This tended to lend his paintings a very intellectual approach, and sometimes it is difficult to know from a painting when he is being very clever, and when he is working with the 'accidents' which were so beloved by the Dadaist school of painting, with which he is sometimes linked. This interest in philosophy has tended to make some of Ernst's paintings very difficult to understand, and the following observations should make this quite clear.

One of the most obscure of Ernst's paintings is that to which he gave the enigmatic title, 'Of this Men Shall Know Nothing'. The picture is built around a number of paintings of eclipse diagrams.

The painting is a surrealistic one that makes brilliant use of eclipse symbolism. In the skies, to the top of the painting, is a curious arrangement of four legs using a lunar crescent as a sort of parachute.

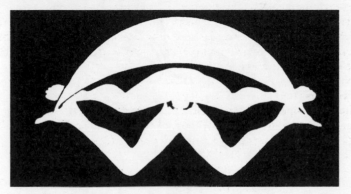

As we can see, the four legs are actually mirror-images of a single pair of legs:

On the earth, below the parachute, is an even more surrealistic group of figures, made up from eclipse and lunar-phase diagrams, each figure constructed with a 'head' made up from a lunar circle which forms part of an eclipse (below). The grid-lines which sketch out these strange figures have been borrowed by Ernst from an eclipse diagram (see figure 16) – as have the forms, constructed from shadows and penumbras. The central figure has a severed hand lying across the circle which marks its breast.

In the foreground is what appears to be a pile of offal: if a mirror is laid along the bottom of the picture, to reflect this 'offal', it is revealed as the innards of a human body. Just as the cosmic parachute is a mirror image, this physical plane is designed to be a mirror-image. Just so, the Moon is a reflection of the Sun, and is visible to the earth only by virtue of the light which the Sun bestows upon it.

The secret meanings in this disquieting picture have already been examined by some art historians[2] but, as far as I know, its most remarkable content – the eclipse-content, as we might call it – has not been fully revealed until now. The art-historian Elizabeth Legge has shown that the inverted crescent Moon, from which are suspended the two sets of human legs, was itself derived from a nineteenth-century engraving of an eclipse:[3]

Beneath this disturbing union of human legs, suspended from a crescent Moon, are the two human-like eclipse figures, opposite. That to the left seems to be a lunar eclipse diagram, elevated from the earth, so that its shadow falls to a point upon nothing – a reminder that this is actually a cosmic truth, that the Moon *always* projects its shadow. The central diagram is more complex, with what may be a version of an annular eclipse that serves as a face for a semi-humanoid figure, the gigantic hand of which is resting over its body. The circular object in this severed hand resembles (once again) the diagram of an annular eclipse.

Both the 'head' and lower circle of this figure cast shadows, suggesting that they are cosmic bodies – perhaps the Moon and Sun, or Moon and Earth? I do not suppose that the identity of these circles is all that important: what is of interest, however, is that the details are quite clearly

165

based on the familiar eclipse–diagrams found in astronomy textbooks. It is very likely that Ernst took as his model for the eclipse diagram an engraving in a book of astronomy, printed in 1883 (figure 16).[4]

Ernst painted his picture in 1923. In March 1923 there was an eclipse exactly upon his Saturn.

SATURN IN THE CHART OF ERNST: 11.40 VIRGO
LUNAR ECLIPSE OF 3 MARCH 1923:   11.37 VIRGO

It is very interesting that the severed hand in the diagram (below) has been interpreted as a reference to the protective gesture of Venus, hiding her private parts from the casual gaze.[5]

In fact, Max Ernst's own notes to this picture[6] tell us that the severed hand 'shields the earth', and that Ernst was consciously painting the Moon as it 'goes at great speed through its phases and eclipses'. The fact is that the hand seems to rest on the stomach area of the shadow body of the central figure. This part of the body – the belly, the womb, and the feminine private parts – are ruled by the zodiacal sign Virgo in the traditional images of zodiacal man and woman (figure 17).

Here we have a most interesting picture – it was painted in the year when an eclipse affected the life of the painter in a most personal way. The picture portrays both lunar and solar eclipses. One of the eclipses involves a symbolism linked with Virgo. The actual eclipse which affected the life of the artist was in Virgo . . . I am not sure what conclusions to draw from all this material, yet it is clear that this remarkable picture is deeply autobiographical. Did Ernst know what was influencing his chart? Did he have some knowledge of astrology? Or was he tapping into the Cosmos with the aid of the artistic sensibility? I do not know the answers to these questions, yet the painting remains one of my favourites from among Surrealist art. As far as I know, it is the only painting of any distinction to incorporate eclipse-diagrams as an integral part of a composition.[7]

The painting was dedicated to the French writer André Breton, and may celebrate the fact that, after some years of trying, Ernst had finally succeeded in obtaining a visa to go and live in Paris, the artistic centre of the western world.

This is probably the effect which the 1923 eclipse had on Ernst, but in order to understand how this might be, we need to look at the painting once more.

If we examine the picture again, we shall see that there are two eclipse diagrams, both seemingly depicting lunar eclipses. The quite extraordinary thing is that in October 1922, when Ernst learned that the visa would come through, there was another lunar eclipse which fell upon his chart – upon his creative Sun, in Aries:

SUN IN THE CHART OF ERNST:	12.27 ARIES
LUNAR ECLIPSE OF 6 OCTOBER 1922:	11.52 ARIES

Between this eclipse of 1922 and the second eclipse of 1923, Ernst achieved his desire, and left Cologne for Paris. The theme of the central eclipse diagram, with its emphasis on the stomach, now becomes quite clear – in the astrological tradition, Paris is ruled by Virgo![8]

LUNAR ECLIPSE OF 13 MARCH 1922:	22.15 VIRGO
LUNAR ECLIPSE OF 3 MARCH 1923:	11.37 VIRGO

Anne Frank

Millions of people met their deaths through the ideas and actions of Hitler. Among these victims one in particular is now remembered for her tragic diaries, which somehow survived the Holocaust.

The personal diaries of Anne Frank tell the courageous story of a young German-Jewish girl hiding in an Amsterdam attic from the German soldiers during the Second World War. According to the records, the young girl was finally arrested by the Gestapo in August 1944, and taken to a concentration camp, where she died in March 1945.

Her horoscope (overleaf) was published some years ago.[1] It shows the Sun and Mercury in Gemini, the sign which rules over diary-writing. What the conventional horoscopes do not show is that an eclipse of 1945, which was the cosmological cause of Hitler's death in the Berlin bunker, also brought about the death of this young Jewish girl.

This eclipse of July 1945 was in 17 degrees of Cancer. It fell upon the planet Pluto in Anne Frank's chart:

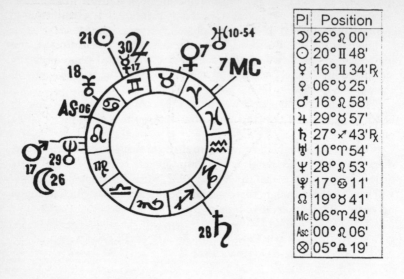

Pl	Position
☽	26° ♌ 00'
☉	20° ♊ 48'
☿	16° ♊ 34' ℞
♀	06° ♉ 25'
♂	16° ♌ 58'
♃	29° ♉ 57'
♄	27° ♐ 43' ℞
♅	10° ♈ 54'
♆	28° ♌ 53'
♇	17° ♋ 11'
☊	19° ♉ 41'
Mc	06° ♈ 49'
Asc	00° ♌ 06'
⊗	05° ♎ 19'

POSITION OF PLUTO IN FRANK'S CHART: 17.11 CANCER
SOLAR ECLIPSE OF 9 JULY 1945:   16.57 CANCER

In mythology, Pluto is the ruler of the Underworld, and it is tempting to read this powerful contact of Pluto with a solar eclipse as marking the transport of Anne Frank to the terrible underworld of the concentration camp, where she met her death.

Vincent van Gogh

We have already looked at the influence of fixed stars in van Gogh's horoscope (see p.87). Perhaps uniquely he had as many as six fixed stars emphasized in his natal chart, which is given opposite.[1] With such a cosmic pressure upon him, it is understandable that Andre Lhote should write of him as 'not merely the most accursed of modern painters, but the only one who was accursed in every way'.[2]

Vincent van Gogh was born at Zundert, 30 March 1853 at 11.20 am.[3] At that time and place, the Ascendant degree was in 22 degrees Cancer, which was exactly on the fixed star Pollux. This means that an extremely powerful star was rising over the eastern horizon at the moment of his birth. To judge from the surviving lists of books he had read, van Gogh was deeply interested in occult things, and I wonder to what extent the obsession with stars, and starry nights, in his later phase of painting was a result of some insight into his own horoscope?

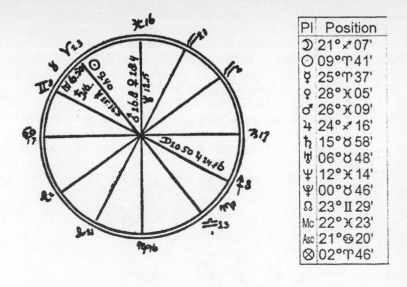

Pl	Position
☽	21° ♐ 07'
☉	09° ♈ 41'
☿	25° ♈ 37'
♀	28° ♓ 05'
♂	26° ♓ 09'
♃	24° ♐ 16'
♄	15° ♉ 58'
♅	06° ♉ 48'
♆	12° ♓ 14'
♇	00° ♉ 46'
☊	23° ♊ 29'
Mc	22° ♓ 23'
Asc	21° ♋ 20'
⊗	02° ♈ 46'

ASCENDANT IN THE CHART OF VAN GOGH: 21.20 CANCER
POSITION OF FIXED STAR POLLUX IN 1853:   21.11 CANCER

Pollux is an orange star, set in the head of the Southern Twin. In the astrological tradition, it is connected with accidents to the face, and there are few astrologers who, on seeing this star on the Ascendant, would not immediately think of Vincent's famous picture of his bandaged head, after he had cut off the lower part of his ear, and delivered it as a gift to a lady of pleasure, Rachel.[4] Pollux is also noted for influencing a violent death under certain circumstances. In Roman times, the name of the star Pollux was sometimes used as an interjection, as 'Pol', and it is perhaps more than a coincidence that the asylum in which Vincent was kept towards the end of his life was located at St-Pol, a mile or so to the south of San Remy.

While Vincent's obsession as an artist is partly linked with the power of Pollux, my own interest in his chart rests upon the position of his Mars. Mars was in 27 degrees Pisces, which happened to be very close to the star Scheat.[5]

MARS IN THE CHART OF VAN GOGH: 26.09 PISCES
POSITION OF FIXED STAR SCHEAT IN 1853:   27.19 PISCES

Scheat is by no means the most evil influence in the heavens – it is an orange star set on the left leg of Pegasus, and it is reputed to bring many accidents. However, several modern astrologers insist that it causes sudden death.[6] Any fame born of contact with Scheat can come after death, for there is nothing in the astrological tradition to insist that this fame should come during the lifetime of the native. Despite only selling two pictures in his lifetime, van Gogh is now one of the most famous of all nineteenth-century painters. The modern astrologer, Elsbeth Ebertin, has suggested that under certain circumstances the star can threaten death by fire, explosion, fire-arms, and so on.[7] These are the things of Mars, and it is reasonable to expect such a finale to life under this star, as incendiary things have always been linked with the fiery planet.[8]

The paintings of stars which Vincent did towards the end of his troubled life are fascinating. The well-known 'Cypresses with Two Figures' is usually seen as representing the Sun on one side of a cypress and the crescent Moon on the other (opposite).

Van Gogh's picture is dominated by a supra-living Sun which swirls in heavily laid impastos, dragging with it all the cosmological stellar life of the skies. The picture is divided vertically by a huge cypress, which seems to be quivering under the impress of the solar life. In the distance, to the right is a house and a horse and cart. In the foreground, two men are walking down the road. The cypress, horse-and-cart, and men do not cast shadows.

The atmosphere is electric – one can almost feel a frisson in the air, as though something of great cosmic moment is occurring. The cypress divides the sky into two areas. That to the left is dominated by the swirling Sun: that to the right is dominated by what appears to be a star – yet it cannot be a star, for it is the same size as the Sun. It must be a Moon, yet the crescent is directed away from the Sun, instead of towards it. This is a surrealistic Moon:

What does this mean? Is the radiant yellow disk not the Sun at all? In my opinion, either Vincent is painting the Cosmos in upheaval, or the radiant yellow disk is not the Sun.

Could it be a star? This is a possible interpretation, as the figures in the painting do not cast shadows.

The 'Sun' and crescent Moon are low in the skies, so we might expect that the painting was either a morning or evening picture. If it is morning, we are looking approximately to the east. If it is evening, we are looking approximately to the west.

In a study of the Sun and Moon in this painting, Frederick Dawe suggested that Vincent was attempting to excite a 'sense of unreality and disquiet in the mind of the spectator' by this unreal and impossible juxtaposition of Sun and Moon.[9] In this interpretation Dawe visualizes the 'sun' and Moon as though they were approaching an eclipse.

The picture was finished in 1889. In that year there were three solar eclipses. Only one of these would be visible in the early morning from southern France, where van Gogh worked at the time: one took place shortly after midday, and the other was at night-time.[10] If the painting is indeed linked with an eclipse, it must be one that took place on 28 June 1889, in 7 degrees of Cancer. This eclipse was total at 09.19 am local time.

However, since (to judge from the painting) the Moon is about two degrees away from direct contact with the Sun, we must presume that the scene depicted was painted almost four hours earlier, and thus quite early in the morning.[11] Of course, I am not suggesting that the picture is itself intended to be a 'realistic' portrayal of a pre-eclipse, yet it is evident that in the year this picture was painted the conditions were right for Vincent to make such a pre-eclipse picture. If this were the subject, then the intensity of the troubled sky and the almost-paranoiac sub-lunar world below would be explained. Van Gogh would be painting something of his own presentiment of his eclipse-influenced death.

Although I do not wish to read too much into this picture, I feel that it is legitimate to pose another question.

Is it possible that *the curious crescent actually shows the Sun in partial eclipse*? If this is the case, then the picture points to a time shortly after 9.19 am local time. If this is a partial eclipse of the Sun, then we must ask, what is the bright 'sun' to the right of the cypress? It cannot be the Sun, which relieves us of the necessity of explaining away the wrongly oriented lunar crescent – so we must assume that it is a star.

This should lead us to ask if there was a powerful star a few degrees to the east of the 1889 eclipse point, in 7 degrees Cancer? The answer is, yes. In 1889 the powerful fixed star Sirius – perhaps the most important star in the ancient heavens – was in 13 degrees Cancer.

POSITION OF STAR SIRIUS IN 1889:   12:33 CANCER

When we contemplate this radiant star in Vincent's picture, we are reminded that even the name Sirius came from the Greek *Seirios*, which meant 'scorching' or 'sparkling'.

Vincent was a genius, and therefore it is foolish to attempt to relate his art to standard norms, yet the fact is that many of his paintings of stars seem to have anticipated Surrealist art, which did not properly develop for almost three decades.

For all his genius and posthumous fame, van Gogh's life as a painter was surprisingly brief, lasting less than five years: his genius seemed meteoric, rather than star-like. Although he had been studying art (under very difficult conditions) for some years before 1885, he did not set up as a fully committed painter until that year, when (with the financial help of his brother, Theo) he rented his own studio in Neuenen. [12] In that same year he moved to Antwerp, and never returned to his home in Holland. In March 1885 his father died. All these important events are reflected in an eclipse which took place on Vincent's Mars, in March 1885.

POSITION OF MARS IN THE CHART OF VAN GOGH: **26.09 PISCES**
SOLAR ECLIPSE OF 16 MARCH 1885:   **26.19 PISCES**

Gordon of Khartoum

Charles Gordon was born at Woolwich (east London) on 28 January 1833, at 9:51 am.[1] His chart is given below.

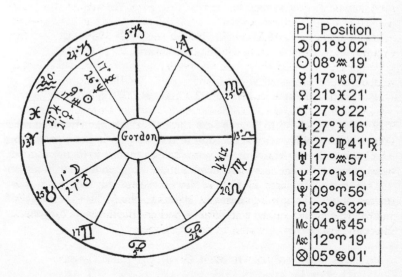

Pl	Position
☽	01° ♉ 02'
☉	08° ♒ 19'
☿	17° ♑ 07'
♀	21° ♓ 21'
♂	27° ♉ 22'
♃	27° ♓ 16'
♄	27° ♍ 41' ℞
♅	17° ♒ 57'
♆	27° ♑ 19'
♇	09° ♈ 56'
☊	23° ♋ 32'
Mc	04° ♑ 45'
Asc	12° ♈ 19'
⊗	05° ♋ 01'

Altogether, it is a fascinating horoscope, with that astrological sign of genius – a number of fixed stars upon his planets.[2] However, one of the most obvious things about the chart is the powerful opposition between the planets Jupiter and Saturn.

Gordon of Khartoum was a remarkable man, with very many accomplishments, but he is now best remembered for the way he died.

In 1884 he was sent to the Sudan, to evacuate the Egyptians caught up in the revolt which had broken out under Mohammed Ahmed, who had proclaimed himself Mahdi. Gordon was besieged at Khartoum, and (to the eternal shame of the British government) the relief force was delayed, arriving at Khartoum only after it had fallen to the Mahdi's troops.

The relief force found that General Gordon had met his death on 26 January 1885, two days before they arrived.

Gordon's death was paralleled by a most extraordinary gathering of eclipses on either side of this date. Indeed, his death was hemmed in by two lunar eclipses, which occurred within six months of each other: during that period another solar eclipse also fell upon one of his planets. This was the sequence, in chronological order:

LUNAR ECLIPSE OF 4 OCTOBER 1884:	12.05 ARIES–LIBRA
ASCENDANT OF GENERAL GORDON:	12.19 ARIES
SOLAR ECLIPSE OF 16 MARCH 1885:	26.19 PISCES
JUPITER IN THE CHART OF GENERAL GORDON:	27.16 PISCES
LUNAR ECLIPSE OF 30 MARCH 1885:	10.06 ARIES
PLUTO IN THE CHART OF GENERAL GORDON:	09.56 ARIES

The solar eclipse of 16 March was the one which had overshadowed Vincent van Gogh's suicide decision to take up painting as a profession (see page 173). General Gordon was a soldier, and it is therefore more reasonable to consider a violent death a more likely ending for him than for an artist. In fact, Gordon's chart predisposed him in a most extraordinary way towards death by stabbing. His Mars – the planet of action, which rules military activities – was on the fixed star Alcyone, in 28 degrees of Taurus.

MARS IN THE CHART OF GENERAL GORDON:	27.22 TAURUS
POSITION OF ALCYONE IN 1833:	27.39 TAURUS

The star Alcyone is in the Pleiades, the *eta* of that beautiful constellation. Elsbeth Ebertin, the German astrologer who studied the asterism in some depth, came to the conclusion that 'the Sun with Pleiades . . . brings a violent death by blows, stabbing and murder'.[3] How much more so would

Mars in this asterism, and on this violent star, bring a violent end.

Records taken from eye-witnesses indicate that Gordon was speared to death by followers of the Mahdi (see above). After he had died, he was decapitated, and his head was sent as a trophy to the Mahdi.[4]

Nell Gwyn

According to the diaries of the astrologer-Mason Elias Ashmole, Nell Gwyn was born on 2 February 1650 (an old-style date), with an Ascendant degree of 24 Capricorn, which implies a time of 6:12 am.[1] Although of very humble birth – and reputed to have begun work in Drury Lane selling oranges – she became one of the most popular actresses of the Restoration period, to the point where John Dryden (the leading dramatist of the day) wrote leading parts into his plays, to display her talents. She was not only a great beauty (figure 8), but was possessed of an alert and intelligent wit. In modern times, she is chiefly remembered as the mistress of King Charles II, by whom she had two children.

It is interesting to compare the two charts for Nell and King Charles[2] because, as is usually the case between lovers, they have degrees in common. One of the distinguishing features of the chart of Charles II was that his Sun and Moon were in conjunction in Gemini. Nell Gwyn had a conjunction of Uranus and Neptune exactly opposite Charles's own conjunction. Nell's chart is given overleaf.

175

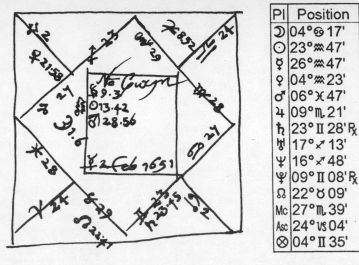

Pl	Position
☽	04°♋17'
☉	23°♒47'
☿	26°♒47'
♀	04°♒23'
♂	06°♓47'
♃	09°♏21'
♄	23°♊28' ℞
♅	17°♐13'
♆	16°♐48'
♇	09°♊08' ℞
☊	22°♉09'
Mc	27°♏39'
Asc	24°♑04'
⊗	04°♊35'

MOON IN THE CHART OF CHARLES II:	20.41 TAURUS
PLUTO IN THE CHART OF CHARLES II:	21.58 TAURUS
DRAGON'S HEAD IN THE CHART OF GWYN:	22.09 TAURUS

The Jupiter of Nell's chart (in 09.21 Scorpio) was opposite the King's own Venus (in 08.26 Taurus) – an almost classical case of lover-mistress arrangement. According to most reliable accounts, Nell (who was then at the height of her fame in the Drury Lane company) became mistress to Charles in 1669. On 30 April of that year there was an eclipse of the Sun exactly across these degrees:

JUPITER IN THE CHART OF GWYN:	09.21 SCORPIO
VENUS IN THE CHART OF CHARLES II:	08.26 TAURUS
SOLAR ECLIPSE OF 30 APRIL 1669:	10.15 TAURUS

So successful was Nell's acting career that it would be pointless to list the conjunctions and eclipses which raised her to fame. It would perhaps be more instructive to look back to her twenty-eighth year, which was preceded by no less than three eclipses in the space of one month, between 14 October and 15 November. One of these eclipses had a profoundly tragic effect on the actress.

Nell Gwyn's mother, who shared Nell's splendid house in London (and who was very partial to alcohol) fell into a fishpond in Chelsea and drowned on 29 July 1679.[3] This tragedy was reflected in Nell's chart by an eclipse of the Sun on her Dragon's Tail.

176

SOLAR ECLIPSE OF 14 NOVEMBER, 1678: 22.26 SCORPIO
DRAGON'S TAIL IN THE CHART OF GWYN: 22.09 SCORPIO

Henry VIII

Although several versions of the chart of King Henry VIII of England
have survived, I have found the data recorded towards the end of Henry's
life by the Italian astrologer, Luca Gauricus, to be the most accurate.[1]
Gauricus was one of the great sixteenth-century authorities on
predictions by means of eclipses.[2] A modern version of this chart is given
below, alongside a figure taken from a plate of engraved horoscopes by
Ebenezer Silby (figure 18).

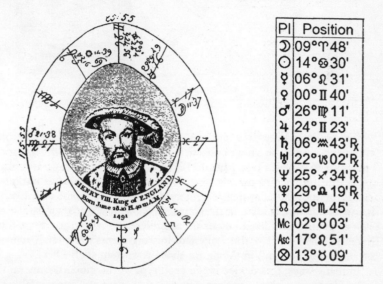

Pl	Position
☽	09° ♈ 48'
☉	14° ♋ 30'
☿	06° ♌ 31'
♀	00° ♊ 40'
♂	26° ♍ 11'
♃	24° ♊ 23'
♄	06° ♒ 43' ℞
♅	22° ♑ 02' ℞
♆	25° ♐ 34' ℞
♇	29° ♎ 19' ℞
☊	29° ♏ 45'
Mc	02° ♉ 03'
Asc	17° ♌ 51'
⊗	13° ♉ 09'

In 1509, Henry became King of England, and also married Catherine of
Aragon – the first of his famous serial marriages. It would be surprising if
such an important year in his own life – as in the history of England – were
not reflected in his chart. In fact, on 12 November of that year there was
a solar eclipse which fell upon his Dragon's Head, which is the index of
good fortune.

DRAGON'S HEAD IN THE CHART OF HENRY VIII: 29.45 SCORPIO
SOLAR ECLIPSE OF 12 NOVEMBER 1509: 29.32 SCORPIO

Henry's chart seems particularly susceptible to changes generated by, or
paralleled by, the eclipses, but the destiny of a sixteenth-century king of

England might not be of much interest to us, did it not take us into rather interesting byways of eclipse-lore. To appreciate this aspect of Henry's chart, we need to look at the *camera obscura* which was being developed during his lifetime.

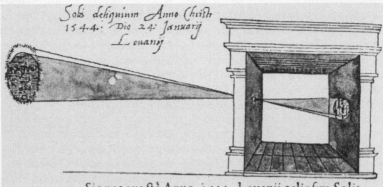

Sic nos exactè Anno .1544 . Louanii eclipſim Solis obſeruauimus , inuenimuſq; deficere paulò plus q̃ dex-

Leonardo da Vinci was one of the first people to record his personal experiences with the camera obscura which, we shall discover, has some relevance to eclipses (see page 194).[3] The camera obscura is an optical apparatus designed to permit a human observer to sit inside a darkened room, on one wall of which is projected an inverted image of the outer world (see picture below). In the sixteenth century, scientists were already experimenting with lenses as an aid to projection, but it is quite possible that the small hole in the Italianate-looking camera (the Italian word means simply, 'room') in the figure above is without such a lens.

In many ways, this device is the prototype of the modern camera: the only difference with the ancient device is that there was not available the technology to permit the observer to record the light on paper and fix the image.

So intrigued were Renaissance astrologers and astronomers by solar and lunar eclipses that, long before the telescope had been made by the Dutchman optician, Hans Lippershey, in 1608, they made special arrangements to view them by means of the camera. Indeed, the camera was certainly used as an aid to making accurate drawings of eclipses. It is known that in the sixteenth century, artists would record the phenomenon by drawing the rapidly changing image – presumably making notes of the time during the various stages of the eclipse. As far as I know, none of these early eclipse-drawings have survived, but a woodprint of such a record being made has been preserved.

The earliest known illustrations of the camera obscura, dated 1545 (opposite), show an attempt being made to view a total eclipse of the Sun which was visible from Louvain, in 1544.[4] The eclipse fell in 13.31 of Aquarius at 09:20:30 local time.

In fact, there were four eclipses in 1544, and one contemporary astrologer had predicted that the year would be 'very opulent' save for these four eclipses, and a great conjunction of Mars and Saturn in the February of that year.[5]

I assume that the astrologer would have been interested in the fate of his own Emperor, Charles V, whose chart was widely available at that time.[6] At the moment of the solar eclipse of January 1544, warlike Mars had been opposite Mars in the birth-chart of the Emperor!

MARS AT SOLAR ECLIPSE OF 24 JANUARY 1544:   26.17 SCORPIO
MARS IN THE HOROSCOPE OF CHARLES V: 24.20 TAURUS

This knowledge would have been sufficient for an astrologer working in 1544 to see the direction which Charles would be taking. However, we are even more privileged, as we now have access to planetary positions unknown in the sixteenth century. Even more belligerence might have been expected from the direct conjunction between the warlike Mars and the dark planet Pluto in the Emperor's horoscope:

MARS AT SOLAR ECLIPSE OF 24 JANUARY 1544:   26.17 SCORPIO
PLUTO IN THE HOROSCOPE OF CHARLES V: 25.19 SCORPIO

What is interesting to us is that if this astrologer had looked at the horoscope of Henry VIII, King of England, he would not have seen such a warlike intention from the eclipse. Even so, Henry also went to war in this year. The reason why the astrologer would not have seen it was because the planet Uranus had not yet been discovered, and it was this disruptive planet which was involved in the eclipse.

In 1544, Henry VIII invaded Scotland (not for the first time), capturing both Leith and Edinburgh. Not content with making war in Britain, he lent support to the Emperor Charles V, and also invaded France, capturing Boulogne in the process. These warlike excursions were reflected in Henry's chart, through a planetary contact which would not be understood until the last 200 years. The lunar eclipse which had been visible in England shortly after sunset on 4 July 1544 fell across his Uranus:

URANUS IN THE CHART OF HENRY VIII: 22.02 CAPRICORN
LUNAR ECLIPSE OF 4 JULY 1544:   21.53 CAPRICORN

179

Emperor Hirohito of Japan

The horoscope of Hirohito, who became Emperor of Japan in 1926, is given below.[1] He was born in Tokyo, 29 April 1901 at 10:10 pm.

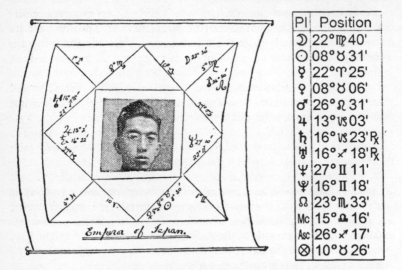

Pl	Position
☽	22°♍40'
☉	08°♉31'
☿	22°♈25'
♀	08°♉06'
♂	26°♌31'
♃	13°♑03'
♄	16°♑23'℞
♅	16°♐18'℞
♆	27°♊11'
♇	16°♊18'
☊	23°♏33'
Mc	15°♎16'
Asc	26°♐17'
⊗	10°♉26'

Emperor of Japan.

We must see this figure as what may be the last personal chart of a great ruler who could realistically be regarded as being representative of the country over which he ruled. In a very real sense, Hirohito was the last of a dynasty of rulers widely regarded as divine: his chart was therefore symbolic of Japan as a whole. Not surprisingly, in view of the power of the Emperor, and the importance of the country over which he ruled, there were a remarkable seven fixed stars in his chart.[2]

When Raphael cast the horoscope of Hirohito, in 1924, Pluto had not yet been discovered. In fact, Pluto later proved to be the most important of planets in regard to Hirohito's undeniable regal qualities, since at his birth the planet had been exactly on the powerful fixed star Rigel. In the astrological tradition, Rigel was reputed to bring great riches, lasting honours and military success.

The absence of Pluto caused difficulties for Raphael, when he attempted to interpret Hirohito's chart. The astrologer's attention had been drawn to the planet Neptune, which was setting in the west of Hirohito's chart. This, along with certain lunar factors, Raphael saw as the shadow of 'some dreadful devastation befalling his land and his people'.[3] Although Raphael did not mention this, the basis of such a prediction must have rested upon the fact that in Hirohito's chart Neptune was exactly upon the fixed star Betelgeuse.

POSITION OF STAR BETELGEUSE IN 1901:	27.22 GEMINI
NEPTUNE IN CHART OF HIROHITO:	27.11 GEMINI

This star, the alpha of Orion, is set in the right shoulder of the constellational giant, almost like a badge of office. Under normal circumstances, the star brings great military honours and martial prowess, but its influence is particularly susceptible to the planet through which its rays shine. While it rarely brings a violent death, it does attract strange changes in mid-life.

'Mid-life' for Hirohito was marked by the years of the Second World War, which Japan entered with a bang at Pearl Harbor in 1941. It is not surprising that this attack, which brought the United States into the war, took place under the influence of an eclipse which operated on degrees in both the chart of the Japanese Emperor, and in the chart of his enemy, the President of the United States.

The Japanese attack on American shipping in Pearl Harbor began on 7 December 1941. Of course, the planning for this invasion had taken several months, and it is interesting to observe that the event was reflected precisely in the Emperor's chart in the lunar eclipse of March 1941, which took place exactly upon his Moon, in Virgo.

MOON IN THE CHART OF HIROHITO:	22.40 VIRGO
LUNAR ECLIPSE OF 13 MARCH 1941:	22.36 VIRGO

In his reading of Hirohito's chart, published in 1924, Raphael had mentioned that Mars would lead Hirohito to undertake 'a military expedition towards a distant State, where his forces will clash with two other military parties, each opposed to the other'. Raphael's recognition of the coming war between Japan and the United States may have been based on the fact that Betelgeuse was in Gemini, the ruler of the United States.[4]

MARS IN THE CHART OF HIROHITO:	26.31 LEO
POSITION OF STAR ALPHARD IN 1901:	25.55 LEO

Alphard was in former times called Cor Hydrae, or the heart of Hydra, because of its position in this constellation. It is a most curious star for it is traditionally supposed to bestow great wisdom and artistic appreciation, yet it is also reputed to threaten violence and scandals.

Undoubtedly, the most terrible thing which Japan experienced while under the rule of Hirohito was the devastation of the two atomic bombs which led to the end of the war. Given my thesis that eclipses lie behind most dramatic events in history, we should not be surprised to find this event also linked with eclipses on a sensitive point in the horoscope of the

Emperor – which is to say on the horoscope of Japan.

The atom bombs which destroyed Hiroshima and Nagasaki were dropped in August 1945. The events were reflected in the Emperor's chart in two consecutive eclipses in months previous to and after the month in which the bombs were dropped.

SOLAR ECLIPSE OF 9 JULY 1945:	16.57 CANCER
SATURN IN THE CHART OF HIROHITO:	16.23 CAPRICORN
DROPPING OF THE TWO ATOMIC BOMBS:	6 AND 9 AUGUST 1945
LUNAR ECLIPSE OF 19 DECEMBER 1945:	26.51 GEMINI
POSITION OF STAR BETELGEUSE IN 1901:	27.22 GEMINI
NEPTUNE IN THE CHART OF HIROHITO:	27.11 GEMINI

This data irrefutably demonstrates Raphael's predictive genius, for he had written of 'violent stars' that shadow 'some dreadful devastation befalling his land and his people'. One of the things which Raphael must have observed, twenty years before the event, was that President Roosevelt had exactly the same Geminian influence in his chart:

MARS IN THE CHART OF ROOSEVELT:	27.01 GEMINI

In fact, Roosevelt had died in April 1945, but it was he who had sanctioned the use of the atomic bomb in the war against Japan.

While the idea of the divine rule of monarchs seems to have disappeared as a living idea from Europe some time in the seventeenth century, it continued in Japan until 1946. In that year – consequent to the upheavals and horrors of the World War, and the two atomic bombs which had been dropped on his country – Emperor Hirohito, who could trace his dynasty back over two thousand years, renounced his divine status. This was a remarkable act of a remarkable man, and it is, of course, reflected in his chart through an important eclipse.

This event of 1946 – unique in modern history – was signified in Hirohito's horoscope by an important eclipse on his Jupiter. The eclipse fell not merely upon the regal planet Jupiter, but on the fixed star Ascella which was on Hirohito's Jupiter at birth.

SOLAR ECLIPSE OF 3 JANUARY 1946:	12.32 CAPRICORN
JUPITER IN THE CHART OF HIROHITO:	13.03 CAPRICORN
POSITION OF STAR ASCELLA IN 1901:	12.15 CAPRICORN

The star Ascella, set in the shoulder of the bowman Sagittarius, is a highly beneficial star which reinforced Hirohito's fortune and happiness. In symbolical terms, this he sacrificed for what he foresaw was the good of his country.

Jupiter, which in ancient times had been the leader, indeed the 'Father', of the ancient gods, was eclipsed.[5] After Hirohito had renounced his divine status, Japan acquired a new constitution based on the democratic principle, rather than upon divine *fiat*.[6]

Adolf Hitler

Occasionally, there strides across the stage of history an individual who leaves little but destruction and chaos in his wake: such are the Genghis Khans and Napoleons of our world. These individuals often seem somehow larger than life, and astrologers recognize that such people always have a number of evil stars emphatic in their charts. A striking example from the twentieth century was Adolf Hitler, whose chart is given below. He was born at Braunau at 6:30 pm, on 20 April 1889.[1]

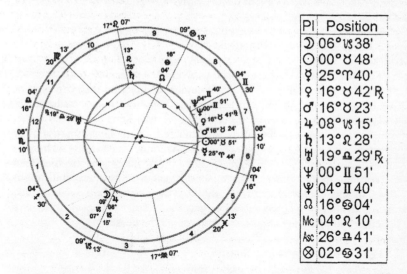

Pl	Position
☽	06° ♑ 38'
☉	00° ♉ 48'
☿	25° ♈ 40'
♀	16° ♉ 42' ℞
♂	16° ♉ 23'
♃	08° ♑ 15'
♄	13° ♌ 28'
♅	19° ♎ 29' ℞
♆	00° ♊ 51'
♇	04° ♊ 40'
☊	16° ♋ 04'
Mc	04° ♌ 10'
Asc	26° ♎ 41'
⊗	02° ♋ 31'

In some ways, his chart looks almost benign. An astrologer might be forgiven for seeing it as the horoscope of a mediocre individual – perhaps something of an obsessive talker who was indolent, and certainly emotionally cold.[2] The truth is that it is almost impossible to understand Hitler's destructive imput into the world, and the discord he sowed, without reference to the fixed stars which dominated his chart. It is equally impossible to understand the nature of his death without reference to a fixed star and an eclipse.

In fact, the most extraordinary thing about the chart is the considerable number of fixed stars – all of evil import – that lie behind it. His Moon, Mercury, Pluto and Dragon's Head were all on fixed stars, three of which were evil. Only Al Pherg does not promise a violent death.

In view of this constellation of stars, we should examine their influences, to see what we can learn about Hitler the monster, who seems to have hidden so well behind his mediocre chart. Let us start with Facies.

MOON IN THE CHART OF HITLER:	06.38 CAPRICORN
POSITION OF STAR FACIES IN 1889:	06.46 CAPRICORN

Facies is a nebula (Messier number M 22), or cloud of stars, set in the face of the constellation Sagittarius in some star-charts, but near his drawn bow in others. The nebula is important to astrologers because it is almost on the ecliptic. In the astrological tradition an emphatic Facies brings accidents and a violent death, with injuries to the face or eyes.

MERCURY IN THE CHART OF HITLER:	25.40 ARIES
POSITION OF STAR AL PHERG IN 1889:	25.16 ARIES

The double star Al Pherg is in the silver cord which connects the tails of the two fishes of Pisces. Its mythological connection with the head of the Egyptian god Typhon expresses its dark nature, though traditionally it has none of the explosive violence of the other stars in Hitler's chart. The fact that it is on the Führer's Mercury reflects upon his famous power as a persuasive and hypnotic orator, for Mercury is an index of human speech and ability to communicate. This star adds tremendous determination and power to whatsoever planet it touches. One might think of this energy aimed from the bow of the man-horse Sagittarius, always confident of achieving its target: the recipient is never quite sure whether the message comes from the man or the beast.

PLUTO IN THE CHART OF HITLER:	04.40 GEMINI
POSITION OF PRIMA HYADUM IN 1889:	04.15 GEMINI

Primum Hyadum is in the constellation Taurus, being the chief star among the group of the Hyades. For all the Hyades were the half-sisters of the gentle Pleiades, they are traditionally linked with violence – perhaps because they are placed in the forehead of the cosmic Bull. They induce a fierce attitude, and danger of poisoning. Because Pluto is such a newly discovered planet, its influence when placed on this star has not been sufficiently studied, but we may liken it to a more violent equivalent of Neptune, the reading for which is a sudden and unexpected death.

The star Wasat is set in the right arm of the Twin, and is actually a double star, one white in colour, the other purple. These combine their influences to make one of the most evil stars in the heavens (second only to Algol – see page 92). As we have seen, the star is reputed to create violence and 'destructiveness as a first principle'. It is traditionally connected with liquid poisons.

Pope John Paul II

In his fascinating account of the life of Pope John Paul II, Michael Walsh mentions a time in the youth of Karol Wojtyla (the name of John Paul II before he took orders) when he became interested in the stage, and acting became his passion.[1] In one play, entitled *The Moonlight Cavalier*, the actors played special roles as representatives of the signs of the zodiac. The role given to Karol was that of Sagittarius. When I read this account, the chart of Pope John Paul II suddenly fell into place in my mind.

There had been no agreement as to when he had been born, and it had therefore proved difficult to study his chart in any great detail – however, this story from his life suddenly became meaningful: of course, Karol

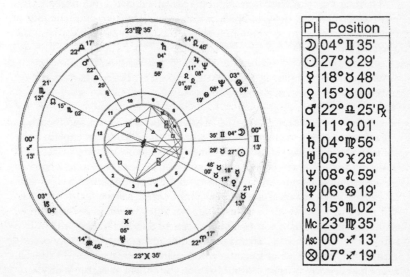

Pl	Position
☽	04° ♊ 35'
☉	27° ♉ 29'
☿	18° ♉ 48'
♀	15° ♉ 00'
♂	22° ♎ 25' ℞
♃	11° ♌ 01'
♄	04° ♍ 56'
♅	05° ♓ 28'
♆	08° ♌ 59'
♇	06° ♋ 19'
☊	15° ♏ 02'
Mc	23° ♍ 35'
Asc	00° ♐ 13'
⊗	07° ♐ 19'

Wojtyla must have had a Sagittarian Ascendant! Only such an Ascendant would account for his gift with languages, and for his legendary world-travels, once he had become Pope. If his Ascendant had been in the first degree of this sign, the resulting zenith would account for his elevation to the papacy, in terms of an eclipse! The search for an eclipse to explain this elevation may seem curious, until one realizes that John Paul II was born on the day of an eclipse.

I have already shown that John Paul II's chart is intimately linked with the horoscope of Poland, where he was born on 18 May 1920.[2] The chart, cast for 8:48 pm, is given on the previous page.

His birth was marked by an eclipse, for on 18 May 1920, there was a solar eclipse in Taurus:

SOLAR ECLIPSE OF 18 MAY 1920:	26.59 TAURUS
SUN IN CHART OF POPE JOHN PAUL II:	27.29 TAURUS

On 13 May 1981, nearly three years after he was elected Pope, an attempt was made on his life by a Turkish terrorist. This assassination attempt was reflected in his chart by a solar eclipse which fell within orb of his Neptune.

SOLAR ECLIPSE OF 31 JULY 1981:	07.51 LEO
NEPTUNE IN THE CHART OF JOHN PAUL II:	08.59 LEO

There are several fixed stars operative in the chart. Undoubtedly, the most noteworthy of these is Spica, which marks the corn in the hands of the celestial Virgin, and which in mediaeval astrology was linked with the Christ-Child.

MARS IN THE CHART OF JOHN PAUL II:	22.25 LIBRA
POSITION OF STAR SPICA IN 1920:	22.43 LIBRA

It is the connection drawn in early Christianity between Jesus and the wheat (which would be made into the flour of the sacred Host) that explains why some of the early woodcuts of the Virgin Mary show her dress decorated with ears of corn (see opposite). The corn is symbolic of the Child who grew in her womb, and who came to Earth from the realm of stars.

The decision that Karol Wojtyla should become Pope – the first non-Italian Pope for 450 years – was taken (as is traditional, behind locked doors in the College of Cardinals) between 14 and 16 October 1978.[3] In a sense, the Cosmos had already made the decision, which was merely ratified by the College of Cardinals, for earlier in the year, on 13 March, there had been an eclipse of the Moon on the zenith of Karol Wojtyla:

ZENITH IN CHART OF POPE JOHN PAUL II: 23.35 VIRGO
LUNAR ECLIPSE OF 13 MARCH 1979:   22.38 VIRGO

The year 1999 should prove to be important for the Pope, as the first lunar eclipse of this year will fall upon the Pope's planet, Jupiter:

JUPITER IN THE CHART OF POPE JOHN PAUL II: 11.01 LEO
LUNAR ECLIPSE OF 26 FEBRUARY 1999:   11.25 LEO

Eclipses have been used by astrologers for centuries to chart the lives of popes. No doubt this is connected with the fact that popes have been seen as the equivalent of Sun-beings – as representatives on Earth of the living Christ, so frequently symbolized in art as a radiant Sun round which the created world circles. This solar symbolism seems to have made the popes especially susceptible to the effects of solar eclipses, which darken the Sun, however momentarily.

Stemming from this eclipse-lore is an intense interest in attempting to predict the date of the deaths of popes – an interest in that final eclipse. Among such records is the well-documented account of eclipse-prophecies pertaining to the death of Paul III.

On the late evening of 22 April 1548, there was a lunar eclipse in 12.12 degrees of Taurus. This was close to the degree of the natal Moon in the chart of Pope Paul III, who was then eighty years old. In consequence of the eclipse (and no doubt because of his advanced age) some astrologers insisted that the year would prove fatal for him. Other astrologers, including Marius Alterius (who was a semi-official poet-astrologer to the Pope) did not agree: he even went so far as to predict that the Pope would live on until 1561.[4] In fact, Paul did die in 1549.

Paul III was both a learned and cultivated man, who has sometimes been described as a secular prince in the Vatican. It was he who commissioned Michelangelo to paint the fresco of *The Last Judgement* in the Sistine Chapel. In view of the close co-operation between the men it is not surprising to find an exact correspondence in their charts. The Sun of Paul III had been in 17.41 degrees of Pisces – exactly upon the Mars of Michelangelo.[5]

Helen Keller

I have not been able to determine the exact time of the birth of Helen Keller, but one thing is sure – that on the day of her birth, in Tuscumbia, Alabama, on 27 June 1880, her Dragon's Head was on 7 degrees of Capricorn. The horoscope, cast for midday, is given opposite.[1]

This degree in Capricorn was of profound importance to the girl, for in 1880 the degree was occupied by the fixed star Facies. Facies is one of the

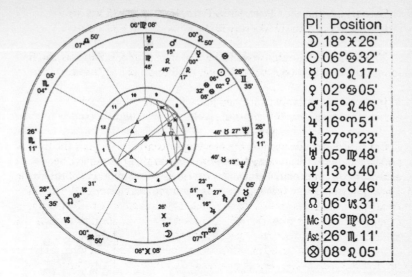

Pl	Position
☽	18° ♓ 26'
☉	06° ♋ 32'
☿	00° ♌ 17'
♀	02° ♋ 05'
♂	15° ♌ 46'
♃	16° ♈ 51'
♄	27° ♈ 23'
♅	05° ♍ 48'
♆	13° ♉ 40'
♇	27° ♉ 46'
☊	06° ♑ 31'
Mc	06° ♍ 08'
Asc	26° ♏ 11'
⊗	08° ♌ 05'

most notorious of the stars (it is actually a nebula in the face of the Archer, Sagittarius), for its role in causing blindness.[2]

On 28 December 1879, there was an eclipse on this degree. Since this was a lunar eclipse, it lay directly across the nodes in Keller's birth chart – an extraordinary and powerful placing.

LUNAR ECLIPSE OF 28 DECEMBER 1879:   06.41 CANCER
DRAGON'S TAIL IN THE CHART OF KELLER: 06.31 CANCER

This powerful contact might presage difficulties enough in the life of anyone, but in the case of Helen Keller the contact was rendered even more problematic, for the eclipse fell upon Facies, thus involved in the pairs of oppositions of nodes and lunar eclipse. The data is:

LUNAR ECLIPSE OF 28 DECEMBER 1879:   06.41 CAPRICORN
DRAGON'S HEAD IN THE CHART OF KELLER: 06.31 CAPRICORN
POSITION OF FIXED STAR FACIES IN 1880:   06.38 CAPRICORN

Helen Keller went blind and deaf at the age of nineteen months, yet, through sheer determination and love for life, she became one of the leaders in the American Foundation for the Blind. Her work, T*he Story of My Life*, first published in 1902, became a best-seller. It is notable that this – the first of several books – was published under the effect of an eclipse which fell on the expansive planet Jupiter of her chart, in 17 degrees Aries.

JUPITER IN THE CHART OF KELLER:	16.51 ARIES
SOLAR ECLIPSE OF 8 APRIL 1902:	17.48 ARIES

Princess de Lamballe

While Princess Diana is the most famous princess to die violently in Paris in modern times, the most famous in the eighteenth century was the Princess of Lamballe.

Marie Therese Louise of Savoy-Carignano, who became Princess de Lamballe through marriage, was born on 8 September 1749, in Turin, Italy. The horoscope below is cast for 1:34pm, local time.[1]

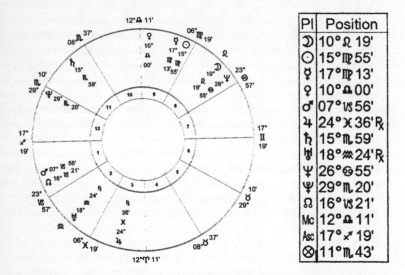

Pl	Position
☽	10° ♌ 19'
☉	15° ♍ 55'
☿	17° ♍ 13'
♀	10° ♎ 00'
♂	07° ♑ 56'
♃	24° ♓ 36' ℞
♄	15° ♏ 59'
♅	18° ♒ 24' ℞
♆	26° ♋ 55'
♇	29° ♏ 20'
☊	16° ♑ 21'
Mc	12° ♎ 11'
Asc	17° ♐ 19'
⊗	11° ♏ 43'

Introduced to the glittering court of Louis XVI, she soon became the confidante and friend of the Queen, Marie Antoinette (whose horoscope is given on page 129). In 1789, the French Revolution began, and a new constitution was proclaimed. Louis XVI was eventually brought to trial for treason. Found guilty, he was executed on 21 January 1793. Lambelle shared in the imprisonment of the royal family, remaining Antoinette's closest friend until she herself was arrested.

In September 1792, the Princess de Lamballe was taken to the Hotel de la Force, then used as a prison, where she refused to take an oath against the monarchy and her royal friends. In consequence, she was handed over to the drunken populace, and after being tortured, was beheaded. Her severed head was carried on a pike through the streets of Paris – the intention of the crowd being to compel the Queen, Marie Antoinette, to kiss it. Fortunately, when this grisly relic was held up to the windows of the rooms in which Antoinette was incarcerated, her guards refused to allow the Queen to look out, to see what the commotion was.

Such a violent death, of one so famous, could scarcely pass by untouched by eclipse. The Princess met her death on 3 September 1792: a solar eclipse fell upon her Jupiter thirteen days later.

SOLAR ECLIPSE OF 16 SEPTEMBER 1972:	24.08 VIRGO
JUPITER IN THE CHART OF PRINCESS DE LAMBALLE:	24.36 PISCES

Leonardo da Vinci

One of the most-quoted adages of fixed-star literature is that stars lift up and throw down – which is to say that the general disposition of stars is to raise the native to eminence, and then dispose of that person unceremonially towards the end of life.

Because so many of the fixed stars are traditionally of a disruptive disposition, one tends to find that the charts of genius reflect lives which are full of ups and downs. As we have seen, the ups are often paralleled by eclipses, and the downs are also marked by eclipses. This seems to be the destiny of those who, for one reason or another, work with the inner tools of genius.

Vincent van Gogh's chart (see page 169) – so tied to fixed stars, and almost obsessed by eclipses – is a very good example of how the stars and eclipses work in what might be called a disruptive way: one gets the impression that such a personality has come to Earth as a plaything of destiny, which has little concern for the personal wishes or suffering of the person concerned. Vincent might with good reason be regarded as a genius nowadays, but I doubt very much if he enjoyed his life very much, or whether he would have been easy to live with. In general, that is the sign of a multitude of fixed-star influences which are buffeted by eclipses.

There are exceptions. One notable one is Leonardo da Vinci, the Renaissance all-round genius, who seemed almost god-like in his knowledge and talents, yet – to judge from contemporary comments – was also a delightful companion.

There has been much dispute concerning Leonardo's horoscope, even though his data has lain for centuries in the archives in Florence.[1] According to these records, deposited by Leonardo's grandfather, Antonio, Leonardo was born on 15 April 1452 at the third hour of the night. In view of the various disputes surrounding this time, I am reproducing below a fair copy of the two lines from the certificate recording the birth of this 'Lionardo':

*Nacque... vnmio nip... figluolo figliuolo mio figliuolo adj 15
dapile- Jnsabato aon—3 dinotte—Ebbe nome lionardo*

1452

A grandson of mine was born, son of S. Piero my son on 15 April – on Saturday – 3 at night. His name Lionardo.

The chart cast for this data, for Vinci near Florence, is given below (also in figure 9):

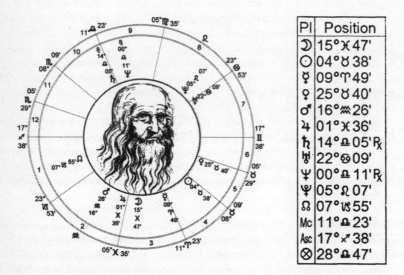

Pl	Position
☽	15° ♓ 47'
☉	04° ♉ 38'
☿	09° ♈ 49'
♀	25° ♉ 40'
♂	16° ♒ 26'
♃	01° ♓ 36'
♄	14° ♎ 05' ℞
♅	22° ♋ 09'
♆	00° ♎ 11' ℞
♇	05° ♌ 07'
☊	07° ♑ 55'
Mc	11° ♎ 23'
Asc	17° ♐ 38'
⊗	28° ♎ 47'

As one might expect of such a genius as Leonardo, there are several other fixed stars in his chart – in fact, no fewer than five prominent stars.[2] It is quite fascinating that each of these five fixed stars are viewed by Ptolemy as representative of the power of the planets Saturn and Jupiter.

From our point of view, perhaps the most interesting of these stars is Skat, which probably takes its name from the Arabic *al shi'at* 'a wish'. It was near this star, on 25 September 1756, that the 'new' planet, Uranus, was seen by Johann Mayer, who thought that he had discovered a new star.[3]

JUPITER IN THE CHART OF LEONARDO:	01.36 PISCES
POSITION OF FIXED STAR SKAT IN 1452:	01.13 PISCES

There is a wealth of material in the star-books about the influence of this star, which is set in the right leg of Aquarius, but almost all readings agree that it brings good fortune and great happiness. In Leonardo's chart, it is with Jupiter, and the reading so deepens the contact with such things as philosophy, religious and arcane lore that the modern astrologer, Vivian Robson, goes so far as to say that it is prominent in Freemasonry.[4] Reading these contacts in Leonardo's chart purely in terms of planetary imput (and without considering the astrological traditions attached to these stars) we find that Leonardo would have in his chart the force of *five* Saturns and *four* Jupiters! This accounts for his famous reclusiveness (Saturn) and for his great dignity and love of beautiful things (Jupiter).

One of the strongest areas in Leonardo's chart is in 16 degrees of Aquarius, where the fixed star Deneb Algedi shared with the star Sadalsuud the degree occupied by Leonardo's Mars.

MARS IN THE CHART OF LEONARDO:	16.26 AQUARIUS
POSITION OF STAR SADALSUUD IN 1452:	15.45 AQUARIUS
POSITION OF STAR DENEB ALGEDI IN 1452:	15.53 AQUARIUS

Deneb is set in the tail of the Goat, Capricorn, and is perhaps the only star in Leonardo's personal galaxy which savours of difficulties. It brings a certain melancholy (always associated with Capricorn) and loss, usually through legal entanglements, reminding us of the many difficulties which Leonardo had with ecclesiastical authorities – mainly through his seeming inability to finish anything.

It was an eclipse on this star – and indeed on the two stars and Mars – which marked what is arguably Leonardo's greatest undertaking – the fresco of 'The Last Supper' in the refectory of the convent church of Santa Maria delle Grazie, in Milan. The commission came to him through the ruler of Milan, Ludovico, who had invited Leonardo to leave Florence to work for him, in 1482. However, Leonardo did not begin work on this fresco until 1495.

In the first month of that year there was an eclipse on the extraordinary gathering of fixed stars and Mars in his natal chart:

MARS IN THE CHART OF LEONARDO:	16.26 AQUARIUS
POSITION OF STAR SADALSUUD IN 1452:	15.45 AQUARIUS
POSITION OF STAR DENEB ALGEDI IN 1452:	15.53 AQUARIUS
SOLAR ECLIPSE OF 26 JANUARY 1495:	15.37 AQUARIUS

One gets the impression that even the stars worked on a grand scale, when concerned with Leonardo's genius. The large fresco, with its opportunities for experimentation in technique, and the chance to study a wide range of facial types and human expressions, suited Leonardo's talents and aspirations perfectly. It is scarcely surprising, in the light of this powerful eclipse-contact, that 'The Last Supper' should become the most famous fresco in the world. Even today, when scarcely a fragment of the original picture has survived the many restorations, it still attracts huge numbers of visitors each week. It is typical of the working of Deneb Algedi that such a fertile invention should not survive. It was never completely finished, and when Leonardo's patron, Ludovico was driven out in 1499, some of the French soldiers who had taken Milan passed their time using Leonardo's painting as an archery target.

Leonardo was one of the first people to write about personal experiences with the camera obscura which has some relevance to the way eclipses were studied (see page 178).

Abraham Lincoln

Another remarkable man who had several fixed stars operative in his chart was Abraham Lincoln, who was born at Mill Creek, Kentucky on 12 February 1809. According to the nineteenth-century astrologer Dr Luke Broughton (who published the chart while Lincoln was still alive), Lincoln was born in the famous log cabin at 2:00 am. Broughton's horoscope, which was published on the cover of a monthly journal edited by the astrologer (figure 5),[1] was reasonably accurate, but I have used a modern chart from a different source, as this includes two planets which Broughton knew nothing about – Neptune and Pluto. For this data, I have also used the birth-time of 2:34 am provided by the Dutch astrologer, 'Libra'.[2]

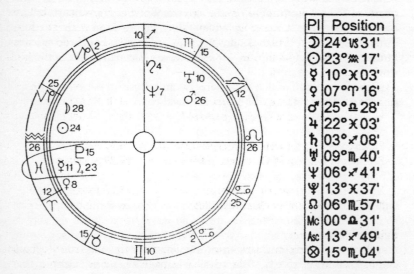

Pl	Position
☽	24°♑31'
☉	23°♒17'
☿	10°♓03'
♀	07°♈16'
♂	25°♎28'
♃	22°♓03'
♄	03°♐08'
♅	09°♏40'
♆	06°♐41'
♇	13°♓37'
☊	06°♏57'
Mc	00°♎31'
Asc	13°♐49'
⊗	15°♏04'

There were four fixed stars operative in the chart of this great man.[3] One of these stars was with Neptune, a planet not known in Broughton's day, yet, in spite of this, the astrologer did manage to predict with reasonable accuracy the date of Lincoln's assassination.[4] Almost certainly, Broughton recognized that the President would be assassinated because one of the fixed stars operative in his chart was Alphecca, which had a reputation for threatening a violent death when on the planet Uranus. This star was exactly upon the Uranus in Lincoln's own chart:

URANUS IN THE HOROSCOPE OF LINCOLN:	09.40 SCORPIO
POSITION OF STAR ALPHECCA IN 1809:	09.37 SCORPIO

Alphecca is not an intrinsically evil star – it is said to bring dignity, honours and certain artistic talents: this is probably why the star is called Gemma (precious stone) by some. However, its nature does seem to change dramatically in terms of the planet or node with which it is associated. This explains why the rather destructive Uranus in Lincoln's chart was a portent of death.

As is so often the case, the threat of a violent death was signalled in the heavens by an eclipse – in fact, by several eclipses. Broughton actually predicted Lincoln's death quite accurately, which suggests he recognized that a series of eclipses would fall on the President's planets between November of 1863 and November 1965, marking the last crowded years of his life, during which (shortly after emancipating the slaves in the states then in rebellion) he conducted the Civil War, fought and won another election, and saw Robert E. Lee surrender to Grant at Appomatox, before meeting his death at the hand of the fanatic, John Wilkes Booth. It is worth looking at these events, bearing in mind that Lincoln was assassinated on 14 April 1865 – approximately half way between the last two eclipses.

SATURN IN THE CHART OF LINCOLN:	03.08 SAGITTARIUS
LUNAR ECLIPSE OF 25 NOVEMBER 1863:	02.36 SAGITTARIUS
DRAGON'S HEAD IN THE CHART OF LINCOLN:	06.57 SCORPIO
SOLAR ECLIPSE OF 30 OCTOBER 1864:	07.29 SCORPIO
MARS IN THE CHART OF LINCOLN:	25.28 LIBRA
SOLAR ECLIPSE OF 19 OCTOBER 1865:	26.19 LIBRA

Princess Margaret
It really is quite extraordinary how often one finds the fixed star Regulus emphasized in the charts of the royals (see page 156). For example, it is

emphatic in the chart of Princess Margaret, who was born on 21 August 1930, at Glamis in Scotland.[1]

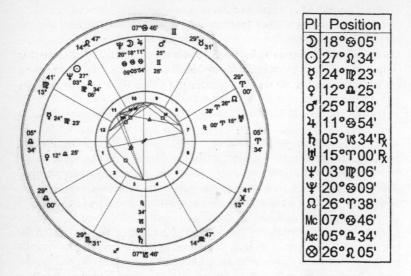

Pl	Position
☽	18°♋05'
☉	27°♌34'
☿	24°♍23'
♀	12°♎25'
♂	25°♊28'
♃	11°♋54'
♄	05°♑34'℞
♅	15°♈00'℞
♆	03°♍06'
♇	20°♋09'
☊	26°♈38'
Mc	07°♋46'
Asc	05°♎34'
⊗	26°♌05'

In 1959, the English astrologer Charles Carter, predicted from a rare transit of Venus over Regulus a wedding 'for a Royal Lady whose natal Sun is very near Regulus indeed'.[2] His meaning was transparent, since when Princess Margaret was born, Regulus had been in 29 degrees of Leo, and her own Sun had been in 28 degrees of that sign.

FIXED STAR REGULUS IN 1930:	28.47 LEO
SUN IN THE CHART OF PRINCESS MARGARET:	27.34 LEO

Margaret's marriage, to the commoner Antony Armstrong-Jones, took place on 6 May 1960 at 11:45 am.[3] Astrologically speaking, the marriage did not have much chance of success, because while the star lifts the native up to honours and good fortune, it also brings ruin, and 'benefits seldom last'.[4] The eclipse which appears to have sparked off the marriage was that of 27 March 1960, which occurred within a degree of Armstrong-Jones's own Venus, in Aries, and on the Ascendant in Margaret's chart.

ECLIPSE OF 27 MARCH 1960:	06.20 ARIES
VENUS IN THE CHART OF ARMSTRONG-JONES:	05.28 ARIES
ASCENDANT IN PRINCESS MARGARET'S CHART:	05.34 LIBRA

Karl Marx

Karl Marx was famously born shortly before a solar eclipse:

MARX BORN 5 MAY 1818, WITH SUN IN:	13.55 TAURUS
SOLAR ECLIPSE OF 5 MAY 1818:	14.09 TAURUS

As one might imagine in a chart of so powerful an individual, his chart is peppered with fixed stars.[1] In spite of this, the curious fact is that the main literary events in his life were dominated not by fixed stars, as by eclipses on his Saturn.

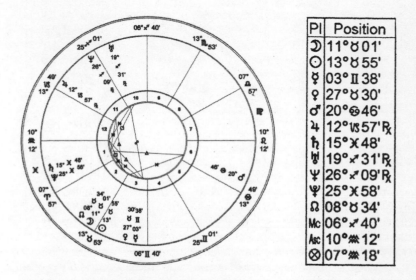

Pl	Position
☽	11° ♉ 01'
☉	13° ♉ 55'
☿	03° ♊ 38'
♀	27° ♉ 30'
♂	20° ♋ 46'
♃	12° ♑ 57' ℞
♄	15° ♓ 48'
♅	19° ♐ 31' ℞
♆	26° ♐ 09' ℞
♇	25° ♓ 58'
☊	08° ♉ 34'
Mc	06° ♐ 40'
Asc	10° ♒ 12'
⊗	07° ♒ 18'

Early in 1848, he and Friedrich Engels published the *Communist Manifesto* – a pamphlet which was to have a profound influence on European political life and thought for the next century or so. In that year, there was an eclipse on the Saturn in his chart:

SATURN IN THE CHART OF MARX:	15.49 PISCES
SOLAR ECLIPSE OF 5 MARCH 1848:	15.09 PISCES

This Saturn degree was of profound importance in Karl Marx's life – as perhaps might be expected of an intellectual of his brilliance (Saturn rules the intellect). When another solar eclipse occurred in this same degree, in 1867, Marx published his most influential work, *Das Kapital*, on which he had worked for almost a decade.[2]

197

SATURN IN THE CHART OF MARX:	15.49 PISCES
SOLAR ECLIPSE OF 6 MARCH 1867:	15.23 PISCES

Marilyn Monroe

Whenever one needs to study stellar and eclipse effects on unfortunate lives, one can do no better than to examine the extraordinary chart of the Hollywood star, Marilyn Monroe. The chart, cast for 1 June 1926 at 09:42 pm in Los Angeles is given below.[1]

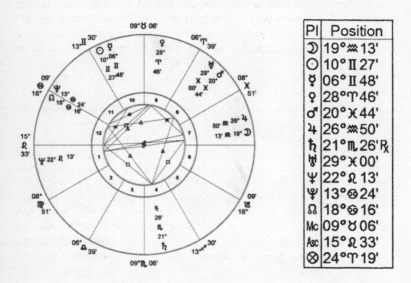

Pl	Position
☽	19° ♒ 13'
☉	10° ♊ 27'
☿	06° ♊ 48'
♀	28° ♈ 46'
♂	20° ♓ 44'
♃	26° ♒ 50'
♄	21° ♏ 26' ℞
♅	29° ♓ 00'
♆	22° ♌ 13'
♇	13° ♋ 24'
☊	18° ♋ 16'
Mc	09° ♉ 06'
Asc	15° ♌ 33'
⊗	24° ♈ 19'

Marilyn's horoscope is remarkable because there were no fewer than three very powerful fixed stars pouring their rays into her life. These were Sirius – perhaps the most famous powerful fixed star in the heavens – Mirach and Unukalhai.

POSITION OF SIRIUS IN 1930:	13.07 CANCER
PLUTO IN THE CHART OF MONROE:	13.24 CANCER
MIRACH IN 1930:	29.25 ARIES
VENUS IN THE CHART OF MONROE:	28.46 ARIES
UNUKALHAI IN 1930:	21.04 SCORPIO
SATURN IN THE CHART OF MONROE:	21.26 SCORPIO

In brief, Sirius brought her wealth and fame, Mirach brought her scandals and the tendency to take drugs, while Unukalhai brought her suicide by poisoning.

In the astrological tradition, Unukalhai with Saturn (as in Marilyn's chart) is reputed to bring 'secret insanity, drug-taking' and suicide.[2]

A person of Marilyn's radiance, beauty and sense of histrionics simply had to have the warm Leo rising, but the main problem with the sign rising in her chart is that it carries with it the illusion-breeding and delusion-making Neptune.

According to my own calculations, she had 16 degrees of Leo on her Ascendant. There were only two eclipses in 1962, the year she died – yet both were on this Leo-Aquarius axis. That of 5 February 1962 was in 16 degrees of Aquarius exactly on her Descendant – the house of relationships.

SOLAR ECLIPSE OF 5 FEBRUARY 1962:	15.44 AQUARIUS
DESCENDANT ANGLE IN THE CHART OF MONROE:	15.33 AQUARIUS

In fact, this eclipse was famous among astrologers, because it was accompanied by an extraordinary gathering of planets in Aquarius – seven planets and the Dragon's Tail. Marilyn's own Dragon's Tail and Moon were involved in this event, which means that she was tied into one of the most interesting astrological happenings of the 1960s.

Heavy and portentous as this eclipse of 1962 undoubtedly was, I feel that the cosmic event which really marked the end for Marilyn was the preceding solar eclipse of 26 August 1961, which took place in 19 degrees of Leo, opposite her own natal Moon, in Aquarius.

SOLAR ECLIPSE OF 11 AUGUST 1961:	18.31 LEO
MOON IN THE CHART OF MONROE:	19.13 AQUARIUS

She committed suicide (some authorities argue that she was murdered) on 4 August 1962.[3]

Wolfgang Amadeus Mozart

There is some dispute about the exact time of Mozart's birth[1] According to my own calculations, he was born at 08.33 pm, in Salzburg (Austria) on 27 January 1756.[2]

Mozart had such a prodigious talent – in his brief life he composed forty-one symphonies and twenty operas, along with scores of sonatas, quartets, and other pieces – that it is difficult to point to a particular year in his short life which marked his most productive period. However, the period between the end of 1787 and 1788 must be among the most prolific of works of genius, for in this short time he composed his three greatest

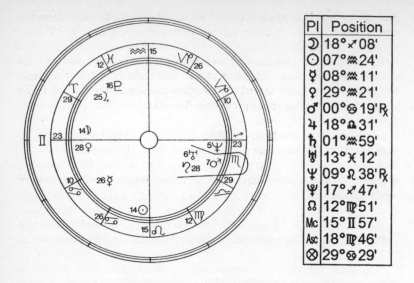

Pl	Position
☽	18° ♐ 08'
☉	07° ♒ 24'
☿	08° ♒ 11'
♀	29° ♒ 21'
♂	00° ♋ 19' ℞
♃	18° ♎ 31'
♄	01° ♒ 59'
♅	13° ♓ 12'
♆	09° ♌ 38' ℞
♇	17° ♐ 47'
☊	12° ♍ 51'
Mc	15° ♊ 57'
Asc	18° ♍ 46'
⊗	29° ♋ 29'

symphonies.[3] This remarkably productive period was initiated by an eclipse on what is undoubtedly the most sensitive point in his chart – the conjunction of Pluto and Moon on his nadir.

SOLAR ECLIPSE OF 9 DECEMBER 1787:	17.36 SAGITTARIUS
PLUTO IN THE CHART OF MOZART:	17.47 SAGITTARIUS
MOON IN THE CHART OF MOZART:	18.08 SAGITTARIUS

Mozart's most remarkable opera was the Egypto–Masonic *The Magic Flute*, with a libretto by Schikaneder and Giesecke. It was first performed in Vienna in 1791.

As any reader might expect by now, a work which was to enthrall the world for over two centuries must have been heralded by an eclipse. As a practised astrologer might expect, an opera which figured the astounding Queen of the Night, who first appears on a throne bedecked with transparent stars, would have to involve a lunar eclipse.[4]

LUNAR ECLIPSE OF 12 OCTOBER 1791:	18.37 LIBRA
JUPITER IN THE CHART OF MOZART:	18.31 LIBRA

One small astrological problem is that 1791 was also the year of Mozart's death. Is it possible that this lunar eclipse of 12 October could have been a harbinger of his death? I think not – the fact that Egypt is itself ruled in astrology by the sign Libra is its own argument for the eclipse being linked with the genius that produced *The Magic Flute*, which was a dramatic representation of the pseudo-Egyptian rites then popular in Masonic circles.

There are other reasons why the October 1791 eclipse was not the signal of Mozart's death. He died on 5 December 1791, the great 'Requiem' which had haunted his last days unfinished. In the following March, there was a lunar eclipse on his Ascendant.

LUNAR ECLIPSE OF 8 MARCH 1792:	19.05 VIRGO
ASCENDANT IN THE CHART OF MOZART:	18.46 VIRGO

A lunar eclipse upon an Ascendant is among the most powerful of all contacts, and under normal circumstances we would have no hesitation in reading from it an end to Mozart's life. However, there is another reason why this eclipse should be linked with his death – Mozart's Ascendant was on a fixed star. This was the star Denebola, the *beta*, set in the tail of the constellation Leo.

LUNAR ECLIPSE OF 8 MARCH, 1792:	19.05 VIRGO
ASCENDANT IN THE CHART OF MOZART:	18.46 VIRGO
POSITION OF STAR DENEBOLA IN 1756:	18.13 VIRGO

Since it was on the Ascendant at his birth, this means that the qualities of Denebola were intimately linked with Mozart's life and genius. It also means that, because it was overshadowed by the solar eclipse of March 1792, it coloured Mozart's death.

At the very beginning of the Western astrological tradition, Claudius Ptolemy told us that the star was of the nature of Saturn and Venus. This is a curious mixture in itself – the dark and melancholic nature of Saturn does not mix easily with the light and vivacious femininity of Venus. However, if we reflect upon it, this really touches the very core of Mozart's music, which is, on the surface light-hearted, yet underneath touched with a sadness – a sadness which is not always sweet. As one might imagine from such contrasts, the star has a dual influence: in the beginning, it lifts to good fortune, but finally brings troubles and sickness. Few people began life with as much promise as the child prodigy Mozart, and few died in such awesome penury, after a lifetime of labour. In fact, Denebola often brings poverty in its train – reminding us of Mozart's constant need for money, and of his final pauper's grave – in spite of efforts made to earn money in legitimate ways. His was a most curious funeral for a Freemason of such fame.

It has been suggested that Mozart was poisoned – though some medical historians have suggested that he died of kidney failure. In fact, the presence of Denebola on his Ascendant does seriously raise the question of poisoning, for this is one of the associations of the star, as of the star Acubens which was on his Neptune.[5] However, modern medical analysis has shown that Mozart died of a streptococcal infection which exacerbated his renal failure, contracted at a Masonic lodge meeting on 18 November 1791, during an epidemic in Vienna.[6]

Michel Nostradamus

The great French prophet, Michel Nostradamus, has fascinated me for a very long time, not least for the use he made of an eclipse at the very end of his own life. He was born on 14 December 1503, at 12:14 pm, in Salon, France. His chart is given below, along with a modern tabulation.[1]

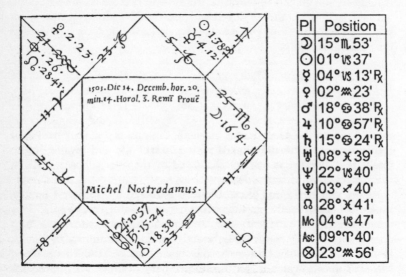

Pl	Position
☽	15°♏53'
☉	01°♑37'
☿	04°♑13'℞
♀	02°♒23'
♂	18°♋38'℞
♃	10°♋57'℞
♄	15°♋24'℞
♅	08°♓39'
♆	22°♑40'
♇	03°♐40'
☊	28°♓41'
Mc	04°♑47'
Asc	09°♈40'
⊗	23°♒56'

In the last years of his life he published almanacs, giving the positions of the planets, weather predictions and so on, along with samples of his curiously written prophetic verses. It is quite evident that when he came to draw up the lists for what was to prove his last almanac, he knew on which day he was going to die. In order to show that he knew the very day, he inserted in the Almanac for 1566 an incorrect placing. A section from this almanac is shown opposite:

One forms the impression from the large round circle alongside the first day of July that there is to be a full Moon, or perhaps a lunar eclipse. The

202

IVILLET.

Par pestilence & feu, fruits d'arbres periront:
Signe d'huile abonder: pere Denis non gueres:
Des grands mourir mais peu estrangers sailliront:
Insult marin barbare: & dangers de frontieres.

1 g Oct.s.Ioan.   ♇ ☉ à 3.h.o.m.ær turbidus..
2 a Visitation.   ♇
3 b s.Tibault..   ♒
4 c s.Vldarich.   ♒ Feu du ciel en naues ardant.
5 d P ier.de lucé.   ♒
6 e Oct.s.Pier.   ♓
7 Fs.Pantesme.   ♓
8 g s.Zenon.   ♈

9 a Oct.ñ.dame.   ♈ ☾ à 17.h.20. min.

symbol indicates the position of the Moon, in Capricorn, and the fact that
it is drawn full, rather than in crescent, indicates that an eclipse (or a full
Moon) is expected on that day.

Yet, Nostradamus was incorrect. He was too proficient an astronomer
and astrologer not to have known very well that the eclipse was not going
to happen until the following day. These are the correct details:

LUNAR ECLIPSE ON 2 JULY 1566:   19.21 CAPRICORN

Nostradamus was found dead – already cold in his bed – by his son, on
the morning of 2 July 1566.[2] My argument is that Nostradamus had
displaced the eclipse in his almanac by twenty-four hours in order to
indicate that this would be a strange day – in fact he called it a day of a
'strange transmigration'. It proved to be the day of his death.[3]

Is there any way that Nostradamus could have known from his own
birth chart that he was likely to die on 1 July 1566? The answer is quite
definitely, yes. I do not want to go into the details of the horoscope, and
how Nostradamus would have interpreted it, for this would take us into
very advanced astrology – however, it is evident that Nostradamus would
have known that the lunar eclipse of 2 July 1566 would fall exactly upon
the Mars of his chart – a very dangerous position.

| LUNAR ECLIPSE ON 2 JULY 1566: | 19.21 CANCER |
| MARS IN THE CHART OF NOSTRADAMUS: | 18.38 CANCER |

In fact, the danger was increased by virtue of the fact that when he was born, in 1503, his Mars had been on the fixed star Procyon:

LUNAR ECLIPSE ON 2 JULY 1566:	19.21 CANCER
MARS IN THE CHART OF NOSTRADAMUS:	18.38 CANCER
POSITION OF STAR PROCYON IN 1503:	19.06 CANCER

The eclipse of 1566 consequently fell not merely upon Mars, but upon Procyon, a star with a ragbag of mixed influences, which include such things as an interest in occult things and astrology, but also danger of death.

While dealing with what we might call the death–eclipse of Nostradamus, it might be as well to discuss the prophecy he made about the year 1999, which some people have linked with the solar eclipse of August.

The eclipse of 11 August 1999 will be in 19 degrees of Leo, and (fortunately) does not fall upon a powerful fixed star. The nearest star to this degree, in 1999, will be Algenubi in 21 degrees of Leo, set in the mouth of the lion. This placing indicates that the orb is far too wide for the eclipse to be linked with the star.

| SOLAR ECLIPSE OF 11 AUGUST 1999: | 18.21 LEO |
| POSITION OF FIXED STAR ALGENUBI IN 1999: | 20.36 LEO |

I mention this because, fairly recently, efforts have been made to link this eclipse with the famous quatrain X.72 from the Nostradamus *Prophecies*. According to some, this verse seems to suggest that a major war ('Mars to reign') might begin after July 1999 – the time specified by Nostradamus in this verse.[4]

The quatrain is now so famously linked in the popular mind with the '1999 eclipse' that it is worthwhile quoting a translation of Nostradamus' strange prophetic verse, reproducing his own punctuation. I give the original French in the footnote.[5]

> The year one thousand nine hundreds ninety nine seven months
> From the sky will come a great King of alarm
> To bring back to life the great King of Angoulmois.
> Before after Mars to reign by good fortune.

*

Whatever this quatrain does mean, I cannot see any connection between it and the eclipses of 1999. Nor does Nostradamus himself appear to draw any connection between the verse and the three eclipses of that year.

A great deal seems to hang upon what Nostradamus meant by 'a great King of alarm', and by that other 'King of Angoulmois'.

In fact, if we choose to stay with the Nostradamus quatrain, we might argue that it is more likely that the prophet refers to the lunar eclipse of July 1999 (the month and year he specified) rather than to either of the solar eclipses of the year.

The lunar eclipse of 28 July 1999 falls on 5 degrees of Leo–Aquarius. In 1999, the star Oculus will be on this degree.

LUNAR ECLIPSE OF 28 JULY 1999:	04.58 AQUARIUS
POSITION OF FIXED STAR OCULUS IN 1999:	04.42 AQUARIUS

Oculus is a small star which takes its name (and even its inclusion in the astrologic stellar lists)[6] from its distinctive placing in the right eye of the constellation Capricorn, the Goat. In the astrological tradition, it is regarded as having a power equivalent to that of Saturn and Venus together, combining a piercing intellect with beauty of form. Although Oculus was included in the star-lists used by Nostradamus, he never referred to it in his writings, and I can only presume that it has nothing to do with the July 1999 prediction.

In the last line of the quatrain Nostradamus mentions one planet by name. This is Mars, which he often uses as a symbol of warfare or general destruction. He tells us that Mars will 'reign' before and after this period. In fact, Mars is in and out of the sign Scorpio throughout 1999, and happens to be in this sign for each of the eclipses. During these periods, Mars is in the sign over which, in the time of Nostradamus, he traditionally had rule.

Mars is not on any significant fixed star on 28 July 1999. Nor is it on a fixed star on 11 August of that year. At the solar eclipse of 16 February, Mars is very close to the fixed star Khambalia. While this has a reputation for violence, it is certainly not powerful enough to have a profound effect, and it is certainly not easy to see why Nostradamus would have troubled to draw our attention to it. Any effect would work only through personal charts which already have this degree occupied.

The star is such a beneficial one that even the disruptive and active Mars becomes relatively harmless when it is placed over it. Thus, when we consider 1999 in terms of the sort of astrology that Nostradamus uses, we cannot arrive at an understanding of what his quatrain means.

In general, Nostradamus' verses cannot be interpreted before an event has actually occurred. If we glance at just one word in the quatrain I have just examined, we may see what I mean. The word Angoulmois has only a most obscure meaning. In sixteenth-century French it was sometimes (though rarely) used as the name for a herb, which was the equivalent of petan, or a kind of tobacco leaf. But this only helps us make sense of the word, or line in the quatrain, if we make the wild speculation that Nostradamus had the idea of tobacco in mind. If this were the case, then the reference could be to the Americas (from whence tobacco was already coming into the European markets – it reached England last, probably the year before Nostradamus died). Could this mean that the prophecy for 1999 is somehow linked with America? If so, we must ask, who is the 'King of America'?

However, the fact is that I cannot remember ever encountering a single prophecy by Nostradamus – who made hundreds of accurate prophecies – which was unravelled before its fulfilment made the quatrain crystal clear. If it is of any help, to those who find themselves confused by this quatrain, I can say that while I have read the prophecies of Nostradamus in the original French several times, and while I have read most of the European literature attached to the Nostradamus predictions, I have absolutely no idea to what the quatrain refers!

Maximilien Robespierre

Of all the terrible reputations earned by violent men during the terrors of the French Revolution, few have equalled that of the lawyer Robespierre. He seems to have been a psychopath hiding behind a very urbane mask: on the one hand he appeared to be an intelligent, respectable and cultured gentleman, with a strong ambition to do well in society. But he was also a scheming, calculating and callous politician, obsessed by revolutionary social ideas which resulted in the period now called 'the Reign of Terror'.[1]

From the moment that Robespierre took his place on the ironically named murder-machine, the Committee of Public Safety, in Paris, the stream of blood flowed so profusely on the guillotine that bodies were sometimes piled ten feet high around the scaffold. It was Robespierre who was responsible for the murder of Louis XVI and Marie Antoinette (see pages 128 and 190.).

Eventually – in the way of things – the violence turned a full circle, and Robespierre was himself sentenced to death on the guillotine, on 28 July 1794. I record the date, because it was an important one in his chart, and one which was reflected by an eclipse.

The chart and data for Robespierre are given opposite.[2] Few men can have had such an uncomfortable set of fixed stars working through their chart.[3]

Every chart has what the Greek astrologers called the anaretic, or 'killer'. This is the planet (or node) which, in the fullness of time, brings

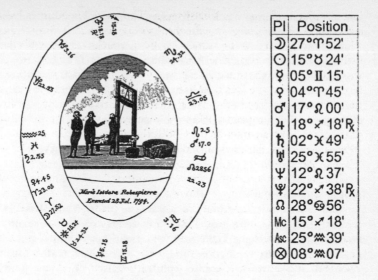

Maria Isidore Robespierre. Executed 28 Jul. 1794.

Pl	Position
☽	27°♈52'
☉	15°♉24'
☿	05°♊15'
♀	04°♈45'
♂	17°♌00'
♃	18°♐18'℞
♄	02°♓49'
♅	25°♓55'
♆	12°♌37'
♇	22°♐38'℞
☊	28°♋56'
Mc	15°♐18'
Asc	25°♒39'
⊗	08°♒07'

the life to an end. In the case of Robespierre, who had the lower part of his face shot away the day before his head was chopped off, this death was what might be called 'violent'.[4] Astrologically speaking this is quite understandable, for the 'killer' was the planet Pluto, not merely because of its connection with death and darkness, but also because in Robespierre's chart it was upon Aculeus:

PLUTO IN THE CHART OF ROBESPIERRE: 22.38 SAGITTARIUS
POSITION OF STAR ACULEUS IN 1758: 22.23 SAGITTARIUS

Although given in the traditional star-lists, Aculeus is actually a Nebula, or cluster of stars, located in the sting of Scorpio. In the astrological tradition, it brings wounds to the face, and affects in particular the eyes – often causing blindness.

On the day of Robespierre's beheading (28 July 1794) this conjunction of Nebula and Pluto was exactly upon his Ascendant:

ASCENDANT IN THE CHART OF ROBESPIERRE: 25.39 AQUARIUS
POSITION OF PLUTO 28 JULY 1794: 25.39 AQUARIUS

Was there an eclipse reflecting this event? The answer is, yes. The year 1794 saw six eclipses – four solar and two lunar. Rather surprisingly, this sequence of eclipses was sealed at either end by two eclipses both of which fell on sensitive points in Robespierre's chart. At the beginning of the year, in January, there was a solar eclipse opposite his Neptune, in 12 degrees of Aquarius.

NEPTUNE IN THE CHART OF ROBESPIERRE: 12.37 LEO
SOLAR ECLIPSE OF 31 JANUARY 1794: 11.56 AQUARIUS

Later in the same year, there was a solar eclipse opposite the planet Saturn of Robespierre's chart, a month after his execution.

SATURN IN THE CHART OF ROBESPIERRE: 02.49 PISCES
SOLAR ECLIPSE OF 25 AUGUST 1794: 02.24 VIRGO

John D. Rockefeller

We have already noted the dramatic working of the fixed star Wasat in the chart of Adolf Hitler (see page 183). Now we may study it in relation to the chart of another remarkable man who, rightly or wrongly, gained for himself a notorious reputation, and who, rather late in his life, was acclaimed as the world's leading philanthropist. This was John D. Rockefeller, who was born at Albany, New York, on 8 July 1839. His chart is a complex one, but what interests us is the fact that his Sun was on the fixed star Wasat.[1]

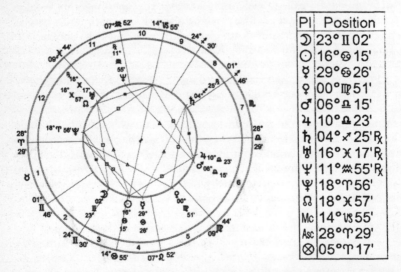

Pl	Position
☽	23° ♊ 02'
☉	16° ♋ 15'
☿	29° ♋ 26'
♀	00° ♍ 51'
♂	06° ♎ 15'
♃	10° ♎ 23'
♄	04° ♐ 25' Rx
♅	16° ♓ 17' Rx
♆	11° ♒ 55' Rx
♇	18° ♈ 56'
☊	18° ♓ 57'
Mc	14° ♑ 55'
Asc	28° ♈ 29'
⊗	05° ♈ 17'

A most interesting thing is that during Rockefeller's lifetime, an eclipse fell exactly upon his natal Sun, and therefore upon Wasat. This occurred at the solar eclipse of 7 July 1861, in 17 degrees of Cancer.[2]

SUN IN THE CHART OF ROCKEFELLER:	16.15 CANCER
FIXED STAR WASAT IN 1839:	16.16 CANCER
SOLAR ECLIPSE OF 8 JULY 1861:	15.50 CANCER

Now, in view of what we saw in Hitler's less fortunate chart, we might ask why Rockefeller could fall under the same influence, and yet not suffer the same dreadful end?

I think that the answer to the question is to do with receptivity in the original chart. Wasat, like most cosmic powers, offers two directions – a positive and a negative. The negative is towards destructiveness and violence, while the positive is towards the study of poisons, in both herbal and purely chemical formulations. Hitler, by virtue of the fixity of his chart, and the gathering of dark stars, was predisposed to react to the eclipse of 1945 in a violent way. Rockefeller was in some ways protected from violence – perhaps because his own Sun was harmoniously linked to the planet Uranus, the planet which rules inventiveness.[3] Instead of responding to the dark side of Wasat, Rockefeller was attuned to the inventive side of Uranus which grasped at the 'chemicals and poisons' associated with the star.

Let us consider what happened to Rockefeller in 1861, the year of this solar eclipse. It was in this year that he and his partner decided to go into business, as investors, with the inventor Samuel Andrews, who had a patent for an economical process for cleaning crude oil – that is, for 'refining', or removing the chemical dross and poisons from it to produce petroleum and various useful by-products. It was this decision which laid the foundation for Rockefeller's meteoric rise to wealth: in less than eighteen years he had obtained control over 90 per cent of the oil refineries in the United States of America.

This examination of Wasat in his chart helps us to understand that while certain fixed stars do predispose towards violence, they may also be received as transforming powers, given the right context. I am not for one moment suggesting that Wasat did not leave its dark-side effects on Rockefeller, or that his chart suggests that he was a perfect human being: indeed, to judge from contemporary accounts, when his business methods became known to the public he was said to be the most hated man in the United States of America. What I can be sure of is that his chart suggests that he was probably the most misunderstood man in that country.

It is partly his attempts to change this opinion of himself, and to organize some proper outlet for his wealth, that leads us to look at yet another eclipse which influenced his life – once again in a constructive way. In 1890, there was a lunar eclipse in Gemini. Rockefeller's own Saturn was directly opposite to this degree, in Sagittarius, and would therefore be affected by its contact.

It was in this year that Rockefeller – by now the richest man in America – began to give away his enormous wealth.[4] After his death, in May 1937, it was publicly announced that he had given away over 530 million dollars to various beneficiaries throughout the world.

Crown Prince Rudolph of Austria

Given the influence of Regulus, which ensures a sophisticated and royal mien, it is perhaps not surprising that it is frequently connected with those of royal birth, or those who are drawn into the orbit of royalty, yet end in tragedy.

Rudolph, the Crown Prince of Austria, an extremely talented and sensitive young man, was deeply interested in literature, and well prepared in many ways to take over the Austrian empire from his father, Francis Joseph. In 1881 he married Stephanie, daughter of the king of the Belgians, but he soon took a couple of mistresses, one of whom was the beautiful seventeen-year-old Baroness Marie Vetsera.

On the morning of 30 January 1889, the two were found dead in the royal hunting lodge at Mayerling, Vienna. I have already discussed some aspects of this tragedy in connection with the chart of Rudolph's father, the Emperor Francis Joseph (see page 79). The official explanation for

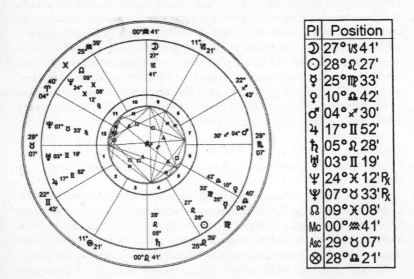

Pl	Position
☽	27° ♑ 41'
☉	28° ♌ 27'
☿	25° ♍ 33'
♀	10° ♎ 42'
♂	04° ♐ 30'
♃	17° ♊ 52'
♄	05° ♌ 28'
♅	03° ♊ 19'
♆	24° ♓ 12' ℞
♇	07° ♉ 33' ℞
☊	09° ♓ 08'
Mc	00° ♒ 41'
Asc	29° ♉ 07'
⊗	28° ♎ 21'

their deaths was that Rudolf had strangled Marie and then shot himself – both being under the impression that the Emperor was about to insist that their liaison should end. However, if it were a suicide, there was something very curious about the way it was hushed up, and by the fact that all those concerned in the event were sworn to secrecy. The official documents on the case were specifically excluded from the State Archives, and while many theories have been published, no one has ever discovered the truth about their deaths.[1]

Rudolph was born on 21 August 1858 at 10:12 pm near Vienna: his chart is given above.[2] His Sun was on the fixed star Regulus.

SUN IN THE CHART OF RUDOLPH:	28.27 LEO
POSITION OF REGULUS IN 1858:	27.35 LEO

Although the Sun and the Moon were to conjunct on the day following the couple's 'suicide', this was not an eclipse. In fact, the eclipse which seems to have sparked off Rudolph's death had taken place earlier in the month, being the lunar eclipse of 17 January. This eclipse had fallen across the Moon in Rudolph's horoscope, in 28 degrees Capricorn.

MOON IN THE CHART OF RUDOLPH:	27.41 CAPRICORN
LUNAR ECLIPSE OF 17 JANUARY 1889:	27.19 CAPRICORN

There is some argument as to when Rudolph began his affair with Marie Vetsera. According to the historian Carl Lonyay, he met her for the first time on 5 November 1888, and subsequent meetings (usually in secret) were arranged by the Countess Larisch in her own apartments.[3] Perhaps it is this meeting, which so deeply affected both their lives, which was presaged in the eclipse of July of that year, when it fell on the Prince's zenith. However, I do not wish to join the ranks of the scenarists, film-makers and playwrights in believing that Rudolph, who had another mistress at the time, and who had known the girl in a sexual sense only for a few days, regarded her as the love of his life.[4]

LUNAR ECLIPSE OF 23 JULY 1888:	00.44 AQUARIUS
ZENITH OF THE CHART OF RUDOLPH:	00.41 AQUARIUS

Although by its nature, astrology is concerned with life, and with the coming into being (as the ancient hermetic texts would put it), astrologers sometimes do cast and interpret death charts. The one cast for the early morning of 30 January 1889 suggests murder rather than suicide. Indeed, there is no trace of a suicidal or murderous tendency in Rudolph's chart.[5]

The star Regulus, which dominates Rudolph's chart lifts to greatness, even into royalty, yet, as the great mediaeval astrologer Guido Bonatus wrote, after all this wonderful elevation, 'yet still, whatever of all this happens, it signifies that the Native shall die an unhappy death'. This is not a promise of suicide, or that the native will commit murder! The fixed star Bellatrix which was on Rudolph's Jupiter, the North Asellus on his Saturn, and the Prima Hyadum on his Uranus both threaten a violent end – but none of these suggests suicide and committing murder. In other words, from a brief count of the threat writ in the fixed stars alone, it is clear that Rudolph would meet a violent end. There is not a trace of any suggestion of violence to self or others.

Working with progressions for a death–chart, I arrived at a time of 6:30 am. It was claimed that the suicide-to-be ordered breakfast from his servants, before strangling his mistress and shooting himself.

Warren de la Rue

The earliest satisfactory photograph of an eclipse was taken in Spain in 1860 by Warren de la Rue, a British astronomer, who was the inventor of photo–heliography.

De la Rue was born in Guernsey, on 18 January 1815; unfortunately, the exact time of birth is not known. However, I have erected a chart, cast for the midday of his birthdate, and give this below. While the four angles on this chart are unlikely to be of much value in the following horoscopic commentary, the planetary positions (save for the Moon) are sufficiently accurate for me to draw certain very interesting conclusions.

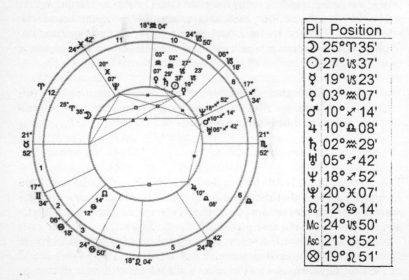

Pl	Position
☽	25° ♈ 35'
☉	27° ♑ 37'
☿	19° ♑ 23'
♀	03° ♒ 07'
♂	10° ♐ 14'
♃	10° ♎ 08'
♄	02° ♒ 29'
♅	05° ♐ 42'
♆	18° ♐ 52'
♇	20° ♓ 07'
☊	12° ♋ 14'
Mc	24° ♑ 50'
Asc	21° ♉ 52'
⊗	19° ♌ 51'

There had been a solar eclipse nine days before de la Rue's birth, in 20 of Capricorn, upon his natal Mercury.

SOLAR ECLIPSE OF 10 JANUARY, 1815:   19.32 CAPRICORN
MERCURY IN THE CHART OF DE LA RUE: 19.23 CAPRICORN

The subject of eclipses, and of the Sun and Moon, seems to have pursued Warren de la Rue throughout his life. Indeed, as we shall see, the chart above reveals that there were some very interesting connections between his birth and the eclipse he so famously photographed in 1860.

De la Rue's entire life seems to have been oriented around the Sun, Moon and eclipses. In 1850, he had constructed his own 13-inch reflecting telescope, which he mounted in Canonbury (London), and used to make careful drawings of the Moon and various other celestial bodies. In his own study of what he called 'Celestial Photography', de la Rue tended to discount his own achievements, reminding his readers of the combined efforts of the American astronomers William Bond and Fred Whipple, who had been the first to make a photographic picture of any celestial body.[1] These two scientists took a daguerreotype picture of the Moon, through the great refractor telescope in Harvard Observatory, round about 1850. After seeing this daguerreotype of the Moon, which had been taken in the Great Exhibition in 1851, he turned to the laborious method of wet-collodion process to make photographic records of its surface. In order to take photographs of the Sun, he invented the filter-system which remained for many years the basis of photo-heliography.

His early experiments with lunar photography taught him the importance of using the term 'full Moon' correctly, for with the aid of the camera he discovered that the full Moon is not seen quite so frequently as people imagine.

... for example, about every 29 days it is stated that there is a full Moon, but we see by the photographic picture that there never is a full Moon visible to us, except just before or just after a lunar eclipse, or at all events except when the Sun, earth and Moon are very nearly in the same plane.[2]

The photographs de la Rue took of the July eclipse recorded the red-flame prominences which shot above the dark edge of the Moon during the total eclipse: these, of course, are invisible to ordinary vision because of the normal brilliance of the sunlight.

Some of de la Rue's pictures were so valuable for scientific research that they were still being used in astronomical text-books thirty years later,[3] and led to the more advanced technology used by Professor Harkness, who photographed the total eclipse of the Sun on 29 July 1878, in 6.34 degrees of Leo. If we wish to understand fully this extraordinary correspondence between de la Rue and eclipses, we should observe that in 1860 there were *two* solar eclipses. Both were touched by planets in de la Rue's chart. Let me show the data for the solar eclipse of July, of which he took the historic photographs. We are fortunate that a drawing was made of this dramatic eclipse, with its rich corona and heliographic effects:[4]

This eclipse occurred in very close opposition to de la Rue's own Sun.

SOLAR ECLIPSE OF 18 JULY 1860:	26.06 CANCER
SUN IN THE HOROSCOPE OF DE LA RUE:	27.37 CAPRICORN

The correspondence between the chart and the earlier eclipse of January is even closer, and fell on *two* planets in his horoscope:

SOLAR ECLIPSE OF 23 JANUARY, 1860:	02.17 AQUARIUS
SATURN IN THE CHART OF DE LA RUE:	02.29 AQUARIUS
VENUS IN THE CHART OF DE LA RUE:	03.07 AQUARIUS

One almost gets the impression that Nature herself conspired to draw Warren de la Rue to the eclipse of 1860, which he photographed in Spain, in order to ensure that it was recorded.

Percy Bysshe Shelley

The planet Pluto, which did not enter astrological studies until about 1911, several years *before* it was discovered by astronomers,[1] is now recognized as tending to drag the native down to Earth – almost into the innards of the Earth. In that respect, it reminds one of the mythological story of the rape of Proserpine by the god Pluto, who dragged the girl into the underworld to claim her as his wife. Pluto is concerned with what is hidden below the surface – whether this be the hidden riches of a buried treasure, the inner resources of a sensitive writer, or the hidden workings of diseases in the physical body.

In extremes, it is Pluto which does that final 'dragging below', by signalling death, through its mythological connection with the Under-world. A very clear example of this may be seen in the horoscope of the English Romantic poet Percy Bysshe Shelley. The poet was born on 4 August 1792 in Horsham (Sussex) at about 9:40 pm.[2]

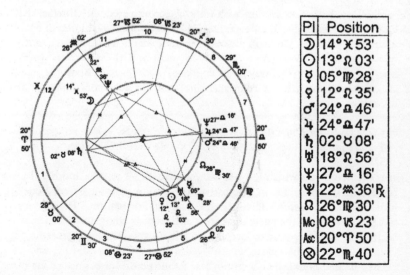

Pl	Position
☽	14° ♓ 53'
☉	13° ♌ 03'
☿	05° ♍ 28'
♀	12° ♌ 35'
♂	24° ♎ 46'
♃	24° ♎ 47'
♄	02° ♉ 08'
♅	18° ♌ 56'
♆	27° ♎ 16'
♇	22° ♒ 36' Rx
☊	26° ♍ 30'
Mc	08° ♑ 23'
Asc	20° ♈ 50'
⊗	22° ♏ 40'

Shelley's brief adult life (he died at the age of thirty) began and ended with eclipses.

In 1811 Shelley eloped with, and married, the young Harriet Westbrook, and afterwards lived for a while at Keswick, in Cumbria. In

July 1814, he eloped with another young lady, Mary Wollstonecraft Godwin. In January 1815, he inherited a useful sum of money, some of which he set aside for Harriet, who had given birth to his son. During this time he was working on his first important poem, *Alastor, or the Spirit of Solitude*. This was published in 1816, and ensured his fame. In the same year, Harriet drowned herself in the Serpentine, London, on 9 November.

The many dramatic and tragic changes of this year were reflected in an eclipse on the penultimate day of 1815 upon his zenith – the House of Career.

SOLAR ECLIPSE OF 30 DECEMBER 1815:	08.07 CAPRICORN
ZENITH IN THE CHART OF SHELLEY:	08.23 CAPRICORN

Shelley was accidentally drowned on 8 July 1822. The solar eclipse of 16 August of that year fell exactly opposite Shelley's Pluto.

SOLAR ECLIPSE OF 16 AUGUST 1822:	23.26 LEO
PLUTO IN THE CHART OF SHELLEY:	22.36 AQUARIUS

Shelley's famous obsession with water was connected with the fact that his Neptune was close to his Descendant, close to the exact union of Mars with Jupiter. The Moon in Pisces has often been used in astrological literature as an explanation for his obsession with water. However, Shelley's Dragon's Tail was in 26 degrees Pisces, exactly upon the fixed star Scheat, which has a reputation for causing accidents linked with drowning.

DRAGON'S TAIL IN CHART OF SHELLEY:	26.30 PISCES
POSITION OF STAR SCHEAT IN 1892:	26.28 PISCES

It is this fixed star which left its stamp on Shelley's psyche and life. In a fair summary of its action, the astrologer Vivian Robson wrote, Scheat 'causes extreme misfortune, murder, suicide and drowning.'[3] Perhaps it is not surprising that the party of writers and friends who passed their days with Shelley off the coast of Lerici gradually formed the uneasy suspicion that he was actually seeking death by drowning – if it could be read so clearly in his chart, then it must have been possible to sense it in his psyche, or in his attitudes.

Frank Sinatra
The following horoscope for Frank Sinatra was cast for 12 December 1917 at 3.00 am, at Hoboken, New Jersey.[1]

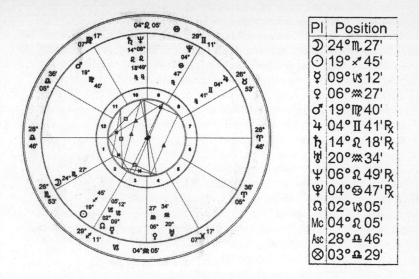

Pl	Position
☽	24° ♏ 27'
☉	19° ♐ 45'
☿	09° ♒ 12'
♀	06° ♒ 27'
♂	19° ♍ 40'
♃	04° ♊ 41' ℞
♄	14° ♌ 18' ℞
♅	20° ♒ 34'
♆	06° ♌ 49' ℞
♇	04° ♋ 47' ℞
☊	02° ♑ 05'
Mc	04° ♌ 05'
Asc	28° ♎ 46'
⊗	03° ♎ 29'

In the chart we see the out-going friendliness of the Sagittarian ('Come fly with me!' is one of Sinatra's most popular songs). This sun-sign combines with the intense and deeply passionate nature of the moon in Scorpio.

There is a fascinating photograph of Frank Sinatra in a still from *Las Vegas Nights* which was made in 1939, and released in 1940.[2] This shows Frank as the lead singer with the Tommy Dorsey Band. In the background is an enormous backset decorated with the constellations around the zodiacal band. Frank Sinatra is standing with Taurus over his left shoulder, and Pisces over his right – which is to say that he is placed directly on the constellation Aries. This is undoubtedly an unintended symbolism, yet the extraordinary thing is that, when the film was being made in 1939, there was an eclipse on 29 degrees of Aries, which fell exactly upon his own Descendant.

SOLAR ECLIPSE OF 19 APRIL 1939:   28.44 ARIES
DESCENDANT ANGLE IN THE CHART OF SINATRA: 28.46 ARIES

Sinatra was famous – if not infamous – for the number of women who passed through his life. Among these was the lovely Mia Farrow, who married Sinatra when she was twenty-one years old, and he was forty-nine.

Mia was born 9 February 1945 at 11:27 am, in Los Angeles. Her data (above) shows her to have essentially an Aquarian nature, but with a tendency to associate with older (or moody) men (Moon and Mars in Capricorn).[3] The pair married on 20 July 1966.

Pl	Position
☽	11° ♑ 41'
☉	20° ♒ 40'
☿	06° ♒ 50'
♀	07° ♈ 21'
♂	26° ♑ 26'
♃	26° ♍ 13' ℞
♄	04° ♋ 22' ℞
♅	09° ♊ 07' ℞
♆	06° ♎ 08' ℞
♇	08° ♌ 50' ℞
☊	16° ♋ 42'
Mc	25° ♑ 59'
Asc	10° ♉ 55'
⊗	01° ♈ 56'

When astrologers compare the charts of lovers, or married couples, they generally find that they have a degree in common: this is the degree which pulls them together in the magic of cosmic destiny. Such a communal degree often tells the astrologer quite a lot about the nature of their relationship, and the communal degree for Mia and Frank is no exception. Mia Farrow's Sun position, in 21 degrees of Aquarius, was on Sinatra's Uranus, which would usually suggest a short-lived relationship, if one lived in the public gaze.

Now, I am not particularly interested in the course of this marriage, which in any case lasted only sixteen months. My interest lies in the eclipse which fell across this communal degree in February 1971.

Sun in the chart of Farrow:	20.40 Aquarius
Uranus in the chart of Sinatra:	20.34 Aquarius
Lunar eclipse of 10 February, 1971:	20.54 Aquarius

In March 1971 Sinatra announced his retirement. In retrospect, we now know that he was to 'retire' several times during his professional life – so many times, indeed, that it became something of a joke. This retirement of 1971 was his first, however, and certainly seemed a wise decision considering the way show business was changing. Uranus is a planet which severs connections, cuts through things – often sheering through tangles which cannot be unravelled. As if to underscore the need to withdraw, the lunar eclipse of the 6 August of the same year also fell on Sinatra's Saturn:

Saturn in the chart of Sinatra:	14.18 Leo
Lunar eclipse of 6 August 1971:	13.42 Leo

Sinatra's farewell concert was on 13 June 1971, in Los Angeles.

George Washington
The early history of the city of Washington DC is intimately bound up with the personality of the first President of the United States, George Washington. Not only did Congress vote to name the city after him, but

he was its moving spirit, both in the selection of the site and in overseeing its planning. In view of this, one should not be surprised to find that his personal horoscope is linked with the foundation of the city by means of eclipses. Of course, when the life and aspirations of an individual are so intimately bound up with the formation of a new nation, it is inevitable that the person's chart should seem somehow larger than life. George Washington's chart is, in fact, one of the most remarkable I know.

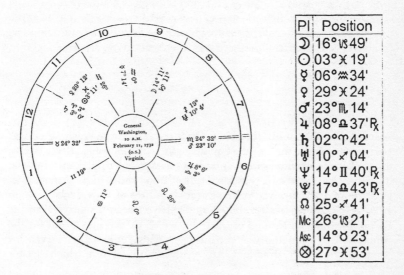

Pl	Position
☽	16° ♑ 49'
☉	03° ♓ 19'
☿	06° ♒ 34'
♀	29° ♓ 24'
♂	23° ♏ 14'
♃	08° ♎ 37' ℞
♄	02° ♈ 42'
♅	10° ♐ 04'
♆	14° ♊ 40' ℞
♇	17° ♎ 43' ℞
☊	25° ♐ 41'
Mc	26° ♑ 21'
Asc	14° ♉ 23'
⊗	27° ♓ 53'

George Washington's horoscope, based on information from the family Bible, is given above.[1] The entry says 'about 10 in the morning', so I have rectified by Washington's death and major events in his life, and have arrived at a birth time of 09:46:30 in the morning, on the old style date of 11 February 1732.

When the preliminary surveys of Washington DC were begun, in 1790, there was a solar eclipse visible from the Potomac over the site where the Capitol building would be raised.[2] The eclipses in the years on either side of this time, and relating to the chart of George Washington himself, were in some ways even more remarkable. An eclipse took place at the time when he was negotiating purchase of the land, and planning the city, and another eclipse took place on exactly the same degree at his death. Let us look at the first of these two in detail.

George Washington (who had started his professional life as a surveyor) did a preliminary survey of the site for Washington DC in 1790, while he was staying in Georgetown. It was this survey that convinced him the site would be ideal for the new federal city of the United States of America. On 6 November 1790, there was an eclipse in 15 degrees of Scorpio, on Washington's Descendant.

SOLAR ECLIPSE OF 6 NOVEMBER 1790:   14.34 SCORPIO
DESCENDANT IN THE CHART OF WASHINGTON: 14.23 SCORPIO

In fact, George Washington's relation to eclipses is utterly remarkable – well beyond that which one may expect of genius. For example, near the time of the foundation of the White House (the first official building to be erected in Washington DC) there was an eclipse on his Saturn.

SOLAR ECLIPSE OF 22 MARCH 1792:   02.49 ARIES
POSITION OF SATURN IN CHART OF WASHINGTON: 02.42 ARIES

What has been described as 'the most catastrophic [day] in all Anglo-American history', was 9 July 1755. On that day, George Washington was so enmeshed in the thick of the famous fight at Monongahela River twelve miles from Fort Duquesne, that he had his clothing ripped with bullets, his hat shot off, and two horses shot dead from under him.[3] Afterwards, he attributed his survival to 'the miraculous care of Providence', yet an astrologer, with no less reverence, might have traced his survival to the Part of Fortune. At the end of the fight, which turned into a rout for the Americans, Washington was the only surviving senior officer: even his commanding officer, Braddock, had received wounds from which he later died.

LUNAR ECLIPSE ON 20 SEPTEMBER 1755:   27.01 PISCES
PART OF FORTUNE IN CHART OF WASHINGTON: 27.53 PISCES

In some cases, even relatively minor events – such as a threat to property – are reflected in an eclipse. In 1781, shortly before the battle of Yorktown, the British sloop *Savage* sailed far enough up the Potomac to direct her guns upon Mount Vernon, which was by then his home. There was a very real risk that Washington's estates would be destroyed, and that the area would return to British rule. Washington's estate manager provided the British ship with provisions, to stay the guns, and thus saved the property. Washington was furious with him, for he would rather have seen his house destroyed than to have dealt with the enemy. In cosmic terms, the threat had been a very real one, and was marked in the skies by an eclipse: the lunar eclipse of 8 April was close to his Pluto. Perhaps if it had been in a closer orb, it might have killed him:

LUNAR ECLIPSE OF 8 APRIL 1781:   19.17 LIBRA
POSITION OF PLUTO IN CHART OF WASHINGTON: 17.43 LIBRA

Given the greatness of the man, it is not surprising that even Washington's death was attended by an eclipse. George Washington died on Tuesday, 30 April 1799. Five days later, there was an eclipse on his Ascendant degree, on the same axis which had witnessed his selection of the site for the federal city, in November 1790.

SOLAR ECLIPSE OF 5 MAY 1799:   14.27 TAURUS
ASCENDANT IN THE CHART OF WASHINGTON: 14.23 TAURUS

Conclusion

As I have already indicated, it is clear that thousands of people will gather in the southern tip of England on Wednesday, 11 August 1999, to watch the much-heralded total eclipse of the Sun. Many gathering there will be wondering what effect (if any) the eclipse will have on their own lives. In most cases, the answer to this question is, little effect unless you are a remarkable person.

I have given several examples of how the beneficial influences of solar eclipses work into the lives of individuals. From these examples, it is easy to see that, generally speaking, the solar effect is always good for creative enterprises: the solar pours constructive energies into the realm governed by the contact it makes with the relevant degree in the personal chart. One has the impression that the solar eclipse works into the lives of those people who are fortunate enough to carry questions in their hearts or minds, and who (perhaps unconsciously) seek answers to such questions in the higher cosmic realms. The solar contact often brings such revelatory answers that the overall effect is to change the life of the person concerned.

Perhaps the souls and spirits of those watching the miracle of an occluded Sun will soar, and no doubt those who are fortunate enough to witness it will feel that the journey to watch a phenomenon lasting only 2 minutes and 23 seconds was worthwhile.

Those who have the time to reflect upon the experience afterwards may well carry a feeling of the almost inconceivable majesty of the Cosmos, sensing behind the inexorable movement of Sun, Moon and Earth a power that is directed not mechanically, but with that grace and calm which is the hallmark of a spiritual activity. If this is the realization – that mankind dwells within a living organism, rather than within a giant and soulless clock – then the experience of that Wednesday in August 1999 will certainly have proved to be worthwhile. However, this sense of wonder at the Cosmos should really be a consequence of any solar or lunar eclipse, and we might therefore ask if there will be anything special about this eclipse which marks it out from any other?

The answer is, no. Although a great deal of nonsense has been written about the sixteenth-century prophet Nostradamus, and the erroneous belief that he foretold things about the solar eclipse of 1999, there is nothing of extraordinary significance in this eclipse. Save, of course, that it is rare in being visible in parts of Europe and the southern tip of England.

By now, anyone who has read this book will recognize how the secret influences of this eclipse will be transmitted, for its power will work into humanity *only in the usual way of eclipses*. In short, it can have a significance for certain individuals only if the degree in which it is located happens to correspond to a degree in their personal horoscope.

The eclipse of 11 August 1999 will fall in 18.21 Leo, and will last 2 minutes and 23 seconds. A similar eclipse, though not visible in England, occurred within living memory of many people, on 11 August 1961. This eclipse fell in 18.31 Leo – which is to say that it was less than ten seconds of arc away from the 1999 point. Since it lasted almost three times as long as that which is to take place in August 1999, it was, in terms of astrological theory, much stronger. This 1961 eclipse would have a far more powerful influence upon individual charts than the 1999 equivalent.

The one thing these two eclipses have in common (besides a proximity to the same precise position in the zodiac) is the date – 11 August. This date is the one sure standard to which an astrologer may point with confidence, even without access to the personal chart. In general, the birth date (regardless of year) offers a useful clue to the position of the Sun. On the 11 August of any year the Sun passes through, or touches, 19 degrees of Leo, though this can be affected by place of birth and even by time of birth. Because of the nature of the calendar, a contact may sometimes also be established with that same degree on 12 August. For example, the solar eclipse of 12 August 1942 fell on 18.46 Leo.

This means that anyone now alive, and born on either of those days (in any year), may have a chart with the Sun on the same degree of the solar eclipse of 1999. That – without access to the personal chart – is *all* that one can know about the likely effect of this eclipse. Even the precise nature of this effect on those born on 11 August (of any year) must remain a mystery without access to the chart. How the eclipse will interact with this solar position depends very much upon the nature of the chart itself.

Are there any examples of well-known individuals born on the 11 August, with the Sun close to this exact position of the solar eclipse of 1999?

There are of course a great number of interesting people who were born on this day, but one literary figure who is of particular interest to astrologers is the American writer, Alex Haley, who was born on 11 August 1921. Haley, the author of the best-selling fictionalized history of his African origins, *Roots*, was born with the Sun very close to 18.31 Leo. Since Haley died in 1992, any question of an influence from the 1999 eclipse is irrelevant. However, as our own interest lies in the influence of 19 Leo, it is interesting to observe that the eclipse of 1961 which fell in this degree seemed to have changed Haley's life fundamentally. The eclipse seems to have divided his life into what may be called a classical 'before and after'. In the years leading up to the eclipse, he worked as a cook in the United States Coast Guard. In the years after 1961 he began to write, and became incredibly successful. This is a very dramatic example of how an eclipse, falling on a natal Sun (that is, the birthday position), can radically change a human life for the better. As a matter of further interest, I should observe that Haley's death, in 1992, was paralleled by the solar eclipse of 30 June, which fell directly upon his Pluto.[1]

An example of a famous birth on the following day – 12 August – which one might reasonably expect would be linked with this eclipse degree, is the American film director, Cecil B. de Mille, who was born in 1881. However, his chart reveals that by the time he was born the Sun had moved along the zodiacal belt more than one degree, which means that in terms of our concern with the eclipse of 1999 it becomes irrelevant to his chart. I mention de Mille because his birth date is an interesting example of how even within the passage of a single day, the profound influence of an eclipse can be lost. Even so, it is worth recording that Cecil B. de Mille's chart was not without its eclipse influences. For example, his first block-busting success, the early version of the biblical epic, *The Ten Commandments*, was released in 1923. In this same year, the lunar eclipse of 3 March fell on the same degree as his Uranus.[2]

As we might imagine from the sample chart of De Mille, by the following day (13 August) in any year, the Sun will have moved to a position where the eclipse of 1999 could have no direct effect at all. I could take as an example of this the chart of Fidel Castro, the Cuban revolutionary, who was born on 13 August 1926. By this time, the Sun had moved *just* out of the degree orb allowed for eclipse influences.

Because Castro is such a remarkable individual, it is inevitable that other eclipses should play an important role in his life. An example of an effective eclipse in Castro's life was that which influenced the military USA action against Cuba, now called the Bay of Pigs – an invasion which took place in 1961. This event was paralleled by a lunar eclipse (on 2 March of that year) which fell exactly upon Castro's Mars – a typical sign of difficult conflict. None of the operative eclipses in his life appears to have anything to do with the position of his Sun (that is, the birth date) however, which implies that Castro should be unaffected by the 11 August 1999 eclipse.

I mention Castro's chart because, while it is reasonably certain that he will not be affected by the August 1999 eclipse, it is very likely that 1999 will bring major changes for him, due to the working of another eclipse. The solar eclipse of 16 February 1999 falls on 27.08 Aquarius, right across the same degree occupied by Castro's Neptune – a planet which generally brings about significant spiritual changes.

The three charts we have glanced at have been selected to show that the eclipse of August 1999 can have a profound influence (in the case given above, a very beneficial change), for those whose birthdays fall in or close to the date in question. Beyond this, it is absolutely impossible to make any statements about the effect of the eclipse on the lives of individuals. I write this knowing full well that some popular books of astrology have made dire predictions of a most outrageous kind, which really can have no connection with serious astrology. In view of this, I can do no better than conclude with a warning – in modern times there are far too many people practising and even writing about what they happily call astrology who have insufficient knowledge of the subject. Though there is no law against this, it is tantamount to someone practising medicine without having troubled to go to medical school, or seeking qualification. It is for this reason that I have to warn readers to take with a pinch of salt any prophecies they may encounter regarding the future effect of the eclipse of 1999 – or indeed of any eclipse – without it being related to a well-established chart of an individual. Any other approach to prediction by eclipses can be nothing more than foolish – and even dangerous – guesswork.

Table of Eclipses in Text

Below are listed all the eclipses mentioned in the preceding text, given in zodiacal order, with date, zodiacal position, and the name of the personal chart to which the eclipse refers.

03 Ari.	– Sol. Ec. 22 Mar 1792:	02.49 Ari. – Washington
05 Ari.	– Sol. Ec. 25 Mar 1819:	04.30 Ari. – Blake
07 Ari.	– Sol. Ec. 27 Mar 1960:	06.38 Ari. – Margaret
12 Ari.	– Lun. Ec. 6 Oct 1922:	11.52 Ari. – Ernst
13 Ari.	– Lun. Ec. 4 Oct 1884:	12.05 Ari. – Gordon
15 Tau.	– Sol. Ec. 5 May 1799:	14.27 Tau. – Washington
18 Ari.	– Sol. Ec. 8 Apr 1902:	17.48 Ari. – Keller
19 Ari.	– Lun. Ec. 12 Oct 1791:	18.37 Ari. – Mozart
25 Ari.	– Sol. Ec. 15 Apr 1847:	24.39 Ari. – Brontë, e.
29 Ari.	– Sol. Ec. 19 Apr 1939:	28.44 Ari. – Sinatra
02 Tau.	– Lun. Ec. 25 Oct 1855:	01.21 Tau. – Brontë, c.
04 Tau.	– Sol. Ec. 24 Apr 1800:	03.33 Tau. – Beethoven
04 Tau.	– Lun. Ec. 25 May 1994:	03.37 Sag. – Clinton
08 Tau.	– Sol. Ec. 26 Apr 1892:	07.05 Tau. – Shaw
10 Tau.	– Lun. Ec. 30 Apr 1809:	09.10 Tau. – Beethoven
10 Tau.	– Sol. Ec. 10 May 1994:	19.49 Tau. – Clinton
11 Tau.	– Sol. Ec. 30 Apr 1669:	10.15 Tau. – Gwyn
11 Tau.	– Lun. Ec. 3 Nov 1827:	10.29 Tau. – Beethoven
13 Tau.	– Lun. Ec. 6 Nov 1911:	13.00 Tau. – Titanic
22 Tau.	– Lun. Ec. 11 May 1892:	21.37 Tau. – Shaw
24 Tau.	– Lun. Ec. 15 Nov 1872:	23.17 Tau. – Emerson
28 Tau.	– Sol. Ec. 17 Apr 1912:	27.05 Ari. – Titanic
29 Tau.	– Sol. Ec. 20 May 1966:	28.55 Tau. – Speck
03 Gem.	– Sol. Ec. 25 Nov 1882:	02.38 Gem. – Emerson
05 Gem.	– Lun. Ec. 26 Nov 1890:	04.23 Gem. – Rockefeller
09 Gem.	– Sol. Ec. 30 May 1946:	08.48 Gem. – Ribbentrop
09 Gem.	– Sol. Ec. 30 May 1946:	08.49 Gem. – Hiroshima
19 Gem.	– Lun. Ec. 9 Dec 1992:	18.12 Gem. – Clinton

24 Gem.– Lun. Ec. 16 Dec 1815:   23.47 Gem. – Byron
27 Gem.– Sol. Ec. 17 Jun 1890:   26.07 Gem. – Van Gogh
29 Gem.– Sol. Ec. 20 Jun 1955:   28.05 Gem. – Bardot
05 Can. – Lun. Ec. 26 Jun 1805:   04.48 Can. – Blake
07 Can. – Lun. Ec. 28 Dec 1879:   06.41 Can. – Keller
16 Can. – Sol. Ec. 8 Jul 1861:   15.50 Can. – Rockefeller
17 Can. – Sol. Ec. 9 Jul 1945:   16.57 Can. – Frank
17 Can. – Sol. Ec. 9 Jul 1945:   16.57 Can. – Hitler
17 Can. – Sol. Ec. 9 Jul 1945:   16.57 Can. – Hiroshima
19 Can. – Sol. Ec. 11 Jul 1991:   18.59 Can. – Vincent
27 Can. – Sol. Ec. 18 Jul 1860:   26.06 Can. – De La Rue
28 Can. – Lun. Ec. 17 Jan 1889:   27.19 Can. – Rudolph, Prince
28 Can – Sol. Ec. 20 Jul 1982:   27.42 Can. – Diana, Princess
05 Leo – Sol. Ec. 27 Jul 1832:   04.27 Leo – Emerson
09 Leo – Sol. Ec. 1 Aug 1943:   08.03 Leo – Atomic Energy
12 Leo – Lun. Ec. 26 Feb 1999:   11.25 Leo – John Paul II
14 Leo – Lun. Ec. 6 Aug 1971:   13.42 Leo – Sinatra
17 Leo – Lun. Ec. 6 Feb 1822:   16.59 Leo. – Beethoven
19 Leo – Sol. Ec. 11 Aug 1961:   18.31 Leo – Monroe
19 Leo – Sol. Ec. 11 Aug 1999:   18.21 Leo – Nostradamus
24 Leo – Sol. Ec. 16 Aug 1822:   23.26 Leo – Shelley
30 Leo – Sol. Ec. 22 Aug 1979:   29.01 Leo – Diana, Princess
01 Vir. – Lun. Ec. 19 Feb 1905:   00.34 Vir. – Potter
03 Vir. – Sol. Ec. 25 Aug 1794:   02.24 Vir. – Robespierre
08 Vir. – Sol. Ec. 31 Aug 1913:   07.49 Vir. – Potter
08 Vir. – Sol. Ec. 26 Feb 1998:   07.55 Vir. – Clinton
10 Vir. – Sol. Ec. 2 Sep 1997:   09.34 Vir. – Diana, Princess
12 Vir. – Lun. Ec. 17 Mar 1923:   11.37 Vir. – Ernst
15 Vir. – Sol. Ec. 7 Sep 1858:   14.37 Vir. – Burton
19 Vir. – Lun. Ec. 9 Mar 1849:   18.19 Vir. – Brontë E.
20 Vir. – Lun. Ec. 8 Mar 1792:   19.05 Vir. – Mozart
23 Vir. – Lun. Ec. 13 Mar 1979:   22.38 Vir. – John Paul II
24 Vir. – Sol. Ec. 17 Sep 1830:   23.39 Vir. – Emerson
25 Vir. – Sol. Ec. 16 Sep 1972:   24.08 Vir. – Lamballe, Princess
02 Lib. – Lun. Ec. 22 Mar 1913:   01.17 Ari. – Duncan
11 Lib. – Lun. Ec. 30 Mar 1885:   10.06 Lib. – Gordon
16 Lib. – Sol. Ec. 9 Oct 1847:   15.28 Lib. – Brontë, C.
20 Lib. – Lun. Ec. 8 Apr 1781:   19.17 Lib. – Washington
27 Lib. – Lun. Ec. 19 Oct 1865:   26.19 Lib. – Lincoln
29 Lib. – Sol. Ec. 19 Apr 1958:   28.34 Lib. – Bardot
30 Lib. – Lun. Ec. 23 Oct 1790:   29.50 Lib. – Banneker
07 Sco. – Sol. Ec. 31 Oct 1902:   06:58 Sco. – Potter
08 Sco. – Sol. Ec. 30 Oct 1864:   07.29 Sco. – Lincoln

10 Sco.	– Sol. Ec. 2 Nov 1967:	09.07 Sco.	– Diana, Princess
15 Sco.	– Lun. Ec. 4 May 1966:	14.02 Sco.	– Potter
15 Sco.	– Sol. Ec. 6 Nov 1790:	14.34 Sco.	– Washington
28 Sco.	– Sol. Ec. 20 Nov 1835:	07.26 Sco.	– Andersen
30 Sco.	– Sol. Ec. 12 Nov 1509:	29.32 Sco.	– Henry VIII
03 Sag.	– Lun. Ec. 25 Nov 1863:	02.36 Sag.	– Lincoln
07 Sag.	– Sol. Ec. 29 Nov 1826:	06.46 Sag.	– Blake
07 Sag.	– Sol. Ec. 28 May 1900:	06:47 Sag.	– Lautrec
09 Sag.	– Sol. Ec. 30 Nov 1853:	08.29 Sag.	– Renoir
13 Sag.	– Lun. Ec. 3 Jun 1928:	12.37 Sag.	– Disney
18 Sag.	– Sol. Ec. 10 Dec 1806:	17.25 Sag.	– Banneker
18 Sag.	– Sol. Ec. 9 Dec 1787:	17.36 Sag.	– Mozart
20 Sag.	– Sol. Ec. 11 Dec 1852:	19.20 Sag.	– Van Gogh
20 Sag.	– Sol. Ec. 12 Dec 1871:	19.44 Sag.	– Bismark
21 Sag.	– Sol. Ec. 12 Dec 1890:	20.05 Sag.	– Vincent
22 Sag.	– Lun. Ec. 12 Jun 1881:	21.22 Sag.	– Alexander II
09 Cap.	– Sol. Ec. 30 Dec 1815:	08.07 Cap.	– Shelley
11 Cap.	– Sol. Ec. 1 Jan 1805:	10.16 Cap.	– Blake
13 Cap.	– Sol. Ec. 3 Jan 1927:	12.29 Cap.	– Duncan
19 Cap.	– Lun. Ec. 11 Jul 1824:	18.38 Cap.	– Blake
19 Cap.	– Lun. Ec. 11 Jul 1824:	18.38 Cap.	– Byron
20 Cap.	– Sol. Ec. 10 Jan 1815:	19.32 Cap.	– Byron
20 Cap.	– Sol. Ec. 10 Jan 1815:	19.32 Cap.	– De La Rue
20 Cap.	– Lun. Ec. 2 Jul 1566:	19.21 Cap.	– Nostradamus
21 Cap.	– Sol. Ec. 12 Jul 1889:	20.36 Cap.	– Franz Joseph
22 Cap.	– Lun. Ec. 4 Jul 1544:	21.53 Cap.	– Henry VIII
30 Cap.	– Lun. Ec. 22 Jul 1804:	29.38 Cap.	– Blake
01 Aqu.	– Lun. Ec. 23 Jul 1888:	00.44 Aqu.	– Rudolph, Prince
03 Aqu.	– Sol. Ec. 23 Jul 1860:	02.17 Aqu.	– De La Rue
09 Aqu.	– Sol. Ec. 19 Jan 1482:	08.32 Aqu.	– Leonardo
12 Aqu.	– Sol. Ec. 31 Jan 1794:	11.56 Aqu.	– Robespierre
16 Aqu.	– Sol. Ec. 26 Jan 1495:	15.37 Aqu.	– Leonardo
16 Aqu.	– Sol. Ec. 5 Feb 1962:	15.44 Aqu.	– Monroe
21 Aqu.	– Lun. Ec. 10 Feb 1971:	20:54 Aqu.	– Sinatra
22 Aqu.	– Lun. Ec. 11 Feb 1952:	21.19 Aqu.	– Bardot
06 Pis.	– Sol. Ec. 25 Feb 1952:	05.43 Pis.	– Bardot
23 Pis.	– Lun. Ec. 15 Sep 1875:	22.23 Pis.	– Blavatsky
27 Pis.	– Sol. Ec. 16 Mar 1885:	26.19 Pis.	– Gordon
27 Pis.	– Sol. Ec. 16 Mar 1885:	26.19 Pis.	– Van Gogh
28 Pis.	– Lun. Ec. 20 Sep 1755:	27.01 Pis.	– Washington

Notes

Eclipses and Us

1. Nigel Lewis, *The Book of Babel, Words and the Way we See Things*, 1994, p. 272.

2. From *Della Composizione del Mondo di Ristoro d'Arezzo, Testo Italiano del 1282* in the Enrico Narducci (Milan) edition of 1864. Ristoro's observations typify the quality of mediaeval star-gazing and available tables, for the eclipse did not take place 'in 20 degrees of Gemini'. Of course, Ristoro had no satisfactory way of observing the time accurately, which explains his phrase, 'about the sixth hour'. The eclipse took place at 12:38 pm in 18.51 Gemini, which means that had Ristoro used his own observations in personal horoscopy, he would have been wrong in the subsequent predictions. Mercury was in Taurus, about 20 degrees from the Sun, and would have been visible. Ristoro's Italian is very stylish, and I have tried to reproduce in translation something of its terse excitement.

3. My conviction that the eclipse mentioned by Peter of Abano is the same as that mentioned by Ristoro is based on the fact that Peter finished his *Conciliator* in his native Padua in 1310, and in it mentions the solar eclipse as having occurred about 70 years previously. A total eclipse of the Sun visible in Europe clearly left its mark for a very long time. It had, of course, happened over a decade before Peter was born. For background material, see 'Peter of Abano', in Lynn Thorndike, *A History of Magic and Experimental Science*, 1923, vol. 11: for date of his mss. p. 879, for mention of eclipse, p. 897.

4. In fact, we have only Plutarch's word for the notion that Theoclymenus was writing about an eclipse at all.

5. William Lilly, *Annus Tenebrosus, or the Dark Year. Or Astrologicall Judgements upon two Lunar Eclipses and one admirable eclips of the Sun, all visible in England, 1652.* 1652. p. 49.

6. From the title page of *Annus Tenebrosus* – n. 5 above.

7. For Dante, this power is 'the love that moves the Sun and the other stars'. – see note 83 below.

8. The story is told in a bibliographic note to the Regiomontanus *Calendarium* in the Maggs brothers' catalogue, *Manuscripts and Books on Medicine, Alchemy, Astrology & Natural Sciences*, 1929. The story may even be true: the eclipse

took place shortly after sunset, with the Moon in 20 degrees Gemini, which means that it would have been visible at the latitudes Columbus was in.

9. This is the Reverend William Wyatt Gill, a missionary who delighted in recording the influence of Christianity on his barbarian subjects: see for example, *From Darkness to Light in Polynesia*, 1894. For the eclipse, see 'Eclipse of the Sun as seen in the South Seas', p. 703.

10. The Claudius edict seems to have been the work of the astrologer Balbillus. See Frederick H. Cramer, *Astrology in Roman Law and Politics* 1954, pp. 114 ff.

11. Robert Stawell Ball, *The Story of the Heavens*, 1890 edn, p. 41.

12. In 1913, there were five eclipses – three solar and two lunar: 22 March lunar eclipse in 01.16 Libra; 6 April solar eclipse in 16.20 Aries; 31 August solar eclipse in 07.48 Virgo; 15 September, lunar eclipse in 22.05 Pisces; 30 September, solar eclipse in 06.26 Libra.

13. Of course, this eclipse is not the first to be mentioned in literature. For example, it has been suggested (see Schoch *Observatory*, xlix, 1926, pp. 19-21) that the solar eclipse of 16 April 1178 BC (which was total at Ithaca) is the one mentioned by Homer in *Odyssey*.

14. From an early date, the Babylonians appear to have been able to take into account the various inequalities of motion of Moon and Earth which are now called the anomalistic month and year.

15. Archilochus, *Fragment* 74.

16. The date of Archilochus' birth has never been established. However, it seems that he took part in the colonization of Thasos, *circa* 708 BC, which means that he may have witnessed the total eclipse of 14 March 711 BC. This may be the one mentioned in his poem.

17. In mediaeval astrology, the Sun rules the right eye, the Moon the left. In the ancient Egyptian mythology, the Moon is sometimes called the 'left eye of Horus'. It was believed that, in a lunar eclipse this is swallowed for a short time by a sow. On a far more exalted level of philosophy, Goethe recognized that the eye itself was formed from sunlight.

18. *Pythian Odes* 9. Some scholars think that the Ode was composed as early as 474 BC.

19. Plutarch (recording Tarutius' opinion), *Romulus*, 12, 5-6. He was conceived in the first year of the second Olympiad, in the month of Choeac, on the 23rd day, and in the third hour.

20. Plutarch, *Romulus*, 12, 4. This account does not agree with that given by Cicero, in *De Divinatione*, 2, 47, 98. See F.H. Cramer, *Astrology in Roman Law and Politics*, 1954, p. 65.

21. See Pliny *Historiae Naturalis*, book ii, 9. Other people claim that Thales predicted the eclipses of 610 BC, 603 BC and 584 BC.

22. For the Thales observations, see J. L. E. Dreyer, *A History of the Planetary Systems from Thales to Kepler* in the re-titled Dover edition of 1953, pp. 12-13

23. The wood-engraving by Le Campion is from the Nonesuch Press edition of *Herodotus*, 1935.

24. Herodotus, *Historia*, vii 37.

25. I interpret the figure as representing Clio because of the mariginal text below the illustration in the Nonesuch edition of 1935. This mentions that Herodotus established the specialist meaning of the word 'History'.

26. For the mediaeval astrologer, the most ominous thing, alongside the eclipse, was the conjunction of the superiors – that is, the threatening conjunction of the planets Mars, Jupiter and Saturn.

27. For a survey of the astrology of Geoffrey of Meaux (the Ganifredus de Meldis of the Latin catalogues) see Lynn Thorndike, *A History of Magic and Experimental Science*, vol. III, pp. 280 ff.

28. The dog-Latin reads: '*eclipsis lune universalis cum magna mora 18 die marcii una hora post ortum lune ad longitudinem Oxonie*'. See Thorndike, *op. cit.*, III p. 283.

29. This was true at the beginning of the eclipse: by 9:28 the Moon was in 06.30 Libra, by which time Venus had moved from Aries into Taurus.

30. The Sun and Mercury were in Aries, and Venus had only just slipped into the first minutes of Taurus, so these would seem to observers to be bunched together in Aries. Mars, Jupiter and Saturn were in Aquarius – the last two still in the all-important Grand Conjunction which the mediaeval astrologers regarded with such awe.

31. See Thorndike, *op. cit.*, n. 27, vol. III, p. 290. I think, however, that this issue is not one of measurement: Geoffrey of Meaux was calculating the duration of the eclipse, and he probably had no way of checking if his calculations were correct. Other astrologers did not calculate the eclipse to last quite so long.

32. The original manuscript, written by, or copied from, Geoffrey of Meaux, is preserved in the Bodleian as Digby 176. Of course, Geoffrey did not call it the 'Black Death'. This name came later, and was probably a reference to the black spots which grew alongside the tumours on the bodies of victims. Geoffrey called it the *pestilentia*.

33. The Latin was *minutae bestiolae*. The quotation, pertaining to the conjunction of 1345, is from Trithemius *Chronicon Hirsauagiense* II, pp. 204–5 in the 1690 edition.

34. Rudolf Steiner discussed the ancient attitude to eclipses – and indeed to Sun and Moon – in a number of lectures. Perhaps the most pertinent reference (in so far as it relates to questions put to the Cosmos during eclipses) is in the first of four lectures Steiner delivered in Dornach (Switzerland) on 25 June 1922. This was published in an English translation as the first of four chapters in *Human Questions and Cosmic Answers*, 1960.

35. An interesting catalogue of the main difficulties which the megalithic builders would have in regard to recording and measuring the precise positions of the Moon is given in E. C. Krupp, *Echoes of the Ancient Skies, The Astronomy of Lost Civilizations*, 1983, pp. 41 ff.

36. This particular plate was reproduced in H. S. Jones, *General Astronomy*, 1922.

37. An excellent account of Hawkins' researches into what has been called the 'Neolithic computer' – and, incidentally, into Fred Hoyle's interesting developments of the Aubrey hole theories – is given in Peter Lancaster

Brown, *Megaliths, Myths and Men, An Introduction to Astro-Archaeology* 1976, Chapter VI: 'Stonehenge and Eclipses', pp. 115 ff.

38. Paul I. Micallef, *Mnajdra, Prehistoric Temples, A Calendar in Stone*, 1990.

39. Tim O'Brien, *Light Years Ago, A Study of the Cairns of Newgrange and Cairn T Loughcrew, Co. Meath, Ireland*, 1922. Although I have based the accompanying diagrams on drawings and photographs I made at Loughcrew, some years ago, the solar engineering is based on the photographs given by Tim O'Brien, *op cit.*, p. 50 for 15 and 16 September.

40. Tim O'Brien, *op. cit.*, p. 51.

41. See G. R. S. Mead, *Thrice-Greatest Hermes, Studies in Hellenistic Theosophy and Gnosis*, 1964 edn, vol. 1: Plutarch, 'The Mysteries of Isis and Osiris', XLIV, P. 224.

42. The notion that the Star of the Magi was an astral phenomenon unlinked with the ordinary stars is widespread in alchemical and esoteric Christian literature: see for example, Fulcanelli, *Le Mystère des Cathédrales*, pp. 52 ff.

43. From *The Book of Chilam Balam of Chymayel*.

44. Wansey, *Stonehenge*, 1796.

45. The woodcut is from De Valdes, *Uso de los Antoios para todo genero de vistas . . .* , 1623.

46. Rodney Collin, *The Theory of Celestial Influence*, 1971 edn, p. 115. See also Appendix Two, p. 353.

47. See for example R. T. Rundle Clark, *Myth and Symbol in Ancient Egypt*, 1978 edn, pp. 219 ff.

48. The monochrome painting is entitled 'The First Hour of the Night', and is presently in a private collection.

49. For a good description of capillary-dynamolysis, with a brief survey of its history, see Agnes Fyfe, *Moon and Plant, Capillary Dynamic Studies*, 1975 edn.

50. This interesting drawing is taken, with kind permission, from F. Gettings, *Dictionary of Astrology*, 1985.

51. See L. Kolisko, 'The Total Eclipse of the Sun, 15th February 1961', in Kolisko, Stifter and Steiner, *The Sun Eclipse in Scientific Experiments*, 1978.

52. Alfred John Pearce, *The Text-Book of Astrology*, 1911 edn, p. 327.

53. Zadkiel's *Almanac* for 1882, pp. 15 ff, relating to the solar eclipse of that year.

54. For the parallels drawn between these eclipses and earthquake disasters, see A. J. Pearce, *op. cit.*, p. 375.

55. The constellation is now named Monoceros. It is believed to have been charted by the German astronomer Jakob Bartschius in the seventeenth century, though it is likely that it appeared in earlier maps as a horse (without a horn), its form being derived from a Persian stellar sphere.

56. James was born on 19 June 1566. A version of his horoscope (cast for 18 June 1566) is given in John Gadbury's *Collectio Geniturarum*, 1662: the glaring inaccuracies in this chart have been carried over into Leo's *Notable Nativities*.

57. The Lunar Dragon in Indian is represented in the names of the nodes, Rahu and Ketu, and in Arabic astrology as Zawzahr.

58. The late mediaeval term for the Dragon's Tail, *katababazon*, seems to have come (via the Arabian astrologers) from the Greek, yet it is not a word one finds intact in the modern Greek lexicons. The word may have been linked with that used in the Mysteries of the Great Mother – *katabasis* – which took on a different meaning in the Christian Mysteries. The word is also linked with the Greek *kataballo*, which was again used in the Mysteries in connection with the Divine Frenzy of the *orgias*. Both these specialist meanings (which later developed into less specialist, yet connected meanings) were linked with certain lunar influences. The general idea of 'going down' and of something distinctly unpleasant is expressed in the astrological reading of the descending node, for it is quite certainly linked with a stellar influx of karma, and (incidentally) with the idea of the descent into incarnation from the lunar sphere, which was one of the mysteries taught in the ancient Mystery Centres of the Great Mother.

59. A. Kircher, *Ars Magna Lucis*, 1631, p. 410.

60. *Karma* is the law of spiritual consequences, which implies that every deed, whether good or evil, will find its balancing consequence, unfoldment and redemption in some future effect.

61. At apogee the umbra falls short by as much as 20,300 miles.

62. This is the path of the total eclipse. The penumbral or partial eclipse covers a much wider area, sometimes up to a thousand miles or so in width.

63. For a recent version of the Karl Marx eclipse story, see J-L Brau, Helen Weaver and Allan Edmands, *Larousse Encyclopedia of Astrology*, 1977, p. 101.

64. The term 'sensitive degrees' can be misleading, for it is applied both to a degree occupied by a planet, nodal point or angle, as well as to the degree marked by an eclipse. The theory of eclipses is based on the idea that the cosmic sensitive degree (that is, the eclipse) merges in an explosive way with the horoscopic sensitive degree (that is the degrees occupied in the chart itself).

65. A close sensitive degree was created by an eclipse in 1986. It is of interest to astrologers who study historical cycles because it is near a degree which was repeated exactly in the years 1734 and 1753. The following data sets out the position clearly:

    1986 9 APRIL 19.07 ARIES
    2005 8 APRIL 19.06 ARIES

    1734 12 OCT 19.15 ARIES
    1753 12 OCT 19.15 ARIES

    In 1734 war broke out between the French and the Holy Roman Empire, over territorial disputes in Italy. In 1753, the 'seven–year war' broke out between the French and the English, over territorial disputes in North America (the ownership of Ohio).

66. See for example almost any edition of Alan Leo's *Modern Astrology*, in which eclipses continue to be interpreted in this way.

67. Lilly, *op. cit.* Later, Lilly insists that the English are not the only nation who should show concern at 'those great Catastrophes which will appear after this so famous Eclips'.

68. Lilly, *op. cit.*, p 47.
69. Lilly, *op. cit.*, p 18.
70. The data for Tromp's death-chart is merely of antiquarian interest, as few modern astrologers would interpret charts in this way, or permit this latitude of orb. The data was:

POSITION OF URANUS IN THE CHART OF TROMP: 21.47 ARIES
POSITION OF PLUTO IN THE CHART OF TROMP: 20.53 ARIES
MARS AT LUNAR ECLIPSE OF 25 MARCH 1652:   24.20 ARIES

In terms of seventeenth-century astrology, the orb for the two 'modern' planets would have been wide enough to accommodate the 2 degrees because they would have been empowered by their conjunction. The orb is acceptable to modern astrologers for different reasons: the rules of interpretation permit two conjuncting planets a wider orb than a single planet.

71. The date (but certainly not the data) was taken from M. E. Jones *The Sabian Symbols in Astrology*, 1953, ex. 195.

72. How *does* an astrologer find out when an eclipse will fall on a specific degree – for example, on this 29.55 axis in the chart of Prince Charles? To determine the date, time and zodiacal position of an eclipse, the astrologer will either make a computer search in a graphic ephemeris, or will consult one or more of several tabulated lists of eclipses. Several tables have been published, with the astrologer in mind. Useful for examining eclipses in zodiacal order are those in Neil F. Michelsen, *Tables of Planetary Phenomena*, 1990, in the 1993 revised edition. For general background information for eclipses from 1800 to 2000 inclusive, one useful work is Hugh MacCraig, *The Ephemeris of the Moon*, 1951, revised 1969. The tendency nowadays, however, is for astrologers to use the more easily available computerized astrological systems, which usually incorporate graphic ephemerides that cover thousands of years. I have checked all the eclipses given in this book against both published eclipse-tables and against the WinStar Plus Matrix Software, 1995, with the Graphic Ephemeris update.

73. On 20 June 1796 there was a lunar eclipse on 29.46 Sagittarius. On 21 June 1853 there was a lunar eclipse on 29.37 Sagittarius.

74. This means, of course, that Prince William was born with an eclipse in his chart.

75. Blake's knowledge of alchemy seems to be derived mainly from his reading of the Rosicrucian alchemist, Jacob Boehme, which he knew through the translations of William Law.

76. Johann Daniel Mylius, *Philosophia Reformata*, 1622, pl. 9.

77. Andreas Libavius, *Alchymia*, 1606.

78. Johann Conrad Barchusen, *Elementa Chemiae*, 1718.

79. Because Rossetti was so widely read, it is impossible to give a specific source for his knowledge that Gabriel was the angel of the Moon. However, the list furnished by Trithemius (and transmitted in part by Agrippa in his *De Philosophia Occulta*, 1534) is classical. In the 1503 *Calendarium Naturale*

Magicum Perpetuum (section Seven), Trithemius listed Gabriel as the angelic equivalent of 'Luna regina coeli' (Moon, queen of the heavens).

80. The proximity of the Moon to the Dragon's Tail is almost sufficient evidence of this.

81. This was given, without data, in Leo's *Notable Nativities* no. 436, taken from *Modern Astrology*, VII, p.501. A discussion led by Jean Overton Fuller, on 21 November 1966, agreed the Ascendant set out in *Notable Nativities*; I have rectified (that is, amended according to astrological principles) this time to 00:47 am. Although this was not the purpose of the rectification, it does have the effect of bringing Neptune directly to the Ascendant.

82. Elizabeth Siddal was already dying of tuberculosis.

83. The final lines in the three parts of Dante's *Commedia* were as follows. In *Inferno*: '*e quindi uscimmo a riveder le stelle*' (And thence we came forth to gaze once more upon the stars).In *Purgatorio*: '*Puro e disposto a salire alle stelle*' (Pure and ready to leap towards the stars). In *Paradiso*, what is probably the most famous line in Italian poetry: '*l'amore che muove il sole e l'altre stelle*' (The love that moves the Sun and the other stars).

    For the Italian, I have used the Daniele Mattalia edition of *La Divina Commedia*, 1960.

84. I wonder if Rossetti (learned as he was in esoteric ideas) knew of the idea of the 'path of the arrow'? This is one of the arcane names given to one of the 22 paths of the Cabbalistic Tree of Life, and connects Yesod with Tiphereth. In the Hermetic Order of the Golden Dawn, this path was linked with the Tarot card, Temperance. In her perceptive essay on the symbolism used by W. B. Yeats, Kathleen Raine recognizes that this is the Way of Sacrifice. See K. Raine, *Yeats, the Tarot and the Golden Dawn*, p.40, 1972.

Rules for Interpreting Eclipses

1. For the astrological data, see Marc Edmund Jones, *The Sabian Symbols in Astrology*, 1953, ex. 281. For the background to Disney's career, see Bob Thomas, *Walt Disney, An American Original*, 1976: Disney's birthdate is given on p. 24.

2. *Steamboat Willy* opened at the Colony Theatre, New York on 18 November 1928, and was a sensation. For some reviews, see Thomas *op. cit.*, n. 1, p. 96.

3. See *Astrology*, vol. 39, no. 2, 1964, p. 70.

4. A considerable number of horoscopes have been cast for Beethoven's birth.

5. The underlying tragedy of Beethoven's financial life was not lack of patronage, so much as the fact that there were no copyright laws to protect his work. He was on friendly terms with almost all the crowned heads of Europe, and it is extraordinary that so few of these individuals intuited his poverty and tried to remedy it.

6. Note for example the conjunction between Saturn and Moon in the chart of Franz Joseph of Austria shown next: this contrasts with the conjunctions between Saturn and Jupiter, and Uranus and Pluto, in Disney's chart. All these factors play a part in the final consequences of an eclipse becoming operative in a chart, for the eclipse activates not merely the degree upon which it falls so much as the entire horoscope.

7. To be precise, he was born at Schonbrunn, Vienna: see Henri de Weindel, *The Real Francis-Joseph, The Private Life of the Emperor of Austria*, 1909, p. 28

8. I have selected the chart from my files, but omitted to note the source of data. It is, however, a rectified chart.

9. For most of the above information, I am indebted to Roger Vadim, *Bardot, Deneuve and Fonda*, in the English translation by Melinda Porter, 1986.

10. See John Walker (ed.), *Halliwell's Filmgoer's Companion*, 1989 ed., p. 55.

11. See for example, Josephine Ransom, *A Short History of the Theosophical Society*, 1938, pp. 76 ff.

12. See 'Formation of the Theosophical Society', in H. P. Blavatsky, *Collected Writings*, vol. 1, 1874-8, pp. 121 ff. We should observe that Madame Blavatsky seems to think that the idea of the society was first mooted in July 1875 (see *op. cit.*, p.124).

13. Blavatsky's chart is one of the enigmas of astrology. She herself was fairly vague about her time of birth, and the situation *vis a vis* astrology is summarized in Leo's *Notable Nativities*, no. 018. Some of the astrologers who have seized on the data circulating from Theosophical sources have misread the Russian calendar, which still adhered to the Julian system until 1914, which means that several of the Blavatsky charts are outrageously incorrect. The one I provide is rectified, and is very similar to that given by Jones in *Sabian Symbols*, ex. 103.

14. This is done by means of 'progressions' and 'transits', see pages 263 and 264.

15. For notes on R. J. Morrison, see Ellic Howe, *Urania's Children. The Strange World of the Astrologers*, 1967, pp. 33 ff. Several of Morrison's eclipse predictions are mentioned in Alfred John Pearce, *The Text-Book of Astrology*, 1911 edn.

16. Later, a series of eclipses took place in Gemini for three years before an earthquake in 1929, which almost completely destroyed the city.

17. This was in 16 degrees of Gemini.

18. As will emerge from the following text, mediaeval eclipse-interpretation was based on the reading of horoscopes cast for the moment of eclipse. Although this ancient method has persisted into modern times, it is more usual now for astrologers to read eclipses in terms of degree significance.

19. See for instance, William Lilly, *Annus Tenebrosus, or the Dark Year*, 1652.

20. To judge from the famous birthdays listed in Sian Facer (ed.), *On This Day, The History of the World in 366 Days* (see entries for March 30) this seems to be the case.

21. The data was publicized at a meeting of the Astrological Lodge, on 25 September 1967, by Ronald Davison. See *Astrology*, vol. 41, no. 4.

22. This is not a rule that I will apply in any of the case histories discussed in this book. However, as one of the rules of eclipse-interpretation, it must be stated.

23. I have not been able to determine her birth-time from official records. However, the Ascendant proposed by the astrologer, Stanley Gritton, in *Astrology*, vol. 40, no. 4, 1966-7, p. 130 seems to be fairly reasonable (save that Beatrix was born in London, not in Westmorland). My own rectified

chart is cast for London on 28 July 1866, at 2:14 pm, when Pluto was close to her Descendant (delayed marriage), Sun in house of publishing, Venus and Mercury on house of career (writing), and Saturn rising (influence of father). The transits and progressions for this chart seem to reflect well in her life – especially in regard to her love life.

24. See Margaret Lane, *The Tale of Beatrix Potter*, 1946.
25. This view is supported by her biography. See Margaret Lane, *op. cit.*, 1968 edn., p. 108.
26. See 'Curious Horoscopes: Matricide', in *Modern Astrology*, vii, 1897, p. 185. The chart is repeated in *Notable Nativities*, as No. 071.
27. The influence of fixed stars in the astrological tradition has a long history. Some useful twentieth-century books on the subject include, Vivian E. Robson, *The Fixed Stars and Constellations in Astrology*, 1923; this gives the position of the stars for 1920, and offers a useful list of astrological traditions concerning the main stars. Elspeth Ebertin, *Die Bedeutung der Fixsterne*, English trans., *Fixed Stars and Their Interpretation* (1971), is marred by some unfortunate slips in both English and stellar positions. However, it offers useful tables designed to calculate the movement of stars due to precession, and lists 73 stars with positions for 1900, 1920, 1937 and 1950, along with a few sample horoscopes which link with specific stars. The information in Chacornac, *Astrologie, Études Scientifiques*, 1936, under the editorship of André Boudineau (1971 edn), is useful for its accurate summary of the ancient traditions (including the Ptolemaic) and its grouping of the stars into constellations for ease of reference. The last two titles provide useful bibliographies for anyone who wishes to delve into the history of fixed-star interpretation.
28. William Lilly, *op. cit.*, p. 30.
29. See for example J. E. Gore, *The Wonders of Space*, 1894, pp. 141 ff.
30. Ovid, *Metamorphoses*, IV, ll. 618 ff.
31. For a useful study of the various names given to the constellations and the stars, see Allen, *Star Names, Their Lore and Meaning*, 1963 edn. For the various names given to the constellation Perseus, see pp. 329 ff.
32. For a useful list of the gems, herbs and sigils of the mediaeval fifteen stars, see Joan Evans, *Magical Jewels of the Middle Ages and the Renaissance*, 1922; 1976 edn, esp. Appendix G, p. 246.
33. The name Hamal seems to be from *al ras al hamal*, 'the head of the sheep', though in Arabic astrology Hamal and its variants are also used to denote the entire constellation.
34. The interest in eclipses, and the eclipse-equivalents, the full Moon is still alive in certain forms of astrology in the United States: see the astrological magazine, *The Mountain Astrologer*, for example December/January issue 1998-9, p. 53, 'Gemini Full Moon – December 3' by Ted PanDeva Zagar. This issue also contains an interesting article by Corrie Cooperman, 'The Saros Cycles and the Eclipses of 1999'.
35. For a brief account of Morrison, see Ellic Howe, *Urania's Children, The Strange World of the Astrologers*, 1967, p. 47.
36. This is standard procedure in advanced predictive astrology: see for example,

Ronald Davison, *The Technique of Prediction*, 1990 reprint of 1971 edn.

37. His successor, A. J. Pearce, studied his method in considerable depth, and formulated the rules used by Morrison with remarkable clarity. It is Pearce who emphasizes that the nature of the event is determined by the nature of the planet close to the eclipse. See *The Textbook of Astrology*, p.226.

38. Morrison was writing in 1864, but the work in which the prediction appears, *Zadkiel's Almanac for 1865*, was not published until the end of 1864, in preparation for sales in the following year.

39. The 1784 position was 27.44 Libra: the 1865 eclipse was on 26.18 Libra.

40. The exact time of Palmerston's birth was not known to Morrison, who therefore speculated a noon-time chart. However, the astrologer A. J. Pearce, in *The Textbook of Astrology*, had (with good astrological reason) taken for granted that the Sun was *hyleg* – that is, 'the supporter of life' in the chart. The eclipse did not reach its full until 5:29 pm on 18 October, but on the previous day the Moon was within orb of conjunction with the Sun.

41. Morrison seems to have used a noon-day chart, which gave the Moon as 12.27 Capricorn.

42. The prediction was certainly not made by Morrison merely with the December eclipse in mind: he must have examined the progressed chart for that year, and noted that the progressed Venus would conjunct the Dragon's Head on the progressed Ascendant.

43. Ellic Howe gives the relevant section from the *Daily Telegraph*, op. cit., pp. 44-5.

44. The modern history of the charts for Eire is complex (see for example Nicholas Campion, *The Book of World Horoscopes*, 1996 edn., pp. 145 ff) but in my opinion the modern conflicts go back to the Kilkenny declaration of 1642. Morrison also used the chart of the declaration of Irish independence made at noon, 24 October 1642, at Kilkenny. At that time Mars in 12 degrees Taurus opposed Moon, Mercury and Uranus in 12 degrees of Scorpio. This powerful opposition was reflected later in the chart for 1 January 1801, which records the formal constitution of Irish union with Great Britain. In this the opposition between Mars (remarkably, again in 12 Taurus) and Neptune (in 19 Scorpio) would be activated by the eclipse of 1846. In this latter chart, the eclipse took place less than three degrees from the Dragon's Head, in 8 degrees of Taurus.

45. A. J. Pearce had recorded that Morrison made the prediction from the position of Jupiter, but this was not true. Without the eclipse being taken into account, the conjunction of Jupiter with the radical mid-heaven would not have signalled the end of the war. See Pearce, *op. cit.*, pp. 326 ff.

46. I have borrowed the data from the English version of C. Aq. Libra's Dutch masterpiece, in translation, *Astrology. Its Technics & Ethics*, 1917, pp. 192 ff. Libra included in the work a special study of the charts attached to the *Titanic*, and included charts of a passenger, W. T. Stead, and of Captain Smith, born on 27 January 1850, at Handley (time unknown). This material was derived from the English astrologer, Walter Gorn Old, better known as 'Sepharial'.

47. Quoted by Libra, *op.cit.*, n. 46, pp. 193 ff.

48. Besides the four fixed stars discussed below, the powerful and evil Scheat was on Mars, and Polaris was on Pluto.

49. See W. Lord, *A Night to Remember*, 1956.

50. The chart survived in Charles E.O. Carter, *The Astrology of Accident, Recent Investigations and Research*, 1932, p. 47. From the information given, I have reconstructed the chart in a form which suggests a birth in northern England (perhaps Liverpool?) on 2 June 1878 at 5:30 am. His Neptune was in 08.31 Taurus. The Dragon's Head in the *Titanic* chart was 08.28 Taurus. There was little chance that poor Hartley would have survived the sinking, even if he had not played on with British stiff upper-lip: his Pluto was on the destructive fixed star, Algol, and his Mars was on the violent Wasat.

51. Mirach is not a particularly evil star, unless it is with one of the malefics, such as Saturn. My point merely is that Mercury with a fixed star is permitted a wider orb than Mercury alone.

52. Marc Edmund Jones, *The Sabian Symbols in Astrology*, 1953, p. 116.

53. Ronald C. Davison was a very fine astrologer indeed, and the author of some excellent books on the art. His observation is found in the journal he edited for many years, *Astrology*, under 'Mass Murder in Chicago' in vol. 40, no.4, 1966–7, p. 130.

54. The data, derived from the American Federation of Astrologers' Bulletin, was given by Davison, *op. cit.*

55. Davison, *Astrology*, vol. 41, no. 4, 1967, p. 130.

56. Besides Skat, Polis and Antares, which I shall discuss here, Renoir had Khabalia on his Mars, in 5 degrees of Scorpio.

57. Another example of paralysis linked with Antares is the chart of Dr Rudolf Kassner, who was born with Mars on this star, and who had to use crutches all his life. This case is quoted in Ebertin (1971), p. 71.

58. Although the opposition between Mars and Mercury is significant, the chart may only be understood by the baleful influence of fixed stars, of which Han (discussed below) is paramount.

59. Lautrec is said to have been born 'at night-time' on the 24 November 1864, at his parents' chateau in Albi. My rectifications, against major events in his life, suggest a birth-time of 9:56 pm. In fact, my commentary on the effects of eclipses in his life does not involve angles or nodal points, so even if my rectification were to be regarded as questionable, the general drift of my argument is undeniable.

60. I have taken the dates of his accident from Maria Cionini Visani, *Toulouse-Lautrec*, in the 1968 English translation, p. 5.

61. It is interesting that his death should appear to be recorded with greater exactitude than his birth: this is a curious thing for an aristocrat – for a person who was in effect the last heir to the nobility of Provence. His parents had been first cousins, and this is usually given as an explanation for the poor condition of his bones. The exactness of his death-time helped in rectification, as Mars (in 5.30 degrees of Scorpio) was exactly on transit over his natal nadir (he died at home, in the arms of his mother).

62. Lilly, *op. cit.*, p. 72.

63. The sniping between John Gadbury and William Lilly has been dealt with

in several histories of seventeenth-century astrology. See for example, Derek Parker, *Familiar to All. William Lilly and Astrology in the Seventeenth Century*, 1975, pp. 252 ff.

64.   In 1627 Regulus was in 24.38 Leo, so Gadbury was allowing more than the permitted orb of one degree. It is interesting to note the pride with which the astrologer William Frederick Allan (who used the pseudonym Alan Leo) recorded his chart, which had Regulus on his Ascendant. Leo (being a Leonine) had no reluctance in displaying his chart in his many books on astrology: for example, see his *The Progressed Horoscope*, 1964 edn., p. xvi.

65.   In Cromwell's chart (figure 7) Mars and Saturn are in opposition across the lunar nodes of the 1652 eclipse chart. This somewhat dramatic demonstration of Cromwell's power cannot possibly have been missed by Lilly. It was not unusual for seventeenth-century astrologers to emphasize the fixed stars in their charts: for example, John Gadbury in *The Nativity of the Late King Charles*, 1659, p. 8, mentions the star which lifted him to royalty (Basilikos, or Regulus) and the star which eventually overlooked his beheading (Algol).

66.   In the modern star-maps, Alpheratz is the alpha of the constellation Andromeda, located in the maiden's hair. However, the Arabic (from whence came the two names Sirrah and Alpheratz) Al Surat al Faras, 'the navel of the horse', indicates that it was once located in the body of the flying horse Pegasus.

67.   Prince Otto von Bismarck was born near Stendal on 1 April 1815, at 1:00 pm. His Sun was in 10.55 Aries, while in 1815 Alpheratz was in 11.43 Aries. The chart given in M. E. Jones, *Sabian Symbols*, 1953, pp. 366-7, no. 99, is inaccurate in some details: for example (relevant to my own analysis, above), Neptune is out by almost a degree.

68.   Ribbentrop was born 30 April 1893 at Wessel on the Rhine, at 10:35 pm. Elsbeth Ebertin, *Fixed Stars and Their Interpretation*, 1971 edn., p. 13, claims that the star Alpheratz was on his MC, which is incorrect. She also claimed that Lenin's Mars was on Alpheratz, but this was not the case: Lenin's Mars was in 14.30 Aries. In 1890, the year of his birth, Alpheratz was in 12.46 Aries.

69.   See Isabelle M. Pagan, *From Pioneer to Poet, or The Twelve Great Gates*, 1911, 3rd edn., of 1930, p. 287.

70.   His chart is remarkable because of its distribution of fixed stars. The star Scheat is on his Sun; Caphir on his Moon, Algenib on Mercury; Alpheratz on Saturn (I deal with this influence in the text), and Polis on the conjunct Uranus and Neptune (a placing which influenced a whole generation of brave men who helped build and maintain the Empire).

71.   I have taken the data from Byron Farwell *Burton, A Biography of Sir Richard Francis Burton*, 1963, p. 8, but the time (not the place) given by Farwell is from the autobiographical sketch mentioned by Pagan (1911), which wrongly gives Burham House, Hertfordshire, as the place of birth. The horoscope given by Alan Leo in *Notable Nativities* n. 356 is slightly incorrect, yet remarkably accurate in the sense that it was a rectified chart, to an uncertain time, and a wrongly recorded birth-place. Alongside my own data, I have given the Pagan (1911) chart.

72. Achernar is the only star in the cosmic river which is of first magnitude.
73. The more widely used Arabic name is Al Nahr, which also means 'the River'. See Allen, p. 217.
74. Fawn M. Brodie, *The Devil Drives, A Life of Sir Richard Burton*, 1968 reprint, p. 312.
75. Brodie (*op. cit.*, n. 76) p. 323. The poem which Burton wrote in his diary about his experience with the bird is reproduced on this page.
76. Ronald C. Davison, *The Technique of Prediction. The New Complete System of Secondary Directing*, 1955, in the 1990 revised edn., p. 123.
77. I have taken Einstein's chart not merely because of its intrinsic interest, but also because it has been so thoroughly studied (and rectified) by some of the finest modern astrologers. In addition, the chart was subjected by Ronald Davison to minute predictive examination in *The Technique of Prediction*, and the reader who might be interested in advanced predictive techniques may feel inclined to follow up the more recondite developments in the chart by following Davison's own arguments.
78. Eridanus was the celestial river into which Phaeton plunged, after having set the world on fire with the sun-chariot of his father, which he was unable to control. This explains why some of the stars in the constellation (including Achernar) are linked with accidental drownings.

It is very interesting (given the connection drawn between the star and scientific knowledge) that Ptolemy did not mention it in his Almagest, even though he would have been able to see it from his native Alexandria. As Allen *op. cit.*, points out, this argues that Ptolemy's catalogue was not entirely based upon observations, but was based on the lost catalogue of Hipparchus, who worked at Rhodes, from which island Achernar was not visible.
79. His natal Moon was in (12 Cancer) conjunct with Achernar. The astrologer Elsbeth Ebertin, *op. cit.*, mentions alongside these classical examples of Einstein and Goethe the charts of Prince Rainier III, General Franco, and the stigmata-possessor, Therese Neumann, who also had Achernar emphatic.
80. For an interesting account, written in layman's terms, see Nigel Calder, *Einstein's Universe*, 1979, p.67.

Charts of Some Famous Individuals

Alexander II
1. His birth data, taken from A. J. Pearce's *Urania* 1880, is more easily available in Alan Leo's *Notable Nativities*, no. 738, where, however, the date of his death is wrongly recorded. The Ascendant given in this source is 5 degrees of Leo, the MC, 7 Aries.
2. On the day of his assassination, the Dragon's Head was on 22.49 Sagittarius. In the natal chart his Sun had been exactly upon the Dragon's Head, in 8.21 Taurus. On the day of his death, Venus was 7.34 in Taurus, on his natal Sun and node: Pluto was less than 3 degrees from his natal Mercury, and the Sun was less than 3 degrees from his natal Pluto.

Andersen
1. I have taken the data from his autobiography *The Story of My Life* in the English translation of 1871.
2. The dreamer-poet's planet Neptune was in trine with Venus. His Dragon's Tail was on Procyon – not a particularly delicate placing, but one which increases the Mercurial nature (for better or for worse). Because of the Mars-Mercury contact the star increases interest in hidden or occult things. It can intensify a love of theatre and literature, and may tend to drive the native restlessly from place to place. However, the star apart, the strong Piscean nature (Venus trine Neptune, and Pluto in the sign) lies behind most of his creative genius. It is not usually realized that Andersen died ultimately of an accident – he fell out of bed, and never really recovered: significantly, this happened close to the time when the last of his fairy-stories were published, in the Spring of 1872. On 4 August, 1875 (the day of his death) Mars was exactly on the radical Dragon's Tail, on 21.58 Cancer, on his Procyon.

Marie Antoinette
1. The evil star in Antoinette's chart was the *alpha* of constellation Libra, called the South Scale in modern astrology, but in Antoinette's day, more usually Zebenelgenubi, which means approximately, 'the south claw' – in reference to the Scorpion's claws, of which it once formed part.
2. Besides the Southern Scales, with which I deal below, the fixed star Achernar was on her Uranus, Sabik on her Pluto, and Acubens on her Neptune.
3. Ebenezer Sibly, *The Science of Astrology, or Complete Illustration of the Occult Sciences*, 1790, pl. 21. Although the time of her birth is known to within a few minutes, there are a very large number of variant charts for Marie Antoinette. I have used as the basis for my own rectification the data given by George Wilde and John Dodson, *A Treatise of Natal Astrology*, 1894, p. 156, which is based on a birth time of 7:30 pm, in Vienna, with a Moon in 20.50 Libra.

   The reason why Sibly reproduced his rather gruesome engraving (which I have reproduced in figure 4) was allegedly to 'teach the curious reader how to distinguish the astral testimonies portending a violent death from those which foreshew our natural dissolution'. Among the seven influences portending death which Sibly noted was the presence of the 'violent fixed star Chaelae' on Louis' Moon. In his chart, the Moon is on 13.15 Libra. It is unlikely that you will find a fixed star Chaelae in the modern reference books. The Latin name goes back to ancient times, when Libra was regarded as part of the claws (chelae) of Scorpio. There were two Chelae in the old star lists, one a beneficent planet, the other thoroughly evil: these are respectively, the *beta* and *alpha* of constellation Libra, and were formerly called Zubeneschamali and Zubenelgenubi, respectively (see n. 1, above). From the description of this Chaelae as 'a violent fixed star', you would presume that Sibly has in mind the alpha, which is the evil one of the two. This is now called the Southern Scales which I view as being operative on Marie Antoinette's Venus, and the significator of her death. The thing which Sibly

241

has observed (and has perhaps tripped over) is the close correspondence between the Venus of Marie Antoinette (11.24 Scorpio) and the Moon of Louis (13.15 Scorpio). This is a classical relationship for a married couple, but I do not think it has much to do with Louis' execution, for he did not die under the impress of the 1793 conjunction of Sun and Moon.

The fixed star is now listed as being in 15.04 degrees of Scorpio. Allowing for precession, it would have been in 11.40 degrees of Scorpio in 1754. This suggests that Sibly has made a mistake in linking it with Louis' chart, for he gives Louis' Moon in 13.15 degrees of Scorpio. An orb of such magnitude simply cannot be allowed for fixed star contacts. These points do tend to invalidate Sibly's assessment as to why Louis died a violent death.

4.   The Sibly data seems to have been different from that used in the interesting collection of charts for French royalty in André Barbault, *Traité Pratique d'Astrologie*, 1961. I have used this Barbault data for the chart alongside the data tabulation. Barbault gives the chart on p. 265, and that of her murderer, Robespierre on p. 266.

5.   Elsbeth Ebertin, *Fixed Stars and Their Interpretation*, in the English translation of 1971, p. 65.

Banneker

1.   David Ovason, *The Zodiacs of Washington DC*, 1999.

2.   The date, in the earliest known specimen of Banneker's handwriting, is recorded on the flyleaf of a Bible he had acquired. This book was in the possession of one of his descendants when inspected and recorded by the historian Tyson prior to 1854. The inscription reads:

I bought this book of Honora Buchanan the 4th day of
January, 1763. B.B.
Benjamin Banneker was born November the 9th, in the year of
the Lord God, 1731.
Robert Banneker departed this life July the 10th, 1759.

From this last piece of information, and from the date of Banneker's own death, I have been able to rectify the chart. At his death, Sun was in transit over the natal Pluto, Venus one degree from opposition to natal Saturn, Neptune one degree from radical Saturn. At his father's death, Uranus was within one degree of opposition to radical Jupiter.

3.   By far the best work on Banneker is that by Silvio A. Bedini *The Life of Benjamin Banneker*, 1972. In this context see p. 129. As Bedini records, Banneker's engagement in the survey was described by Jefferson in a letter to the Marquis of Condorcet, dated 31 August 1791. By this time, Banneker had left the project: he had worked on the survey from early February to the end of April, 1791: see Bedini, pp. 126 ff. It is likely that the project proved too much for his advanced age: at the time, he was 60 years old.

4.   See Bedini (*op. cit.*, n. 4) pp. 107 ff.

5.   In fact Banneker gave positions for fourteen fixed stars in his almanacs.

6.   Besides Princeps he had the beneficial Zaniah and Bellatrix, on his Jupiter and Neptune, respectively, each of which promotes a keen intellect. If my own calculations are correct, he had the beneficial Agena on his Zenith –

which probably accounts for his remarkable advancement in social terms. The star Unukalhai (on his Venus) and Dirah on his Dragon's Tail are surprising, because I can find no trace of their influences in his life.

7. See André Boudineau (ed.), *Les Étoiles Fixes*, 1971, p.87.

Beethoven

1. As the musicologist, Robert Haven Schauffler, admits in his *Beethoven*, 1939, even the exact date of Beethoven's birth is not known for sure. However, he was certainly christened on 17 December, and in the light of the local contemporaneous custom which held that children should be baptized within twenty-four hours of birth, the date seems to have been 16 December. Inevitably, in view of this uncertainty, a considerable number of horoscopes have been cast for Beethoven's birth. The version I give is based on the data given in *American Astrology* and reprinted in *Astrology, The Astrologers' Quarterly* vol. 41., no. 2, 1967, p. 47. I have rectified this chart by a few minutes to fit the most important events in Beethoven's life and work.

2. This reminds us of the storm which witnessed Byron's death in Greece, three years earlier – see page 145.

Blake

1. *Urania: or the Astrologer's Chronicle, and Mystical Magazine*, no. 1, 1825. The horoscope, which was cast by John Varley, has been used widely by modern writers on astrology, even though it contains several minor errors. A careful comparison between the chart I reproduce on page 134 and the accurate tabulated data alongside is essential.

   The chart given by Alan Leo in *Notable Nativities*, no. 195, introduces even more errors.

2. See *Jerusalem* – the lunar eclipse is plate 33, the solar plate 70, as given in A. C. Swinburne's *William Blake. A Critical Essay*, 1906 edn. For a good analysis of the poem, see pp. 208 ff.

3. There were also a solar eclipse in Cancer on 17 July 1814, and two in Capricorn on 10 January 1815 and 30 December 1815. However, these do not appear to have the same symbolic poetic force as the two of 1805.

4. The natal horoscope of Blake, cast initially by John Varley (see n. 1 above), is not quite correct for the time he states. As 27 degrees Cancer (Ascendant degree) is important to Blake, I assume that either Varley's tables or calculations were slightly out. The famous Varley chart is cast for 07:34 pm, and not 07:45 pm, as Varley's own notes indicate. Accordingly, I have cast my own table for the earlier time.

5. John Varley was author of the *Treatise on Zodiacal Physiognomy*, 1828, of which only the first part was published. In his day, Varley was better known as a watercolourist than as an astrologer. However, he does appear to have introduced Blake to the youthful Robert Cross Smith, the original 'Raphael' – astrologer, author and almanac-maker whose pseudonym name still appears in the annual *Raphael's Almanacs*. Smith had already brought out the weekly periodical, *The Straggling Astrologer* in June 1824. This ceased publication in October of the same year, and is now much sought after by

historians of astrology, if only for the engravings. For Varley's exploits with Uranus, see A. T. Story, *James Holmes and John Varley*, 1894, pp.247 ff.
6.   Samuel Palmer was among his disciples.

Brontë, Charlotte
1.   I have taken the birth time (but not the data) from Marc Edmund Jones, *The Sabian Symbols in Astrology*, 1953, ex. 134.
2.   The tell-tale transits for the middle of August include that of the Sun in Leo to an opposition to radical Saturn, and that of Mars in Taurus to a conjunction of Jupiter. The progressions for August 1847 reveal the progressed Mercury in Gemini conjunct the Dragon's Head (and thus in contact with the star Bellatrix), and the progression of Jupiter to the MC.
3.   This is presumably because the star was worked into her life in a creative way through the lunar nodes.

Brontë, Emily
1.   I have taken the birth time (but not the data) from Marc Edmund Jones, *The Sabian Symbols in Astrology*, 1953, ex. 135. The well-written biography by Winifred Gerin, *Emily Brontë, A Biography*, 1971, does not give the time of birth: however, she does record that the date was recorded in the diary of a friend of the girl's parents, Elizabeth Firth.
2.   'Virtual Suicide' is the title of chapter xxxi (pp. 355 ff) in Virginia Moore's beautifully crafted biography, *The Life and Eager Death of Emily Brontë*, 1936.

Byron
1.   In fact, there are several other eclipse influences in Byron's fascinating chart. For example, the lunar eclipse of 22 August 1812, which was on Byron's Saturn, corresponded with the death of his mother. I have selected for study those eclipses which, besides being instructive, seem to represent most clearly the destiny of this remarkable man.
2.   Given the considerable debate in astrological circles about the correct time of Byron's birth, I decided to rectify the chart against known events in his life. I was surprised to find that the birth time I arrived at was only 1 minute earlier than that used by Byron's contemporary, the astrologer John Varley (see note 1, under Blake, p. 243), who had published a figure cast for a birth-time of 1:18 am. This time is also very close to that given by Dr. L. D. Broughton in the United States, in *Elements of Astrology*, p. 324. See also Leo's *Notable Nativities*, nos. 723 and 752. I have used for the representative horoscope that which appeared in the useful work by George Wilde and John Dodson, *A Treatise of Natal Astrology*, 1894.
3.   These three stars seem originally to have been the Al Ashfar, or eyebrows, of the Arabian star map of Leo. The Latin text which accompanies the woodcut mentions these stars ('*in capite stellas tres*') without giving their names. Such crude woodcuts are rarely accurate maps, but the stars do appear to correspond to the *eta*, *mu* and *lambda* of the modern system. The epithet 'The one who rends' given to the devourer Algenubi is not a

translation of the Arabic, and I have been unable to trace its source – though it is certainly very old.

4. See for example Leo's *Notable Nativities* (no. 185): Leo seems to have taken it from Zadkiel's *Horoscope*, for it contains similar errors. The interesting fact is that the child's Mars (in 20.23 Aries) falls exactly upon her father's Part of Fortune, a pathetic synastry given their histories.

5. See Leslie A. Marchand, *Byron, A Portrait*, 1971, p. 453.

6. William Parry, *The Last Days of Lord Byron*, 1825, p. 128.

King Charles I

1. An excellent survey of such predictions is contained in Ann Geneva, *Astrology and the Seventeenth Century Mind: William Lilly and the Language of the Stars*, 1995.

2. For an account of the Nostradamus predictions of the beheading of Charles, see David Ovason, *The Secrets of Nostradamus*, 1997, pp. 206 ff.

3. The woodcut horoscope reproduced is that given by Gadbury in his *The Nativity of the late King Charls Astrologically and Faithfully Perfomed . . .*, 1659. I suspect that the precise birth time is not from any official record, but marks the attempt of astrologers to ensure that the royal star Regulus was rising on the Ascendant, as Gadbury indicates, with his Greek version of the name, Basilikos, upon the angle. Gadbury was showing his royal affiliations with this word, which means 'kingly' or 'ruler'. In the later *Collectio Geniturarum*, 1662, the Ascendant of Charles is marked with the name of the star as Cor Leonis.

4. The woodcut figure for the eclipse of 11 August 1645 is from Lilly's *The Starry Messenger*. The eclipse took place on the New Style date of 21 August.

5. William Lilly, *An Easie and Familiar Method Whereby to Judge the effects depending on Eclipses*, 1652. I have edited the abbreviations and sigils to accommodate modern readers.

6. John Gadbury, *op. cit.*, p. 66.

President Clinton

1. For this data, see David Maraniss, *First in His Class*, 1995, p. 21. At his birth, Clinton was named Blyth: his mother was already a widow, as his father had died in a car accident on 17 May 1946.

2. I cast this originally for 'one hour after dawn' on 19 August 1946, and rectified it according to major events in the life of the President. The cosmic event of February 1998, relating to Clinton's appearance before the Grand Jury, on 17 August 1998, confirms the accuracy of this chart.

3. See *The Starr Report. With Analysis by the Staff of the Washington Post*, 1998.

Copernicus

1. See Junctinus, *Speculum Astrologiae*, 1583. This is the earliest printed chart for Copernicus with which I am familiar.

2. The scheme, set down in manuscript by 1526, was published as late as 1816, under the title of *De monetae cudendae ratione*.

3. Novara is remembered in astrological histories as having accurately predicted his own death, and because he lectured on such astrological techniques as making predictions from eclipses. For brief accounts, see Lynn Thorndike, *A History of Magic and Experimental Science*, 1941, vol. V (sixteenth century).

4. The full title, *De Revolutionibus orbium coelestium*, may be translated as, 'Concerning the revolutions of the celestial orbs'.

5. See for example, Lynn Thorndike, *A History of Magic and Experimental Science*, 1941, vol. V (sixteenth century), pp. 415 ff.

6. Rafal Prinke's horoscope is dated to the announcement of the manifesto of the Polish National Liberation Committee of 22 July 1944 at Chelm, at 10.45 am. Chelm was the first Polish town to be liberated from the Germans by the Soviet army. I have taken Prinke's time from Nicholas Campion, *The Book of World Horoscopes*, 1996, p. 285.

Diana, Princess

1. Lady Diana Spencer's chart has been widely published. I have taken the data from Holden (note 2, below). The most interesting of the various charts for her is in the Winstar computer astrological tradition. I suspect that the chart is inaccurate by about a minute and a half – the time should be 7:43:30 pm.

2. Anthony Holden, *Diana, A Life and a Legacy*, 1997, p. 30.

3. Prince William was born at 09:03 pm on 21 June 1982, in the private Lindo Wing of St Mary's Hospital, Paddington. I have already examined the birth of Prince William in regard to the chart of Prince Charles, on page 63.

4. In 1961 Algol was in 23.36 Taurus. Diana's Venus was in 24.24 Taurus. I record these degrees because there are significant discrepancies in the astrological star lists for the placing of this star: for example, Robert DeLuce *Complete Method of Prediction*, 1969 edn, gives the 1920 position as 23.03 Taurus, while Nicholas Devore, *Encyclopedia of Astrology*, 1947, gives the 1925 position as 25.03 Taurus.

   I have no wish to discuss the Diana chart in detail, but I should point out that the Sun and the MC were also afflicted by unfortunate stellar positions. It seems to me that it is not possible to understand the cosmic reasons for her early death without reference to the fixed stars and eclipses.

5. I call him a prince, since, for all he was god-born, he was of the line of Argolids, through his mother, Danae.

6. Ovid, *Metamorphoses*, IV, 740 ff – in the excellent A.D. Melville translation, 1986 edn., p. 97.

7. In 1961 Regulus was in 29.20 Leo. Diana's Dragon's Head was in 29.43 Leo. Regulus, the *alpha* of Leo, is a triple.

8. Lorenzo was born in Florence on 6 August 1448. His horoscope was drawn up by many astrologers, but the one most widely recognized as being accurate is that cast by Junctinus for his *Speculum Astrologiae* of 1583. Lorenzo's Sun was in 23 degrees of Leo – the same degree as Regulus. According to Junctinus, this was also the degree of his Ascendant.

9. See Vivian E. Robson, *The Fixed Stars and Constellations in Astrology*, 1969 edn, p. 196.

10. She was pronounced dead at 4:00 am, Paris time. For details of her death, see Christopher Andersen, *The Day Diana Died*, 1998 – for the time, p. 13.

Duncan, Isadora

1. Besides the fixed stars I discuss below, Isadora Duncan had the following close contacts: Alpheratz on her Moon, Capulus on her Mercury, Alphard on her Uranus, and Algenib on her Neptune.
2. The chart was cast on the basis of data in Jones, *op. cit.*, 1953, ex. 301, p. 376. My own calculations (set out above) reveal slightly different angles, and Pluto position. The astrologer Hilda Jaffa in her article 'The Life of Isadora Duncan' in *Astrology* vol. 37, no. 4, 1964, p. 122, gives her a birth of 2:30 am.
3. Algol is the *beta* of Perseus, in the decapitated head of the Gorgon Medusa (figure on page 92): it is a spectroscopic binary. The Hebrew astronomers went one step further than the Arabs, and called it Rosh ha Satan (Satan's Head).

    In mediaeval astrological case-histories, the star is often linked with execution by beheading or strangulation. It seems also to have been one of the determinatives of death by burning on the pyre (a judicial death not reserved merely for witchcraft and heresy). In most cases, however, mercy was shown the victims, and they were strangled prior to being burned. When the French guillotine was used for the first time, to behead the highwayman Pelletier, on 25 April 1792, the star Algol played its part. At the time of execution (in Paris) Mercury was within 3 degrees of Algol: Pluto was exactly square to the star, and thus in orb of square to Mercury. Saturn was in opposition to Jupiter.
4. Mary Desti, *The Untold Story. The Life of Isadora Duncan – 1921-1927*, 1929, p. 273.

Emerson

1. From Emerson's *Diary* for 1833.
2. I have based my own computer-generated chart on the time and date given in support of the horoscope in M.E. Jones, *The Sabian Symbols in Astrology*, 1953, ex. 320. However, the astrological data given by this source is incorrect – the Moon is listed as being in Cancer, while it was in Leo. There are other small infelicities, which I have discarded. My rectifications have amended the birth time given by 2 minutes.
3. His Sun was on Prima Hyadum, but the darkness of this star did not appear to become operative until his death (see below), which was preceded by a loss of memory and general decline. I suspect that it was this stellar contact which gave him the ability to see the universal need for transforming darkness into light, through taking personal responsibility for thought and action.
4. In the astrological tradition this is expressed in the adage, 'fixed stars do not cast rays'.
5. The wood-engraving is from C. A. Young, *The Sun*, 1896, p. 251.
6. Quoted by A.J. Pearce, *The Text-Book of Astrology*, 1911 edn., p. 144.

Ernst

1. I have the data from William A. Camfield, *Max Ernst, Dada and the Dawn of Surrealism*, 1993, p.31; however, Camfield does not record the time. In view of this, none of the points I raise in this section on Ernst takes into account such things as angles or the Moon, which might be inaccurate in the figure.

2. See for example Elizabeth M. Legge, *Max Ernst, The Psychoanalytic Sources*, 1989, pp. 84 ff; and F. Gettings, *The Hidden Art*, 1978, pp. 143 ff. Gettings has shown that the offal at the bottom of the Ernst picture may only be understood with the aid of a mirror – it is an image of the innards of the human body. Just so, the legs (outer parts of the human body) in the skies are shown in the form of a mirror image of legs. In this picture, not only is the upper 'reflected' in the lower, in accordance with hermetic principles, but the outer is reflected in the inner.

3. The engraving of the curious lunar eclipse is from *La Nature*, no. 781, 1881, p. 400.

4. My own suspicion is that Max Ernst took his eclipse structure from Amedée Guillemin, *The Heavens: An Illustrated Handbook of Popular Astronomy*. The diagram on p.148 of the ninth revised edition of 1883 corresponds in great detail to the lunar phases in the Ernst picture. This engraving from Guillemin is the one I have reproduced on p. 165.

5. The hand is portrayed in the 'protective' gesture of Venus, hiding her private parts. In this case, however, the hand hovers over the Earth, identifying the globe with Venus, and with something in need of protection.

6. The poetic inscription on the back of the painting is given in full by Legge (*op cit.* n. 1 above), p. 90. This poem makes it quite clear that the theme of the painting is intended to be a reflection on sexuality.

7. Gettings (*op. cit.* n. 1 above), pp. 156 ff, suggested that the arrangement of both the eclipses and the uneclipsed body to the right, was taken from a wood engraving of eclipses and phases of the Moon used in E. D. Babbit's *The Principles of Light and Color*, 1878. Legge had traced it to Camille Flammarion's *Astronomie populaire*, 1880. See however note 4 above.

8. For a list of zodiacal rulerships over countries and cities contemporaneous with Ernst, see A. J. Pearce, *op cit.*, p. 274, under Virgo.

Frank

1. The version I have used is the one given originally in *Les Cahiers astrologiques*, and transmitted to *Astrology*, *The Astrologers' Quarterly*, for publication in vol. 33, no. 3, 1959.

Van Gogh

1. Van Gogh's chart is quite extraordinary, and it seems to me that it is the pressure of these fixed stars which accounts for a great deal of his wayward genius. Certainly, a reading of his chart without reference to this stellar pressure does not make much sense. Here is a data-synopsis of the five contacts which I do not deal with in the main body of the text. Under most circumstances, Vertex alone would be the anaretic, or killer: it is difficult to see how Vincent survived the pressure of this stellar input even to leave

behind the treasures for which he is famous.

MOON IN THE CHART OF VAN GOGH:	21.07 SAGITTARIUS
POSITION OF STAR RASALHAGUE IN 1853:	20.24 SAGITTARIUS
MERCURY IN THE CHART OF VAN GOGH:	25.37 ARIES
POSITION OF NEBULA VERTEX IN 1853:	25.47 ARIES
JUPITER IN THE CHART OF VAN GOGH:	24.16 SAGITTARIUS
POSITION OF STAR ACULEUS IN 1853:	23.43 SAGITTARIUS
NEPTUNE IN THE CHART OF VAN GOGH:	12.14 PISCES
POSITION OF STAR ACHERNAR IN 1853:	13.14 PISCES

2. Quoted by Marc Edo Tralbaut, *Vincent van Gogh*, 1969, p. 340.
3. The horoscope is interesting, for not only was it cast by a Dutch astrologer, but it is also one of the earliest cast for the artist (it was not published until 1917). I have taken it from the frontispiece of charts from C. Aq. Libra, *Astrology, Its Technics and Ethics*, in the English edition of 1917. Libra specified a 10 am birth, but the tabulation I offer is a rectified version of that in F. Gettings, *Fate and Prediction: An Historical Compendium of Astrology, Palmistry and Tarot*, 1980, p. 32.
4. Van Gogh cut off the lower part of his ear in October 1888. Perhaps his best-known picture of his bandaged face is 'The Man with the Pipe', which he painted at the beginning of 1889. This is in the collection of Leigh B. Bloch, Chicago.
5. Betelgeuse is so close to the north-star Polaris in terms of modern projections that it is difficult in practice to distinguish the zodiacal influences of the two stars:

    POSITION OF FIXED STAR POLARIS IN 1853:   26.30 GEMINI

6. See for example Robert de Luce, *Complete Method of Prediction from Genethliac Astrology according to the Western Systems*, 1935 (1969 edn.), p. 116.
7. Elsbeth Ebertin, *Fixed stars and Their Interpretations*, 1971 trans., p. 37.
8. Ptolemy, who recognized its violent nature, said that Betelgeuse was of the nature of Mars and Mercury mixed. The fact that it is a red-orange star has led some historians to assume that colour was the basis of the Martian classification proposed by Ptolemy (who had in fact insisted that the star was 'rather yellow') but my feeling is that the ancients had a different way of assessing the hidden power of the stars than that available today. Of course, Ptolemy did not call it by the later Arabic-derived name: in his *Tetrabiblos* he called it merely 'the star in Orion' – Betelgeuse being the most prominent in this constellation.
9. See Frederick Dawes, *Understanding Vincent van Gogh*, 1976, p. 24. In fact, Vincent did many pictures at this time reflecting the incorrect orientation of the lunar orb towards the Sun. An example is *The Evening Walk* of 1889, now in the Museum of Art, Sãn Paulo, which shows the huge lunar crescent facing away from the Sun, which has set behind cypresses.

10. The data are:

Solar eclipse at 09:24 pm 1 January 1889:   11.43 Capricorn
Solar eclipse at 09:19 am 28 June 1889:   06.47 Cancer
Solar eclipse at 12:51 pm 22 December 1889:   00.56 Capricorn

11. Actually, 4 hours and 9 minutes difference. Were the spatial difference exactly two degrees, then it would have been 05:10 am, and both Sun and Moon would have been very close indeed to the horizon in southern France (given an Ascendant degree of 16 Cancer at that time, with Sun in 7 Cancer). However, it is impossible to gauge from the painting precisely the time or positions.

12. The paintings Vincent produced before 1885 are mediocre, and express no sign of the genius which would be unleashed in the later period, in the south of France.

Gordon

1. I have taken the data and chart from the horoscope given as an example of the Aries type in Isabelle Pagan, *From Pioneer to Poet*, 1911, p. 258. The data was entered into the family bible by Gordon's father, and given in Raphael's *Almanac* for 1879. At that time, General Gordon was still alive, and famous as 'Chinese Gordon' (for his exploits against the Taiping on the side of the Imperial Army) rather than as the 'Gordon of Khartoum', by which name we now remember him.

2. The fixed stars include Alpheratz on his Ascendant, Alcyone on his Mars, Castra on his Pluto, and Procyon on his Dragon's Head. I shall deal here only with Alcyone.

3. Elsbeth Ebertin, *op. cit.*, 1971 English translation, p. 27. On the same page, Ebertin writes that in the chart of Stalin Alcyone was conjunct Pluto: however, this was not true. Stalin's Pluto was in a far more dangerous and cruel location, on the demon-star Algol.

4. The horrors of the last few hours at Khartoum are told in *Cassell's Illustrated History of England*, pp. 54 ff., from which I have taken the illustration on p. 175.

Gwyn

1. Elias Ashmole, vol. 423, f. 103. The date is given by Peter Cunningham, *The Story of Nell Gwyn: and the Sayings of Charles the Second*, 1891, p.2: it is based on the Ashmole papers. Cunningham was one of the few non-astrologer biographers of the nineteenth century to pay attention to the horoscope of his subject. Most of the birth charts I know for Nell Gwyn are cast for London, but according to some historians she was born in Hereford: basing his conclusions on a contemporaneous print, Cunningham concludes that she was born in Coal Yard, off Drury Lane, in London. The chart given by Alan Leo from the Ashmole data in *Notable Nativities* no. 203 is incorrect.

Contemporary records (of which there are many) mention that her chief beauty was her reddish hair, and her saucy manner. On the strength of this,

I would be inclined to change the angles on the Ashmole chart. However, the conclusions I set out are not involved with the angles in any way.

2. Although I have reproduced the pictorial horoscope of Charles II from Ebenezer Sibly, *A New and Complete Illustration of the Occult Sciences*, 1790, this does contain one or two errors. The tabulated data is cast for the New Style 8 June 1630, 01:03 pm, London. I suspect that the oft-quoted earlier chart, cast by Bonatus in *Nunc. Astro. Nat.* in 1687 gave an incorrect lunar sigil.

3. For the drowning of Nell Gwyn's mother (based on the account in the *Domestic Intelligencer*, of 5 August 1679) see Cunningham, *op. cit.* n. 1 above, p. 94.

Henry VIII
1. See Lucus Gauricus, *Tractatus Astrologiae*, 1540 (see also note 2 below). The charts which are sometimes published as alternatives are usually derived from Hieronymus Cardanus, *Opera*, 1663.

2. His book, *Predictions on all Future Eclipses*, does not quite live up to its title: it was based on observations made in Venice, during 1533, and includes much useful information from early sources, such as Ptolemy and Proclus. His Italian work on personal horoscopes, *Trattao di astrologia giudiziaria . . .* formed the basis for his more famous collection of horoscopes which is still used by historians of astrology today, *Tractatus astrologiae iudiciariae de nativitatibus virorum et mulierum . . .* , 1540. Pope Paul III commissioned Gauricus to choose the propitious moment for the laying of the cornerstone of the building around the church of St Peter, in 1543 – widely viewed as a third rebuilding of Rome: see Lynn Thorndike, *A History of Magic and Experimental Science*, vol. V, p. 259.

3. J. P. Richter, *The Literary Works of Leonardo da Vinci*, 1883, I, p.44.

4. To my shame, I cannot recall from which library I obtained this particular image (which is hand-coloured). However, the woodcut is from Gemma Frisius, *Principiis Astronomiae*, 1583. The book gives only the day of the eclipse: I have obtained the exact time by means of a computerized ephemeris.

5. Achilles P. Gassarus, *Prognosticum astrologicum ad annum Christi MDXLIII*, 1544.

6. Several charts for Charles V have survived. That cast by Luca Gauricus, *Tractatus Astrologiae*, 1542, is at least contemporary, and would have been used by the King's astrologers. It is the one I have used here.

Hirohito
1. The data is from one of the most remarkable collections of predictive horoscope readings ever published. The collection appears in the ephemerides, *Raphael's Astronomical Ephemeris . . . for 1924 to 1934*, from Raphael's Astro-Picture Gallery no. 16, p. 41 of the ephemeris for 1928. The chart differs only slightly, in the degrees of angles, to that given in *The Sabian Symbols*, 461, p. 383.

    Each chart in the 'Raphael' series contained a photograph of the native, and a short, yet extremely accurate prediction of the major events in his life. With extraordinary foresight, Raphael elected to include in the ten charts some of the main personalities who would be involved in the coming world war. By this means, prior to 1934, he was clearly predicting the outbreak, development and certain consequences of a war which did not begin until 1939 and ended in 1945.

Among the ten charts from this series of Raphael VII are those for the Prince of Wales – in Raphael's opinion, the chart not 'one which would be expected for a successful Monarch', and the three we shall examine above – the Emperor Hirohito of Japan, Mussolini of Italy, and Franklin D. Roosevelt. Besides the chart for George V, the then-reigning king of Great Britain, Raphael includes that of the Duke of York, the future George VI, whom Raphael recognizes will become king. Two other important charts are those for Ramsey MacDonald, Prime Minister of Great Britain, and Calvin Coolidge, then President of the United States.

2. These were the South Asellus on his Sun, Alphard on his Mars, Ascella on his Jupiter, Sabik on his Uranus, Betelgeuse on his Neptune, Rigel on his Pluto and Agena on his Dragon's Head. I study some of these in the following text.

3. Raphael, *op. cit.*, n. 1 above, no. 16, p. 41.

4. However, it is more likely that it arose from the comparison he made between the charts of the two leaders of these great countries. It is certainly no accident that – given this prediction – he should proceed to reproduce in his series of almanacs the horoscope not only of Hirohito, but also of Roosevelt.

5. Our own word, Jupiter, is from the Greek, *Zeus Pater* (Zeus the Father).

6. As a matter of fact, in his analysis of Hirohito's chart, in 1928, Raphael foresaw that during the life of the Emperor, there would be 'an ever-growing progressive and Democratic Party, which urge on great reforms in the constitution.' See Raphael, *op.cit.*, 1928, p. 41.

Hitler

1. There are several variant charts for Hitler. It seems to have been the German astrologer Elsbeth Ebertin who first researched Hitler's birth time for astrological purposes. Her time of 6:30 pm corresponds fairly closely to the data given in M. E. Jones, *The Sabian Symbols in Astrology*, 1953, ex. 462 (which gives 6:14 pm). The data given by Ebertin seems to be based on the baptismal records, which are notoriously generalized. The difference of 16 minutes does not substantially affect my arguments, which are based on the Ebertin data.

2. Not all astrologers would agree with me: once Hitler began to become powerful in Germany after 1923, his chart was discussed widely, often in quite lurid terms. Elsbeth Ebertin published Hitler's chart (without a known birth time, and wrongly assuming that his Sun was still in Aries) in *Ein Blick in die Zukunft*, 1924, which was sold in mid-1923. He was, she observed, a man 'who could very likely trigger off an uncontrollable crisis'. Ebertin did not name Hitler, but it was evident from the data she gave, and even from

certain references within the text, whom she meant. The fascinating story of Ebertin's involvement with the Führer's chart is told in Ellic Howe, *Urania's Children*, 1967, pp. 88 ff.

Hitler's chart was widely examined in astrological magazines up to the outbreak of the Second World War, which many astrologers predicted: see however my observations in the note to the chart of Hirohito, on page 252, n. 1. The astrologer R.H. Naylor had predicted in June 1939, from comparison between the charts of Hitler and Stalin, that nothing good would emerge from the negotiations between the two: see *Prediction*, June 1939.

Pope John Paul

1. See Michael Walsh, *John Paul II*, 1995, p. 5.
2. In astrological circles, this is termed a very strong chart. The eclipse aside, the most notable feature is the opposition between Uranus and Saturn, which gives a curious tension between conservatism and radicalism.
3. See Peter Hebblethwaite and Ludwig Kaufmann, *John Paul II*, 1979, pp. 8 ff.
4. The lunar eclipse on the night of 22 April 1548 was in 12.12 Taurus. The Moon was in 13.00 Taurus in the first seconds of 28 February 1468, the day on which Alessandro Farnese (the future Pope Paul III) was born.
5. The chart of Paul III was given in Junctinus, *Speculum Astrologiae*, 1583. Michelangelo's chart was also given by Junctinus. This latter, reproduced in F. Gettings, *Fate and Prediction*, 1980, p. 119, shows Mars in 17.17 Pisces, which means that, by the showing of Junctinus, the two planets (Sun and Mars respectively) were separated by just over a degree. Indeed, if the Junctinus chart is accurate, then the lunar eclipse of 1548 was four degrees away from his natal Moon — perhaps this wide orb explains why he did not die in 1583? The relevant horoscopes and predictions of Alterius are preserved in Latin mss. 3689 in the Vatican.

Keller

1. I have taken the birth data from Dorothy Herrimann, *Helen Keller, A Life*, 1998, p. 5, which follows Keller's own details, given in the second paragraph of her autobiography, *The Story of My Life*. The horoscope given by Jones, *The Sabian Symbols in Astrology*, 1953, ex. 514, does not provide a birth time, and seems to be a speculative midday chart.
2. Vivien Robson, *The Fixed Stars and Constellatons*, 1923, says that Facies is of the nature of the Sun and Mars, and that 'it causes blindness, defective sight . . .' Ebertin, in *Fixed Stars and Their Interpretation*, 1971 English trans., p. 71, associated Keller's blindness with the star Antares, but as this star is nowhere near any of the sensitive points on her chart, I presume that she had mistaken Antares for Facies (which she does not list).

Lamballe Princess

1. Her birth is recorded by Georges Bertin, *Madame de Lamballe*, 1901 (in translation by Arabella Ward), p. 15. As the time does not appear to have

been recorded, I have rectified the chart against the somewhat dramatic events of her life.

Leonardo

1. See 'Authentic Horoscope of Leonardo da Vinci' in *Astrology*, vol. 35, no. 2, 1961, which also uses the data recorded by Leonardo's grandfather, converted to 9:48 pm. This data is undoubtedly correct, but both horoscopes given contain inaccuracies: that attributed to Lavagnini in this article is not correct. In my tabulation, I have rectified the time to within a few minutes of the local time given by Leonardo's grandfather.
2. I examine most of the fixed stars in Leonardo's chart on page 192.
3. William Herschel determined that it was a planet in 1781. It is interesting, in view of this contact with Uranus, that Vivian Robson, *The Fixed Stars and Constellations*, 1969 edn., p. 210, should write of the star as influencing a mentality 'far in advance of his time' – a fine summary of Leonardo da Vinci.
4. See Robson, *op cit.* n. 3, p. 210.

Lincoln

1. *Broughton's Monthly Planet Reader and Astrological Journal*, vol. 1., no. 6., 1 September 1860.
2. See C. Aq. Libra, *Astrology. Its Technics and Ethics* in the English translation of 1917. The chart is given, alongside data, in the frontispiece. The chart (which gives a different version of the horoscope) is from F. Gettings, *Fate & Prediction. An Historical Compendium of Astrology, Palmistry & Tarot*, 1980, p. 133.
3. I discuss Alphecca below – the other stars were Terrebellum (on Lincoln's Moon), Algenib (on his Venus) and Han (on his Neptune).
4. For an account of the background to Luke Broughton's prediction of Lincoln's death, see David Ovason, *The Secret Zodiacs of Washington DC*, 1999.

Princess Margaret

1. I have seen several variant times for the birth of Princess Margaret. Example 644 in M.E. Jones, *The Sabian Symbols in Astrology*, 1953, gives precise angles, but no time. In view of this, I have attempted my own rectifications, largely around the event of her first marriage. The transits for the marriage are so classical that I presume the couple had some astrological advice, as Venus and Mercury are conjunct in Taurus, trine to Pluto in Virgo and trine to Jupiter in Capricorn. The astrologer seems to have forgotten the working of the fixed stars and eclipses, however.

    My own rectification of the natal chart suggests that the birth was at 9:50:00 am, which gives Jupiter on the MC, and places the Moon (in 18.05 Cancer) on the star Propus. It also gives an Ascendant of 05.34 Libra, which then makes sense of the radical and progressed charts *vis-à-vis* the marriage.
2. Carter made the prediction on 8 July 1959. See *Astrology. The Astrologers' Quarterly*, vol. 33, no. 3, 1959, p. 73.
3. For an astrological note on the marriage, and on the horoscope of

Armstrong-Jones, see *Astrology*, vol. 34, no. 2, 1960, p. 62.
4. The quotation is from V. Robson, *The Fixed Stars and Constellations*, 1923, p. 196.

Marx
1. The chart of Karl Marx is quite extraordinary in so far as fixed stars are concerned. Menkar is on his Sun, Prima Hyadum on his Mercury, Alcyone on his Venus, Wega on his Jupiter, Rasalhague on his Uranus, Acumen on his Neptune, and Scheat on his Pluto. The wonder is that so many of these lay outside the contact of eclipses during his lifetime: as it is, in 1852 and 1871, Rasalhague was rendered operative by solar eclipse on 11 December 1852 and 12 December 1871, while the usually highly explosive Scheat was made operative by the solar eclipse of 16 March 1866.
2. In 1859 Marx had published the first part of what he intended as a large work, *Zur Kritik der politischen Oekonomie*, but, being unhappy with its structure, he reworked it into the first volume of *Das Kapital*.

Monroe
1. According to Jane Ellers Wayne, *Marilyn's Men. The Private Life of Marilyn Monroe*, 1992, she was born Norma Jean Mortenson, at Los Angeles General Hospital, at 9:30 am, 1 June 1926. I have learned by experience to be suspicious of round-figure times, when they emerge from non-astrological sources, and have rectified the chart for this time against her death. The horoscope given by Alexander Markin in 'Pre-Natal Influences in the Birth Chart' (1977) in *Astrology, The Astrologers' Quarterly*, vol. 51, no. 4, 1977, p. 120, is very close to my own version, with an Ascendant in 14 degrees Leo.
2. Vivian Robson, *The Fixed Stars and Constellations*, 1923, p. 213.
3. See Barbara Leaming, *Marilyn Monroe*, 1998, pp. 422 ff.

Mozart
1. The fact is that for all the intensity of a chart graced with an exact conjunction between Moon and Pluto, and lunar nodes (Dragon's Head and Tail) falling exactly across the Ascendant-Descendant axis, I still feel unhappy about this time. As my chart indicates, I have rectified it by major events in Mozart's life, to 8:33 pm. By this device, I find an explanation for his death, and both progressed and transit charts for the date of death (5 December 1791) – for example, with my amended time, the progressed Sun is on the Dragon's Tail, and the transitting Mars is on the radical Ascendant.
2. Variant charts for Mozart's birth have been around for a very long time, some with such a wide variety of angles that I must presume that his birth time has never really been established. The date, at least, is confirmed by Michael Levey, *The Life and Death of Mozart*, 1971, p. 14. Otherwise, charts vary enormously: for example, Cyrille Wilczkowski, *L'Homme et le zodiaque, essai de synthese typologique*, 1945, gives an Ascendant in 13 Aquarius, with a birth shortly after sunrise; there are however some planetary errors in this chart – notably the position of Mars – so perhaps we may discount it. With

special reference to the opera I discuss, P. L. Beecroft gives an Ascendant of 13 Virgo, to a birth of 08:00 pm: see 'Mozart and "The Magic Flute"', in *Astrology*, vol., 43, no. 4, 1969-70. I have borrowed for my chart-example that given by F. Gettings in *Fate and Prediction, An Historical Compendium of Astrology, Palmistry and Tarot*, 1980, p. 75: this also has 13 degree Virgoan Ascendant.

3. These were, of course, the E flat, the G minor and the 'Jupiter'. The latter nickname is interesting, for no one knows whence it came: it was certainly used in the Edinburgh Festival programme of October 1819, but it was not Mozart's title. The interesting thing is that at the time of the eclipse of 1787, Jupiter was opposite (in 22 degrees Gemini) the radical Pluto-Moon conjunction, while Pluto (in 20 degrees Libra) was only two degrees from his radical Jupiter.

4. The Schikaneder libretto (Act 1, Scene 6) reads *'einem Thron, welcher mit transparenten Sternen geziert ist.'* These would have been the five-pointed Masonic stars associated with Isis. The Queen was the lunar goddess of the ancient world, the prototype of the Virgin Mary.

5. There were other fixed star influences in the composer's chart, and among these the most powerful must have been Acubens on his Neptune. Others include Tejat on his Mars, Foraman on his Jupiter and Acubens on his Neptune.

6. For a thorough analysis of Mozart's last days, and for a detailed examination of his illnesses (based on the analyses of Peter J. Davies) see H. C. Robbins Landon, *1791: Mozart's Last Year*, 1988, esp. 'Myths and Theories', p. 172.

Nostradamus

1. I have taken the chart from my work, *The Secrets of Nostradamus*, 1997 (p. 466), of which the 1998 paperback is entitled *The Nostradamus Code*. I deal with the history of the various charts of Nostradamus in some detail in Appendix 1 of this work. The earliest printed chart I know is that from John Gadbury, *Cardines Coeli*, 1686.

2. David Ovason, *op.cit.*, p. 43.

3. The French *'estrange transmigration'* is in the page from the calendrical column from his Ephemeris, for July, reproduced in Ovason (*op. cit.*), p. 465.

4. I have dealt in full with this curious quatrain on p. 346 of *The Secrets of Nostradamus*, 1997.

5. The French original (first published in 1558) reads:

> *L'an mil neuf cens nonante neuf sept mois*
> *Du ciel viendra un grand Roy d'effrayeur*
> *Resusciter le grand Roy d'Angoulmois.*
> *Avant apres Mars regner par bon heur.*

6. It is such an undistinguished star that Allen in his *Star Names and Their Meanings*, 1899, does not trouble to include it in this encyclopaedic study: the Oculus to which he does refer is an old name for the constellation Corona Borealis.

Robespierre

1. The 'Reign of Terror' is the name given to a period during the French Revolution stretching from March 1793 to the end of July 1794. During this time, power was under the control of the Committee for Public Safety, which Robespierre dominated. During the terror, not only were very large numbers of aristocrats executed, but so also were many of the revolutionaries. Most died by the guillotine, but some were shot and others were drowned.

2. I have rectified the chart (a slight adjustment of a few minutes) given by Alan Leo in *How to Judge a Nativity*, II, 235. The violent death promised in the chart took place when the transit of Pluto was on his Ascendant in 25.39 Aquarius.

3. There were four difficult stars in his chart: besides Scheat, which I shall examine below, Aldebaran is weakly conjunct Neptune, Algenubi is on his Mars, and Aculeus is on his Pluto. The position of Algenubi alone might be cause for concern, as in the astrological tradition this is 'the heartless one', or 'he who rends'. Scheat promises 'extreme misfortune'. Aldebaran promises violent death.

4. He seems to have been shot in the jaw by a young policeman, on 27 July, while vainly trying to persuade people to take up arms on his behalf.

Rockefeller

1. I have taken the birth data from Ron Chernow, *Titan, The Life of John D. Rockefeller, Sr*, 1998, p. 9: Chernow records a birth 'on the night of . . .'. Jones, *op. cit.*, 1953, ex. 799, gives a midnight birth, but gives no source. For this reason, I have avoided eclipse-interpretation involving angles.

2. There was a lunar eclipse on the same degree in 1852, but Rockefeller was still very young, and his physical and spiritual organism was not sufficiently deeply incarnated into the physical realm for him to take advantage of the effects of the eclipse. However, it was in this year that his family moved from Richford, New York, to Cleveland, Ohio. I should perhaps point out that Cancer rules the home.

3. Rockefeller's Sun was in exact trine with Uranus: Sun 16.15 Cancer, with Uranus 16.17 Pisces

4. Just as Rockefeller's Sun was harmoniously related to the planet of originality, Uranus, so his Saturn was harmoniously related to Mars. The eclipse enabled him to combine in a constructive way his power of dissemination (Mars) with the power of conservation (Saturn). His Mars was in sextile to Saturn: Mars 06.15 Libra, with Saturn 04.25 Sagittarius. His Jupiter was also in close trine to Neptune. For all his reputation, Rockefeller had always had a philanthropic side.

Prince Rudolph

1. For the reasonable view that it was a murder, rather than a suicide-pact, see Victor Wolfson, *The Mayerling Murder*.

2. The data was given in a number of astrological magazines after the murder. I have used the horoscope given by the reliable historian (the Chief

Librarian of the British Museum Library) who wrote under the name of A. G. Trent, in his *The Soul and the Stars*, 1894, p. 187.

3. Carl Lonyay, *Rudolph: The Tragedy of Mayerling*, 1949.

4. See Wolfson, *op. cit. n. 1*, p. 85.

5. Some astrologers might claim that the close opposition between Mars and Uranus is of a suicidal disposition: this, they might argue was an increased risk with Uranus upon Prima Hyadum. As a matter of fact, C. E. O. Carter uses precisely this 'inharmonious' example, with specific reference to Rudolph's chart, in his *Astrological Aspects*, 1969 edn., p. 133. He sees in the Mars-Aquarius inharmonious aspect the kind of overbearing selfish impulse of a native who seeks to get his or her own way regardless of the costs, along with a desire for freedom which can externalize as a suicidal tendency. Perhaps it is fair to argue in this vein for a close square aspect, but not for an opposition, which by its very nature is outgoing. Perhaps the contact will invite violence, but I do not think it will sink to self-violence. In addition, the issue behind the Mayerling chart is far more than suicide – it is both suicide and murder – unless of course, one is prepared to argue that Marie Vetsera murdered Rudolph!

De la Rue

1. Warren de la Rue, *Report on the Present State of Celestial Photography in England*, 1860, p. 1 (from the *Reports of the British Association for the Advancement of Science*, 1859). De la Rue was certainly the first to use collodion photography for making pictures of celestial bodies.

2. De la Rue *op.cit*, n. 1 above, p. 140 ff.

3. See Robert Stawell Ball, *The Story of the Heavens*, 1890, p. 41. This plate is from a photograph showing the spots and faculae on the surface of the Sun, taken by Warren de la Rue on 20 September 1861.

4. The wood–engraving is from C. A. Young, *The Sun*, 1896, p. 242.

Shelley

1. In her remarkable study, *From Pioneer to Poet, or The Twelve Great Gates*, 1911, Isabelle Pagan proposed that the ruler of the sign Scorpio should be Pluto, which rules (as she rightly adapts the Ptolemaic phrase), 'the negative side of Mars'. The rulership, but not the sigil she proposed (an inverted symbol for Mars), was adopted shortly afterwards by some Theosophical astrologers.

2. The data, derived from a letter from Shelley's father to the family solicitor, Whitton, was unearthed by Jean Overton Fuller, and announced in a Lodge discussion on 24 February, 1964. See *Astrology*, vol. 38, no. 2, 1964, p. 62. The time seems to be the usual approximate round figure, and I have rectified it to 09:40 pm, to fit events in Shelley's short life. On the whole, it is a lacklustre chart, and it is difficult to understand his genius, save perhaps in terms of the exact conjunction of Mars and Jupiter in 25 Libra in trine to Pluto. For sure, Pluto is very important in Shelley's life.

3. Vivian Robson, *The Fixed Stars and Constellations*, 1923, p. 206.

Sinatra

1. The data for Sinatra and Mia Farrow are from *Horoscope Magazine*: see *Astrology*, vol. 41, no. 2. 1967, p. 49. However, I should record that according to Ray Coleman, *Sinatra. A Portrait of the Artist*, 1995, Sinatra was born 15 December 1915 at Hoboken, New Jersey. The horoscope for this date certainly shows a more outgoing personality, but one which was less complex than that revealed in the 1917 chart. The earlier chart does not explain the relationship with Mia Farrow. His notorious temper is also expressed in the 1917 chart, for this has Sun square Mars, with Moon in Scorpio. For this, and other reasons, I go with the 1917 birth.
2. Coleman, *op cit.*, p. 55.
3. The exact trine between Mars and Jupiter, and the vibrant placing of Venus in Aries, helps her through most difficult encounters, however.

Washington

1. I have taken the data from George Wilde and John Dodson, *A Treatise of Natal Astrology*, 1894, p. 152. This seems to have been derived from Edward Everett's *The Life of General Washington*, 1860, copied from a Bible which had once belonged to Washington's mother, and which recorded the time in old style: 'George Washington, son to Augustine and Mary his wife, was born the 11th day of February 1731/2 about ten in the morning, and was baptized the 3d of April following'. The new style date (22 February 1732) has sometimes been confused by astrologers as an old style. Some of the earlier charts, which were based on that given in *Broughton's Monthly Planet Reader* for September 1861, are very inaccurate.
2. See David Ovason, *The Zodiacs of Washington DC*, 1999.
3. See James Thomas Flexner, *Washington. The Indispensable Man*, 1974 edn., p. 26.

Conclusion

1. Haley's Pluto was in 9.24 Cancer. The solar eclipse of 30 June 1992 fell on 8.56 Cancer.
2. De Mille's Uranus was in 12.38 Virgo: the eclipse of 3 March 1923 fell on 11.37 Virgo.

Glossary

(The words in *italics* indicate cross-references within the Glossary itself.)

AIR One of the four *elements*. The term does not refer merely to the mixture of gases which we breathe: it refers to a condition of nature, in which materiality is expressed in a gaseous state.

AQUARIUS The eleventh sign of the *Zodiac*, for which the sigil is ♒. It is an *Air* sign, traditionally ruled by *Saturn*, but in modern astrology ruled by *Uranus*. It promotes a mental disposition, and often results in eccentricity. The abbreviation used in this book is AQ.

ARIES The first sign of the *Zodiac*, for which the sigil is ♈. It is a *Fire* sign, ruled by *Mars*. It promotes a pioneering attitude, and is usually highly charged with physical energies. The abbreviation used in this book is AR.

ASCENDANT The most important single point in the *horoscope*, marking the degree of the sign of the *Zodiac* which is rising over the horizon at any given moment – usually the moment of birth. It marks the symbolic point of sunrise in a chart.

ASPECT A specific angular relationship between planets or between planets and nodal points (such as the *Dragon's Head*) in a *horoscope*.

CANCER The fourth sign of the *Zodiac* for which the sigil is ♋. It is a *Water* sign, and is ruled by the *Moon*. It promotes an emotional disposition, and tends to give extremes of imagination. The abbreviation used in this book is CN.

CAPRICORN The tenth sign of the *Zodiac*, for which the sigil is ♑. It is an *Earth* sign, and is ruled by *Saturn*. It promotes an austere though discriminative disposition, though often results in a certain rigidity of outlook. The abbreviation used in this book is SA.

CONSTELLATIONS The constellations are the star-patterns in the skies, imaginatively formed from individual stars. Twelve of the constellations bear names very similar to those of the zodiacal signs.

DESCENDANT The cusp of the seventh house of the *horoscope*, linked with the sign *Libra*. This marks the theoretical point of sunset in a chart.

DRAGON'S HEAD The North *Node* of the Moon. The sigil for this node is ☊ and the abbreviation used in this book is DH.

DRAGON'S TAIL The South *Node* of the Moon. The sigil for this node is ☋ and the abbreviation used in this book is DT.

EARTH One of the four *elements*. The term does not refer merely to the soils, rocks and minerals which compose the planet on which we live: it refers to a condition of nature in which materiality is expressed as something solidified, non-fluidic, and heavy.

ECLIPTIC Name given to the imaginary line around the Earth, along which the *Sun* travels. The ecliptic belt is so named because it is along it that eclipses occur. The *Zodiac* (which is conceived as lying beyond the path of the Sun) is formed from the division of the ecliptic into twelve equal arcs of 30 degrees each.

ELEMENTS In ordinary astrology there are four elements, which are conceived as lying behind all created material forms. The solid form is called *Earth*, the fluidic *Water*, the gaseous *Air* and the incandescent, *Fire*.

EPHEMERIS An ephemeris (plural, ephemerides) is a list of planetary positions, usually given for each day of a given year. Some ephemerides list eclipses for the years in question.

FIRE One of the four elements, regarded by many astrologers as the most powerful of the four. The term does not refer merely to the incandescent gas of flame which we see on Earth, but to a condition of nature in which materiality is striving to attain a higher spiritual level of being (sometimes called Warmth).

FIXED STARS This term is something of a misnomer in modern times, for it was originated in a distant past when attempts were made to distinguish between the stars which did not move and those which did (these were the planets). The influence of fixed stars in chart interpretation is of great importance, for their influences are recognized as promoting intense extremes in personality and/or events.

GEMINI The third sign of the *Zodiac*, for which the sigil is ♊. It is an *Air* sign, and is ruled by *Mercury*. The sign promotes rapid mental activity, and usually expresses an intense need for communication of some kind or another. The abbreviation used in this book is GE.

HOROSCOPE A chart erected (usually in a graphic form) for a given moment and place.

261

IMUM COELI Literally, 'the lowest part of the heavens', but in fact the lowest part of the *ecliptic* in relation to a stated place. By definition, it marks the lowest point in the *horoscope* figure. The abbreviation used in this book is IC.

JUPITER In astrology, the beneficent and expansive planet, which is used as an index of how the *native* fits into society. The sigil for Jupiter is ♃. The abbreviation used in this book is JU.

LEO The fifth sign of the *Zodiac*, for which the sigil is ♌. It is a *Fire* sign ruled by the Sun. It promotes creativity and self-development, and is an index of inner warmth and sociability. The abbreviation used in this book is LE.

LIBRA The seventh sign of the *Zodiac*, for which the sigil is ♎. It is an *Air* sign, ruled by Venus. It tends to promote a gentle disposition, and personality traits which seek equilibrium and reconciliation. The abbreviation used in this book is LB.

LUMINARIES The *Sun* and *Moon* are called 'luminaries', or 'givers of light'. The expression is archaic, seemingly going back to a time when it was believed that the Moon was a light-source in its own right.

MARS In astrology, the forceful and active planet, which is used as an index of how the *native* will originate and tackle enterprises. The sigil for Mars is ♂. The abbreviation used in this book is MA.

MEDIUM COELI Literally, 'the middle of the skies', but, in fact, the highest point of the *ecliptic*. It is often called the mid-heaven, or zenith. The abbreviation used in this book is MC.

MERCURY In astrology, the planet of communications, which is used as an index of the native's memory, imitative faculty and speech. The sigil for Mercury is ☿. The abbreviation used in this book is ME.

MOON In astrology, a planet – though, of course, it is recognized as being the satellite of the Earth. The Moon rules over the personality of the *native*, and those factors imbued by education and domestic experiences. The most widely used sigil for the Moon is ☽.The abbreviation used in this book is MO.

NADIR Another word for the *Imum Coeli*.

NATAL CHART The *horoscope* for a particular birth – this is sometimes called the Natus.

NATIVE The human subject of a horoscope – a word derived from the Natus (birth), or nativity.

NEPTUNE In astrology, the sensitive and somewhat nebulous planet which has

262

rule over the Zodiacal sign *Pisces*. Neptune rules such things as artistic and mediumistic experiences. The sigil for Neptune is Ψ. The abbreviation used in this book is NE.

NODES In a very general sense, the Nodes are any non-planetary points within a chart which are for one reason or another emphasized. More specifically, the Nodes of the Moon are the *Dragon's Head* and the *Dragon's Tail*, which are the Ascending and Descending nodes of the *Moon* – the two points where the path of the Moon intersects with the *ecliptic*, or path of the *Sun*.

PART OF FORTUNE A *node* point in a horoscope marking the degree which is the same distance of *Zodiac* arc from the *Ascendant*, as the *Moon* is from the *Sun*. The Part of Fortune is therefore the place where the Moon would be were the Sun rising at the moment of birth. The sigil used in this book is $\otimes$.

PISCES The twelfth sign of the *Zodiac*, for which the sigil is $\mathcal{H}$. It is a *Water* sign, ruled by the planet *Neptune*. It tends to bestow an emotional, poetic and retiring disposition. The abbreviation used in this book is PI.

PLUTO In astrology, the planet which rules the hidden inner realms of mankind, and which is linked with the sexual energies. The planetary influence can be disruptive (being linked under pressure with crime and violence) but also deeply penetrative in terms of perception. The most widely used sigil for Pluto is P but in the tabulations in this book, the sigil Ψ is used. The abbreviation used in this book is PL.

PROGRESSION An astrological technique used to explore the potential within charts with a view to revealing future trends. The notion of 'progressing' the planets and *nodes* of a chart is based on the idea that each subsequent year of life of the *native* is prefigured or reflected in each subsequent day following his or her birth: thus the events revealed in the thirty-fifth year are reflected in the progressed planetary positions of the thirty-fifth day after birth. For another system of reading future trends, see *Transits*.

SAGITTARIUS The ninth sign of the *Zodiac*, for which the sigil is $\nearrow$. It is a *Fire* sign, ruled by *Jupiter*. It promotes the sense of spiritual aspiration and exploration – both in an intellectual sense (by education, for example) and through physical exploration of places and things. The abbreviation used in this book is SG.

SATURN In astrology, this is the planet of limitation, and rules the underlying fears of the *native*. It is also an index of the staying power of the individual. The sigil for Saturn is $\hbar$. The abbreviation used in this book is SA.

SCORPIO The eighth sign of the *Zodiac*, for which the sigil is $\mathfrak{M}$. It is a *Water* sign, ruled by *Pluto*. It is an index of the deeply held passions and obsessions of the *native*, and is linked with the sexual nature. The abbreviation used in this book is SC.

263

SUN In astrology, the Sun is treated as though it were a planet, even though it is recognized as being a star. It rules and reveals the conscious aims of the *native*, and is a good index of his or her sense of selfhood. A strongly placed Sun confers dignity and creativity. The sigil for the Sun is ☉. The abbreviation used in this book is SU.

TAURUS The second sign of the *Zodiac*, for which the sigil is ♉. It is an *Earth* sign, ruled by *Venus*. It is an index of the practical and sensual nature of the *native*. The abbreviation used in this book is TA.

TRANSITS A transit is the passage of a planet or nodal point over a specific degree (usually occupied by another planet or *node*). Astrologers study future and past transits over degrees and planets in the birth chart to see what influences will be working through a chart at the time of transit. This method of prediction differs radically from *Progressions*. An astrologer consulting a chart to see what effects would be anticipated for the thirty-fifth year due to transits will consult a list of planetary positions for that year, and study which planets and nodes transit (and thus spark off) effects within the radical horoscope, or birthchart.

URANUS In astrology, the planet that rules disruption and originality, and under certain conditions is an index of genius. When its influence is particularly strong, it can be very disruptive, and often results in violent events in the life of the *native*. The most widely used sigil for Uranus is ♅. The abbreviation used in this book is UR.

VENUS In astrology, the planet of harmony, love and the arts: it is an index of how the *native* seeks relationships. The sigil for Venus is ♀. The abbreviation used in this book is VE.

VIRGO The sixth sign of the *Zodiac*, the sigil for which is ♍. It is an *Earth* sign, ruled by *Mercury*, and is an index of the thinking, practical and caring predisposition of the *native*: the influence tends to make the native quick-witted, or clever. The abbreviation used in this book is VG.

WATER One of the four elements. The term does not refer merely to the liquid we use, but to a certain condition of nature in which materiality is expressed in a fluidic state.

ZENITH One of several terms for the *Medium Coeli*.

ZODIAC An imaginary belt in the heavens, centred upon the *ecliptic*, yet (in so far as it is located in space at all) beyond the ecliptic. It is divided into twelve signs, each of 30 degrees arc, running in the following order: *Aries, Taurus, Gemini, Cancer, Leo, Virgo, Libra, Scorpio, Sagittarius, Capricorn, Aquarius, Pisces.*

1. One traditional way of representing a solar eclipse is for the artist to show the radiant Sun beneath a darkened lunar globe, as in this engraving of an ancient Sibyl, from Jacopo Guarana's Oracoli, Auguri and Aruspici, *1791.*

2. One traditional way of representing a solar eclipse is for the artist to show the disk of the Sun alongside a crescent moon, with the Moon's radiant pointing away from the sun, in a cosmically impossible orientation. Frontispiece, from Jacopo Guarana's Oracoli, Auguri and Aruspici, *1791.*

3. *The sixteenth-century Florentine astrologer, Francesco Junctinus, in his study. Junctinus was one of the first astrologers to publish, on a large scale, personal horoscopes of the famous, for teaching purposes. Engraving by Leon Trouvé.*

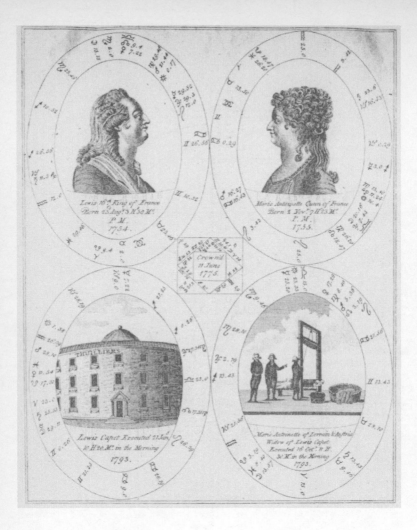

4. The birth-charts and death-charts of King Louis XVI of France and his wife, Marie Antoinette, both of whom were influenced by eclipses. From Ebenezer Sibly, A Complete Illustration of the Occult Sciences, 1812 edn.

BROUGHTON'S
MONTHLY PLANET READER
AND
ASTROLOGICAL JOURNAL.

Vol. 1.   **PHILADELPHIA, SEPTEMBER 1, 1860.**   **No. 6.**

Born Feb. 12th, 1809, at 2 h. 0 m. A. M.

5. Chart of Abraham Lincoln, the 16th president of the U.S.A., cast during Lincoln's lifetime by Luke Broughton, in Broughton's Monthly Planet Reader, *September 1, 1860, as part of a series of predictions relating to the president's life and death.*

6. *The late 19th-century magazine,* Modern Astrology, *which contained many examples of famous or interesting horoscopes, gathered by the editor, Alan Leo. Many of these charts were later published in tabulated form, in Leo's Notable Nativities and More Notable Nativities.*

NATIVITY cast by JOHN PARTRIDGE,
Physician to Her Majesty Queen Elizabeth.

OLIVER CROMWELL,
Born 1H. 4M. 56S. A.M.
April 25th, 1599.
Huntingdon.

*7. The horoscope of Oliver Cromwell, the Lord Protector of England.
From the Vol. VII, 1907 edition of* Modern Astrology.

8. Seventeenth-century engraved portrait of the actress Nell Gwyn, the mistress of Charles II. Nell's birth-chart, inset in the top right, is based on one cast by the astrologer, alchemist and collector, Elias Ashmole.

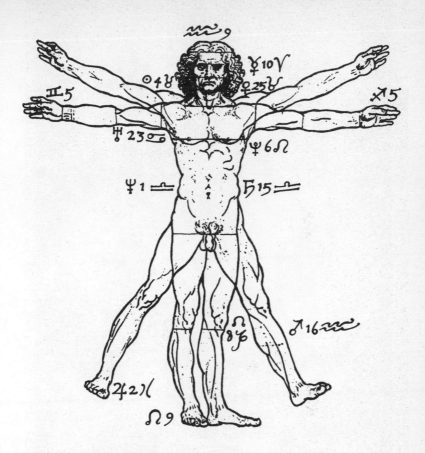

9. *Horoscope of the fifteenth-century Florentine artist, Leonardo da Vinci, with each of the zodiacal placings located near the corresponding part of the body over which the signs have rule. Leonardo's famous drawing is made to correspond to a zodiacal man, similar to the one reproduced in figure 17.*

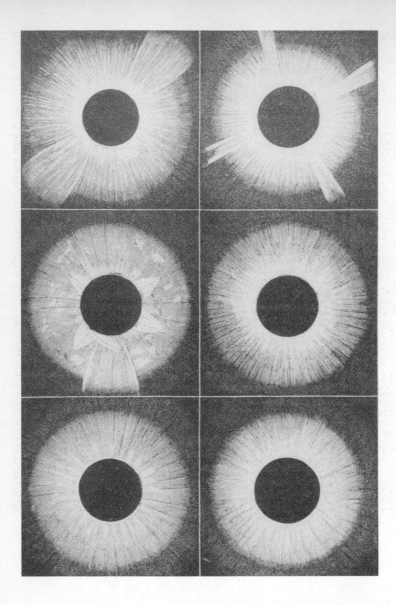

10. Examples of dramatic coronae recorded during solar eclipses in the nineteenth-century. Engraving from C. A. Young, The Sun, *1896.*

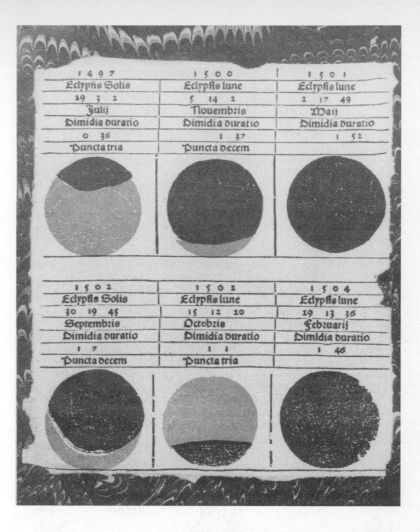

11. *Series of eclipses predicted for the period from 1497–1504, in a book printed in Venice by Ratdolt, based on the eclipse-tables of Regiomontanus. Christopher Columbus is said to have taken this book with him on his last voyage.*

*12. Solar eclipse mentioned by Herodotus, overlooked by Clio, the Muse of History.
Decoration by V. le Campion, from the Nonesuch Press 1935 edition of Herodotus.*

13. Eighteenth century engraving, based on the romantic notion of the Druids as the perpetrators of human sacrifices. Although there is evidence to show that Stonehenge was designed as a predictor of eclipses, there is none to show that the stones were erected by Druids.

And One stood forth from the Divine Family & said

I feel my Spectre rising upon me! Albion! arouze thyself!
Why dost thou thunder with frozen Spectrous wrath against us?
The Spectre is in Giant Man: insane, and most deformd.
Thou wilt certainly provoke my Spectre against thine in fury!
He has a Sepulcher hewn out of a Rock ready for thee:
And a Death of Eight thousand years forgd by thyself, upon
The point of his Spear! if thou persistest to forbid with Laws
Our Emanations. and to attack our secret supreme delights

So Los spoke: But when he saw pale death in Albions feet
Again he joind the Divine Body. following merciful:
While Albion fled more indignant: revengeful covering

His

14. *Plate from William Blake's prophetic poem,* Jerusalem, *printed in 1804–1820.
The Sun and Moon on either side of the bat–like emanation represents
a lunar eclipse.*

278

15. A solar eclipse viewed through one of the trilithon portals of Stonehenge. The three monoliths are reflected in the three figures standing at the portal (these are the scientists, Bacon, Newton and Locke). Print by William Blake, from his poem, Jerusalem, printed 1804–1820.

*16. Nineteenth century engraving of eclipse diagrams, which was probably
the original inspiration for Max Ernst's painting, 'Of This Man
Shall Know Nothing'. From A. Guillemin,* The Heavens.
An Illustrated Handbook of Popular Astronomy. 1883 edn.

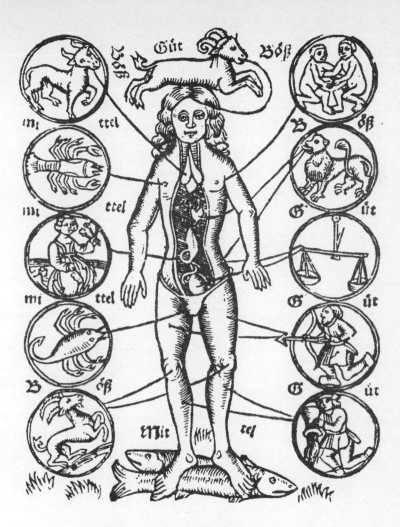

17. Sixteenth century woodcut of Zodiacal Man, showing the traditional rulerships which the twelve zodiacal signs have over the various parts of the body. Aries rules the head, while Pisces rules the feet.

281

18. Engraved horoscopes – mainly of English royalty, including Henry VIII, Mary I and Elizabeth I – from Ebenezer Sibly, A Complete Illustration of the Occult Sciences, *1812 edn.*